AFTERLIFE

AFTERLIFE

POST-MORTEM JUDGMENTS IN ANCIENT EGYPT AND ANCIENT GREECE

Gary A. Stilwell, Ph.D.

iUniverse, Inc.

New York Lincoln Shanghai

Afterlife
Post-Mortem Judgments in Ancient Egypt and Ancient Greece

iUniverse books may be ordered through booksellers or by contacting:

iUniverse
2021 Pine Lake Road, Suite 100
Lincoln, NE 68512
www.iuniverse.com
1-800-Authors (1-800-288-4677)

ISBN: 0-595-34280-9 (Pbk)
ISBN: 0-595-67092-X (Cloth)

Printed in the United States of America

For my Father

Russell Steven Stilwell

Who lived in Justice and Moderation

And faced death with Wisdom and Courage

Contents

Acknowledgements

Afterlife is a revision of the author's doctoral dissertation entitled:

Conduct and Behavior as Determinants for the Afterlife: A Comparison of the Judgments of the Dead in Ancient Egypt and Ancient Greece

The purpose of this revision is primarily to eliminate the type font and line spacing required for a properly formatted Dissertation, making the book more readable, smaller, and less expensive.[1] Secondarily, I have added a brief comparison of conduct and behavior terms as found in Egyptian and Greek religions to those in the later Jewish and Christian religions.

This work could be quite useful for the student or teacher involved in the academic studies of Humanities, Religion or Ethics. This estimation is based on the fact that it has been found to be so by being referenced in other published works subsequent to its completion in the summer of 2000.

There were many people ultimately involved in the creation of *Afterlife*, but here, I would like to express my admiration for and gratitude to the professors on my doctoral committee: Drs. David B. Levenson, Nancy T. deGrummond, David H. Darst, and Shannon L. Burkes.

In spite of their diligence, any remaining mistakes are my own.

---

[1]   In the interest of full disclosure, it is noted that approximately 30 pages of this work have been excerpted for use in a previous book by the author: Stilwell, Gary, *Christianity: 5000 Years of History and Development* (Lincoln: iUniverse, Inc., 2004).

Preface to the Revised Edition

The belief in an afterlife is well attested into the dim past. We have much archeological data that indicates burials were performed over 50,000 years ago that reasonably suggest humans were expecting a continuation of their lives after death. What we do not have is an indication of how one was supposed to achieve that afterlife.

Was an afterlife thought to be available to all people regardless of any personal attributes they might possess? For the distant past, we can't really know for sure.

At what point in time can we know that something was required of a person in order for them to deserve a beneficial afterlife? The earliest written records we have are those of ancient Egypt and, then much more recently, ancient Greece.

Most scholars have claimed that, in the earliest periods, an afterlife was available only for the elite of their society—the Egyptian King in the 25th century BCE *Pyramid Texts* and the Heroes in 8th century BCE Homeric and Hesiodic Greece. Furthermore, it was thought, no special conduct or behavior was demanded of the elite. Rather, they achieved a beneficent afterlife based on their relationship to the gods.

Afterlife argues that this view is incomplete and that from the earliest time periods, both societies believed the gods, primarily *Maat* in Egypt and *Dike* in Greece, were responsible for the proper ordering of the cosmos and that anyone violating that order through improper conduct and behavior would call down upon themselves the most dire consequences—the loss of a beneficent afterlife.

Tallahassee, Florida
January 2005

Introduction

Introductory Comments

In this work we argue that conduct and behavior were believed essential for determining one's post-mortem fate from the earliest historical periods of both ancient Egypt and ancient Greece. It makes the case for a behavior-based judgment of the dead at the dawn of the written record and provides a systematic comparison between the beliefs of the ancient Egyptians and Greeks about the basis for the judgment of the dead.

There have been many volumes written on the ancient Egyptians and Greeks, however, the relatively few that attempt to discuss the religions of both societies in a single work are generally compilations of individual unrelated essays.[2] There are even fewer writers who attempt to investigate the afterlife beliefs of the two societies in the same work. Three scholars who have done so are cited below as important examples.

W. Brede Kristensen's,[3] *Life out of Death*, in contrast with the other two examples cited below, limits his discussion to only the ancient Egyptians and Greeks. His

---

[2]   There are reference works, anthologies and compilations, several of which are cited in this project. Some examples are: J.M. Bremer, Th. P.J. van den Hout and R. Peters, eds., *Hidden Futures* (Amsterdam: Amsterdam University Press, 1994); Hiroshi Obayashi, ed., *Death and the Afterlife* (New York: Praeger, 1992); and E. Hershey Sneath, ed., *Religion and the Future Life* (London: Fleming H. Revell, 1922).

[3]   W. Brede Kristensen, *Life out of Death* (Louvain, Belgium: Peeters Press, 1992). He does, however, make some comments related to conduct with which I take exception: "This Erinys was...not a revenger of a violated law or infringed right" (132); and "The expression [ma-a-t] occurs so often that Egyptian religion would have to be considered as a so-called ethical religion, if ma-a-t really had the same meaning as 'righteousness'. But this is not the case" (58). Thus, he concludes that Egyptian religion is not to be considered an ethical religion. His argument is interesting and somewhat true, but misleading. I will argue that the concept of maat is precisely what Plato was attempting to establish 2000 years later.

primary concern is to compare their eschatological mythology, but he nowhere analyzes conduct and behavior in either society.

J. Gwyn Griffiths',[4] *The Divine Verdict* includes sections on Egypt and Greece along with those on Judaism, Christianity, Near Eastern, Roman, Indian, Iranian and Chinese religions. Griffiths, who has an excellent review of Egypt, covers so much territory that he is limited in space, thus he spends only a few pages on the Greek judgment under the heading: "The Minoan Judges of the Dead" (294-7). This allows only a cursory look at our topic and, therefore, very little attention is given to explicit comparisons of conduct and behavior as it relates to the afterlife.

S.G.F. Brandon's[5] *The Judgment of the Dead* has all of Griffiths' topics in addition to sections on Islam and Japanese religion. Although his work was instrumental in providing an inspiration for me to pursue this subject further, he provides no explicit comparison between the judgments in Egypt and Greece. We also disagree on several particulars.[6]

In light of these examples, we see that many have written about both societies separately and sometimes even together in the same work. These works and others have provided us with valuable information and insights into the issues of Egyptian and Greek religion. However, I have found no one work that focuses on conduct and behavior as determinants for an appropriate recompense in the afterlife for ancient Egypt and Greece or that provides a systematic comparative analysis of the differences and similarities in the views of the two societies. This dissertation attempts to rectify that deficiency. In addition to the analysis, I have provided a catalog of terms that each of our subject societies found important to the quality of their afterlife aspirations.

---

4   J. Gwyn Griffiths, *The Divine Verdict: A Study of Divine Judgement in the Ancient Religions* (Leiden: E.J. Brill, 1991).

5   S.G.F. Brandon, *The Judgment of the Dead: The Idea of Life After Death in the Major Religions*, (New York: Charles Scribner's Sons, 1967).

6   Whereas Brandon allows that metempsychosis is an Orphic doctrine, I will argue that it is not. Also, he apparently has no problem accepting the genuineness of the *Nekyia* in *Odyssey* 11, which leaves room for a Homeric judgment, but nowhere does he discuss the undisputed lines concerning a possible post-mortem judgment in the Iliad. These are not insignificant issues for my analysis. Both because of the importance of the so-called Orphic influence on Plato's myths and because the passages in the Iliad, along with those in the *Nekyia*, provide the best evidence of the antiquity of the Greek judgment of the dead.

This study is divided into four parts. The first part (consisting of chapter 1) surveys and analyzes the views of Plato concerning conduct and behavior as determinants for the afterlife. The second part (chapters 2-5) discusses the comparable views of the pre-Platonic Greeks. The third part (chapters 6-7) examines conduct and behavior as it affects the afterlife in Egyptian religious texts. Part four (chapter 8) provides an explicit comparison of the views of the two societies.

Part One: the Myths of Plato

Plato's work has been analyzed extensively, but usually with regard to his philosophy, and very little scholarly interest has been given to his myths as serious religious texts regarding the judgment of the dead.[7]

Since Plato's eschatological myths are the centerpiece of this inquiry, part one of this four-part study examines the Platonic eschatological myths, and provides a complete catalog and brief discussion of all references in them to conduct and behavior that affects one's fate in the afterlife.

Our first task, then, is to provide a systematic and through analysis of Plato's eschatological myths; it is this section that primarily differentiates this study from the others discussed above. The behavioral terms in the judgment scenes in the various myths of Plato in the *Gorgias, Phaedo, Republic* and *Phaedrus* will provide the benchmark against which all other evidence is compared.

Part Two: The Pre-Platonic Greeks

Part two examines the evolution of the concept of the afterlife from Homer to the Dramatists, also cataloging all references to the afterlife that mention conduct and behavior.

To what extent were conduct and behavior important before Plato? The tendency in much scholarship has been to play down the role of conduct and behavior or to deny that it was important at all. This section will trace a consistent interest in

---

7   Note that the Egyptian texts are truly religious and that the Greek texts for the most part are not. Homer and the Dramatists are literature and Plato is philosophy. The Greek works, however, do reflect the religious attitudes of at least some portion of their society. Therefore we can legitimately aspire to make comparisons once appropriate care is taken to account for likely context and genre.

the topic throughout Greece where there was always a strong undercurrent of belief, even when some intellectuals were denying the afterlife.

This part of the study demonstrates that the concept of reward and retribution in an afterlife, based on conduct in this life, is already found in Homer. However, it is in Pythagorean and Orphic circles of Greater Greece that it reaches its most dramatic development, and from that milieu provides such an enormous impact on Plato.

In Homer, contrary to the claims of some scholars (e.g., Erwin Rohde, *Psyche*, cited in chapter 2), we find an afterlife belief. There is conduct and behavior that figures into that afterlife, and there is a concept of something that continued to exist in the afterlife. After all, Homer says that dead men went to Hades as "something" and the gods punished them for breaking oaths. However, these ideas bore little resemblance to what was to develop over the next three or four hundred years.

Homer never denies an existence after death for anyone. However, this afterlife can range from that of a gibbering shadow or strengthless head to that of an articulate ghost and even to that of a very few heroic personalities being rewarded or punished.

Although there are several passages in the Homeric corpus that speak of an afterlife, only a few appear to indicate any sort of a punishment or reward in that afterlife.

Chapter 3 investigates the Greek works from Hesiod to the Orphic Tablets, including Pindar, Bacchylides, Simonides, Solon, Theognis, Heraclitus, Empedocles and the Eleusinian mysteries.

Here we see that the very little information concerning the afterlife found in Homer did not make much of an impression on his mainland intellectual successors. Hesiod, Solon, Theognis and even the later Democritus represent those thinkers who manifest no belief in a beneficent afterlife. Of course, it seems that all Greeks held to the fact of an afterlife—but in the form of the predominant Homeric concept of undifferentiated shades in Hades.[8]

---

8   The Eleusinian mysteries, contrary to the testimony of the intellectuals, did appear to offer some differentiation, which will be investigated in chapters 3, 4 and 8.

In the western Greek world new ideas were coming to the fore where Pythagoras incorporated, modified and promoted the ideas of the Orphics. Since they believed in the conduct of this life influencing the next one, ethical considerations became more prominent in post-mortem rewards and punishments. Heraclitus, Pindar and Empedocles express these newer ideas in their poetry and thereby set the stage for Plato, who will incorporate them into his own eschatological teachings.

Because of the supposed influence the Orphics had on Plato's myths, one of the more interesting scholarly debates found in this project is that concerning their belief in metempsychosis. Did they hold that belief? We will investigate this issue in this chapter by examining the so-called Orphic tablets of Olbia.

Chapter 4 discusses the Dramatists. Aeschylus and Pindar were born on opposite sides of the Greek world around 520 BCE, just within a generation of the death of Pythagoras. They have both been credited with being the first to posit an afterlife consequence for one's conduct in this life; however, the question of priority is less important than the fact that two Greeks on opposite sides of the Greek world came to a similar conclusion at approximately the same time.

All of the Dramatists both affirm and deny the afterlife in their writings, sometimes in the same work. Upon deeper analysis, we see that although all of the dramatists had much to say about an afterlife, there are actually very few strong statements linking conduct and behavior to the quality of that afterlife. This probably reflects the variety of contesting religious beliefs prevalent in 5th century Greece.

Chapter 5 reaches some conclusions on the Greek authors. Our investigation into the earlier Greek writers has shown that the Pythagorean/Orphic literature of the western Greek world was expounding on concepts such as the immortal soul, the soul's rebirth through cyclic lives and an afterlife consequence for one's conduct while alive. At this same time the mainland Greek intellectuals were still holding on to the predominant Homeric idea that included no beneficial afterlife.

It was in this intellectual environment that the Sophistic movement was creating a morally relativistic society where the laws were being questioned as having no support other that the conventions of the majority. Into this ethical breakdown came Socrates with his ideas of respect for the virtues and the laws, and building on the western Greek concepts of the soul, Plato followed through with support for the laws beyond that of mere convention, explaining in his dialogues and myths that the virtues were based in a much deeper reality.

All of the Greek literature reviewed in chapters 3 and 4 helped set the stage for what Plato later accomplished—some providing ideas in eschatology and others in ethics.

Part Three: The Egyptians

The third part of this study deals with the connection between conduct and behavior and the afterlife judgment in ancient Egypt up to the time of the *Book of the Dead*. An extensive catalog of Egyptian virtues and vices that have afterlife consequences are compiled from the religious texts of the 5th through 18th Dynasties (c. 2700-1200 BCE).

Chapters 6 and 7 investigate the classical judgment of the New Kingdom and the earliest religious texts of the Old and Middle Kingdoms.

After discussing some important concepts concerning the ancient Egyptians as they appear in the Egyptian source texts, four primary questions are examined:

1. What entity is being judged?
2. When did a blessed afterlife become available to all persons?
3. What exactly constitutes the Egyptian judgment of the dead?

Here, it should be noted that the question of the judgment of the dead is nuanced by such factors as: who has an afterlife and who is being judged (King vs. non-royal commoners) and what type of judgment is involved (judicial vs. general). I believe that these factors have historically confused the question and this has led to much divergent scholarly opinion.

4. At what point in the development of the concept of a blessed afterlife did conduct and behavior come to matter?

It should be noted that this is not the same question as—when was the king first judged or when was the commoner first judged or when did conscience first arise?

Thus, our inquiry concerns the link between conduct and behavior and the attainment of a good, bad or no afterlife and asks: Is that link found prior to the 9/10th Dynasty *Instruction for King Merikare*? More specifically, is it found in the Old Kingdom and especially in the 5/6th Dynasty *Pyramid Texts*?

Part Four: A Comparison

In chapter 8, the relationship between conduct and behavior and post-mortem beliefs during these three different phases of Egyptian and Greek development are compared and contrasted:

> The dawn of writing (Homer and *Pyramid Texts*),
> Intermediate texts (pre-Platonics and *Merikare*),
> Final texts (Plato and *Book of the Dead*).

In the earliest periods, the texts dealing with an afterlife appear to be concerned only with the elite: the king in Egyptian 5th Dynasty *Pyramid Texts* and the heroes in Homeric and Hesiodic Greece. This study argues that there is some evidence in the early texts of both societies for a belief that the common people could also be rewarded or punished in an afterlife. In later periods both societies' religious texts dealing with the afterlife exhibit a much more developed democratization.

As post-mortem beliefs became more democratic, conduct and behavior grew in importance. However, from the earliest time periods, both societies believe that the gods, primarily *Maat* in Egypt and *Dike* in Greece, are responsible for the proper ordering of the cosmos and those violations of that order will call down the most dire consequence—the loss of a beneficent afterlife.

General Conclusion

As we shall see, some scholars allow that Homer's people believed in an afterlife but denied that its quality depended on one's conduct and behavior in this life. Many other scholars, of both Egypt and Greece, would agree and deny that moral conduct, as we moderns understand it, mattered significantly in the lives of the people of the earliest period and many also claim that such moral conduct played no part in their beliefs of an afterlife.

This kind of attitude tended to blind others to being able to recognize the values which the ancients held in high esteem and, as we have seen, led many to think that their conduct and behavior was relegated only to magic[9] or ritual initiation or that violations of their moral customs were not thought to be social injustice, but only an affront to the honor of the gods.

Nevertheless, we maintain here that this belief in the gods' punishment for violations of custom was effectively used to maintain order in the believer's society. Without such consequentialist morality, for instance, one could violate his or her oaths with impunity, thereby destroying that order. Whether the belief in retribution is considered in the context of Egyptian *Maat* or Greek *Dike*, it helped control conduct and behavior inasmuch as violations of order were thought to invite a dire punishment.

In the course of pursuing a systematic comparison, this project intends to dispel the kind of thinking that disregards the role of ethics in the religious views of the Greeks of the earliest period and Egyptians, arguing that they were only concerned with 'ritual' or 'magic'.

---

9   For example, in speaking of the Egyptians, Adolf Erman noted that "beside the noble plant of religion flourishes the rampant weed of magic" (Adolf Erman, *Die Agyptische Religion* [Berlin: G. Reimer, 1905], 148); and James Breasted decried the attempts of a "priestly product" to secure moral vindication by magical means. James Henry Breasted, *The Dawn of Conscience* (New York: Charles Scribner's Sons, 1934), 264f.

CHAPTER 1

Conduct and Behavior as Determinants for the Afterlife in Plato's Eschatological Myths

ὁ δὲ ἀνεξέταστος βίος οὐ βιωτός[10]

The above quotation is perhaps one of the most famous of Socrates' sayings. Less well known are the lines that precede this quote:

> If I say that it is impossible for me to keep quiet because that means dis-obeying the god, you will not believe me and will think I am being ironical. On the other hand, if I say that it is the greatest good for a man to discuss virtue every day and those other things about which you hear me conversing and testing myself and others, for the unexamined life is not worth living [ὁ δὲ ἀνεξέταστος βίος οὐ βιωτός] for men, you will believe me even less (*Apology* 37e-38a).[11]

Socrates was interested in examining his and the lives of the citizens of Athens due to the religious skepticism and moral relativism[12] that had been advocated by the Sophists of his day. They had built on the framework of the earlier materialist philosophers who had posited a world of flux and unreliable sense perceptions,

---

10   "The unexamined life is not worth living" (Plato *Apology* 38a).

11   Unless otherwise noted, the translation of the *Apology* will be from G.M.A. Grube, "Apology," in *Plato: Complete Works*, ed. John M. Cooper (Indianapolis/Cambridge: Hackett Publishing Company, 1997). Also note, since many Platonic translations will be taken from Cooper, the reference will hereafter be abbreviated PCW.

12   "Although you [Socrates] claim to be pursuing the truth, you're in fact bringing the discussion around to crowd-pleasing vulgarities that are admirable only by law [convention (νόμος)] and not by nature [φύσις]. And these, nature and law, are for the most part opposed to each other" (*Gorg.* 482e; trans., Donald J. Zeyl, "Gorgias," *PCW*, 827). The Sophists claimed that the laws of society were merely a convention that varied from place to place and since they were relative to time/place customs, were therefore, not binding, as were the natural laws.

and when Socrates came to realize that these teachings were not conducive to the well-being of people, he was led to "abandon them as barren and devote himself to the defense of moral standards. He was convinced that 'justice' and 'courage' were realities."[13] This search for universal definitions would later lead Plato to discover the universal realities in the realm of the Forms.

In Plato's dialogues, Socrates' constant question is: How should men behave? He is not looking for a means of determining if a certain behavior is virtuous or not, but rather what virtue itself is, which "is to be answered not by enumerating virtues but by putting forth characteristics common to virtues."[14]

In the *Apology*, Socrates further says, as he does about most issues, that he is ignorant about life after death. For all he knows it may be either an eternal dreamless sleep or an exit to an afterlife where he can communicate with the heroes and the gods (*Apol.* 40-1). This apparent agnosticism[15] may or may not have attached itself to Plato—it certainly did to his pupil, Aristotle[16]—but Plato uses mythical

---

13 W.K.C. Guthrie, *The Revolution in the Mind* (Westwood MA: Paperbook Press, 1991), 6.

14 See *Meno* 72cd. Laura Grimm, *Definitions in Plato's Meno* (Oslo: Oslo University Press, 1962), 9.

15 Socrates' agnosticism may have resulted from his general denial of knowledge and deStrycker makes a good argument for the Socrates of the *Apology* as having a belief in an afterlife. See E. deStrycker, *Plato's Apology of Socrates*, ed. S.R. Slings (Leiden: E.J. Brill, 1994), 217, 229.

16 Aristotle questioned that the soul is immortal in these lines: "For men knowingly wish for some things that are impossible, such as to rule over the whole of mankind and to be immortal" (*Eudemian Ethics* 1225b, trans., Michael Woods, Aristotle: *Eudemian Ethics* [Oxford: Clarendon Press, 1992], 29); "if anyone were to assert that he was choosing the impossible, he would be considered a fool. But wish can be for the impossible, e.g., immortality" (*Nicomachean Ethics* 1111b, trans., Martin Ostwald, *Nicomachean Ethics* [New York: Bobbs-Merrill, 1962], 58). However, elsewhere he relented on the higher part of the soul, the reason: "But if there is something that remains after, this should be considered. For in some cases there is nothing to prevent this; for example, if the soul is such, not all of it but only the intellect, for it is perhaps impossible for all of the soul to remain" (*Metaphysics* 1070a, trans., Hippocrates G. Apostle, Aristotle's *Metaphysics* [Bloomington: Indiana University Press, 1966], 199); "It is, however, only when separated that it [the soul] is its true self, and this, its essential nature, alone is immortal and eternal" (*De Anima* 429b, trans., Robert Drew Hicks, *Aristotle: De Anima* [New York: Arno Press, 1976], 135).

religious stories handed down to him in order to illustrate and complete his philosophical points. In what is believed to be the first of these religious myths, in the *Gorgias*, Plato relates the myth (μῦθον) as an account (λόγον) that he will tell as being true (ἀληθῆ).[17] Plato's most famous myths are those concerning a judgment in the afterlife.[18]

Plato, in his eschatological myths,[19] claims that there will be a punishment or reward based on whether or not one has been virtuous and attempts to specify what conduct and behavior will result in an afterlife punishment or reward.

Therefore, our initial procedure to discover these conduct and behaviors will be to examine the judgment scenes in the various myths of Plato in the *Gorgias, Phaedo, Republic* and *Phaedrus*.[20] Then, we shall look at some additional

---

17 At *Gorg.* 523a. Cf. 524a-b, 526d, 527a-b. However, the *Phaedrus* at 265b questions the myth's plausibility and the *Phaedo* at 114d is not so sure of its truth since Socrates says: "No sensible man would insist that these things are as I have described them, but I think it is fitting for a man to risk the belief…this, is true about our souls and their dwelling places…and a man should repeat this to himself as if it were an incantation" (114d, trans., Grube, *Plato: Complete Works*, 97). Cf. Dodds, *Plato: Gorgias* (Oxford: Clarendon Press, 1959), 376, 385.

18 For Plato's eschatological myths, see section "Overview of the Platonic Myths" following.

19 This book has been using the term eschatological to denote the myths of interest to us. A debate in late antiquity concerned just what to include. Olympiodorus, in his *Commentary*, claimed that three myths were classified as *nekyia* (an underworld story as in Homer's Odyssey book 11): *Gorgias, Phaedo*, and *Republic*. He claims that Iamblicus included only two, omitting the *Gorgias*. Olympiodorus, *Commentary on Plato's Gorgias*, trans. Robin Jackson, Kimon Lycos, Harold Tarrant (Leiden: Brill, 1998), 46.9. This paper will follow Olympiodorus in including the three *nekyia* and add the *Phaedrus* to the list. The reason is that we are not just interested in the underworld but in Plato's 'otherworld' judgments on the soul.

20 For general treatments of Plato's myths, see (in original chronological order)—Stewart (1905), Frutiger (1930), Edelstein (1949), Zaslavsky (1981), Annas (1982), Brisson (1982): J.A. Stewart, *The Myths of Plato* ed. G.R. Levy (Carbondale: Southern Illinois University Press, 1960); Perceval Frutiger, *Les Mythes de Platon* (Paris: Libraire Felix Alcan, 1976); L. Edelstein, "The Function of the Myth in Plato's Philosophy," X, no. 4 (Oct 1949): 463-481; R. Zaslavsky, *Platonic Myth and Platonic Writing* (Lanham MD: University Press of America, 1981); Julia Annas, "Plato's Myths of Judgement," Phronesis XXVII, no. 2 (1982): 119-143; Luc Brisson, *Platon, les mots et les mythes* (Paris: La Decouverte, 1994).

works[21] of Plato where conduct and behavior is discussed. Finally, we shall look at the opinions of other Greek writers regarding proper conduct and behavior and whether or not they envisioned them affecting reward and punishment in this life and/or in the afterlife.

What Entity is Being Judged?

Ψυχήπᾶσα ἀθάνατος[22]

Phaedrus 245c.

This statement of Plato's is his most direct comment on the major property of the human soul (ψύχη). By the time of Plato, many believed that the soul had acquired the attribute of immortality, although many of Socrates' interlocutors had to be convinced of this fact.[23]

In order to evaluate the impact of conduct and behavior on the afterlife, we need to determine exactly what is being judged in Plato's myths. Generally, it is the

---

21   A great deal of scholarly effort has gone into determining the chronological order of Plato's works. This is important for this study since his myths of the judgment surely evolved over time and we want to see how his eschatological ideas developed. The general consensus is: Plato's early period: *Apology, Charmides, Crito, Euthyphro, Hippias Major, Ion, Laches, Protagoras, GORGIAS, Hippias Minor, Lysis, Menexenus, Republic 1*. Plato's middle period: *Meno, Cratylus, PHAEDO, Symposium, REPUBLIC 2-10, PHAEDRUS, Euthydemus, Parmenides, Theaetetus*. Plato's late period: *Timaeus, Critias, Sophist, Politicus, Philebus, Seventh Letter, Laws*. See: Paul Shorey, *The Unity of Plato's Thought* (Chicago: University of Chicago Press, 1903), 30-40; David Ross, *Plato's Theory of Ideas* (Oxford: Clarendon Press, 1951), 1-10; Terence Irwin, *Plato's Moral Theory* (Oxford: Clarendon Press, 1977), 291-3; Richard Kraut. ed., *The Cambridge Companion to Plato* (Cambridge: Cambridge University Press, 1992), xii; Leonard Brandwood, *The Chronology of Plato's Dialogues* (Cambridge: Cambridge University Press, 1990), passim.

22   Every soul is immortal.

23   Glaucon in *Republic* 608d is surprised at Socrates' claim of the soul's immortality and indestructibility. This is an indication that there was some debate about the immortality of the soul among intellectuals at that time and place, in apparent contrast with the Pythagorean/Orphic ideas coming out of Sicily and western *Magna Graecia*.

immortal soul of the dead person. However, Plato's description of the soul changes; at first it is simple then becomes complex as the myths develop.[24]

Overview of the Platonic Myths

The Gorgias

Context. The *Gorgias* contains the first of Plato's eschatological myths. According to Dodds, "the main ethical thesis of the *Gorgias* is already stated at *Crito* 49b4."[25] The *Crito* is one of the earlier Socratic dialogues and Dodds places the *Gorgias* late in the early works, in part because of its apparent Pythagorean influence. Plato's middle period is when he incorporated Pythagorean ideas, such as reincarnation, in his dialogues. These ideas are absent from his earlier works, so the *Gorgias* is either late in the early period or early in the middle period.[26]

Myth plays an important part in the dialogues of Plato,[27] and explaining their purpose in his dialogues goes back to antiquity. Myth is to be considered neither as allegory nor as the revelation of a higher knowledge. The myths may be grouped into those dealing with metaphysics or science and those dealing with soul or ethics. Human reason can grasp the former through rational knowledge, which is potentially capable of affirmation and certainty. Such is not the case with issues dealing with the soul or ethics.

In the absence of higher revelation, there is no possibility of scientific affirmation and certainty, and rational knowledge must be supplemented with something

---

24   For those readers wanting more detailed information, the Platonic attributes of the soul are examined more extensively in Appendix B: "Additional Investigation of Plato's Psyche."

25   Dodds, Plato: *Gorgias*, 22. Regardless of the consequences to ourselves, "wrongdoing is in every way harmful and shameful to the wrongdoer" (trans., Grube, *Plato: Complete Works*, 43).

26   Dodd's discussion of the date of composition is on his pages 18-30. Irwin agrees with Dodds. Dodds, *Plato: Gorgias*, 18-30; Terence Irwin, *Plato Gorgias* (Oxford: Oxford Press, 1979), 1-8. Gallop's commentary disagrees, placing it in the middle period. The question is: to what extent are there Pythagorean ideas in the Gorgias? David Gallop, *Plato: Phaedo* (Oxford: Clarendon Press, 1990), 74.

27   See the discussions in Edelstein, "The Foundation of Myth in Plato's Philosophy," 463-481, and in Bruce Gottfried, "Plato's use of Myth," in *Plato's Dialogues*, ed. Gerald A. Press (Lanham MD: Rowman & Littlefield Publishers, 1993), 194f.

that speaks to the irrational part of the soul and can arouse one's passions and hopes. All parts, rational and irrational, of the soul must be nourished by philosophy, as Plato claims in the *Timaeus*.[28]

Socrates usually denies that his myths are to be accepted exactly as described, but that one should nevertheless take them as true with a general kind of certainty. In the *Gorgias*, Socrates is not so reticent and more forcefully claims that the myth is a true rational account.

> Hear then, as they say, a very fine rational account (λόγου) which you consider a myth (μῦθον), as I think, but I consider it a rational account; for I shall tell you things I am going to tell as being true (ἀληθῆ)" (Gorg. 523a).[29]

The earlier Socrates had stated that one would do good if one but had knowledge. Now, he recognizes that there are other facets of the soul that may thwart the rational part and must therefore resort to a myth that speaks to the irrational in order to complete the dialectical argument.

Socrates wants to assert his theme that philosophy is superior to rhetoric and he says:

> If I came to my end through lack of flattering rhetoric, I know well that you would see me bearing death easily. For no one fears dying itself, who is not all in all most irrational and unmanly, but he fears doing injustice; for to arrive in Hades with one's soul full of many unjust deeds is the ultimate of all evils. And if you wish, I am willing to tell you a rational account, that this is so (522de).[30]

---

28 "There are three distinct types of soul…each with its own motions…make sure that their motions remain proportionate to each other…provide for it the nourishment and the motions that are proper to it" (*Tim.* 89e-90c, trans., Donald J. Zeyl, "Timaeus," in *PCW*, 1288-9).

29 Cf. *Gorg.* 524ab, 526d, 527ab. See also Irwin, *Plato: Gorgias*, 242. Dodds tends to doubt that Plato believed his myths with an appeal to *Phaedo* 114d, which indeed expresses doubt. However, Dodds softens his doubts with an appeal to the Seventh Letter 335a2 where Plato says that we should seriously believe the logos as a 'truth of religion.' Dodds, *Plato: Gorgias*, 376-7.

30 All Gorgias translations are those of Nichols unless otherwise noted. James H. Nichols, Jr., *Plato: Gorgias* (Ithica: Cornell University Press, 1998), 123;

The myth (523a-527d).[31]

> Now in the time of Cronos there was the following law concerning human beings, and it exists always and still to this day among the gods, that he among human beings who went through life justly and piously, when he came to his end, would go away to the islands of the blessed to dwell in total happiness apart from evils, while he who lived unjustly and godlessly would go to the prison of retribution and judgment, which they call Tartarus (523ab).

The soul will bear the marks of life's experiences. An evil life will show the scars on the soul so that it may be readily judged (*Gorg.* 524c-e). This conception has the soul being judged without a judicial inquiry, approaching something like "a law of spiritual gravity,"[32] where judges are not needed and where the 'judgment' is truly automatic. Nevertheless, three judges who look at the scars, Rhadamanthus, Aeacus and Minos,[33] are stationed in the meadow at a cross-roads where two paths fork off, one to the Isles of the Blest and the other to Tartarus.

Souls are determined by their scars to be curable or incurable and then assigned to the appropriate place in the underworld. The incurables[34] who have committed the most heinous crimes and misdeeds beyond cure are condemned to Tartarus for eternity.[35] The curables are further differentiated by degree of 'virtue' (e.g.,

---

31 A summary of Plato's myths is found at the end of this chapter and a table graphically comparing them is in Appendix D: "Summary of the Four Myths, Table 2."

32 Dodds, *Plato: Gorgias*, 379.

33 This is the only eschatological myth that names the judges, although Plato first names them, along with Triptolemus, at *Apology* 41a. This is the first and simplest of the four myths and I believe that Plato left out the names in later myths because he came to have a different (i.e., automatic, karma-like) judging mechanism in mind. Plato's last work, Laws, has a succinct description of this automatic mechanism at 904b-e.

34 Plato appeals to Homeric precedent by mentioning the famous trio: Tantalus, Sisyphus and Tityus (525e), Cf. *Od.* 11.576-600. At 492e-493d, Plato describes the soul of the intemperate as being forced to carry water in a perforated jar. He also alludes to the possibly Pythagorean and/or Orphic notion of 'our bodies are our tombs' and asks, "if living is being dead, and being dead is living."

35 *Gorg.* 525bc. It is difficult to reconcile Plato's principle that punishment should always be of some benefit with his contradictory eternal punishment. He does allow that the benefit may be, not to the punished, but to others as an example. The Neoplatonists had a real problem with this concept and Olympiodorus in his *Commentary* goes to great lengths to prove that the punishments are, indeed, only purgatorial. Olympiodorus, *Commentary* 50.2-50.4, 317-20. Cf. *Gorg.* 512a, Laws 854cd, 862c.

the virtue of a ruler like Aristides is defined by 'administering justly what is committed to their charge') and each suffers what is fitting (526bc). There is no explanation of the method by which the curables are cured; however, it is offered that they go to the prison in Hades where by suffering and seeing the torment of the incurables they rid themselves of iniquity (525a-c) and presumably eventually enter the Isles of the Blest.[36] Only the philosopher can be admitted directly to the Isles of the Blest.[37] The prison, where purgation takes place, will be an idea taken up by Christianity in its 4th and later centuries in order to solve its own 'judgment of the dead' problems.[38]

In this myth we see that Plato is using a story that appears already to be in the popular milieu: there is a judgment in the afterlife and one is judged according to one's goodness or badness in this life. The myth presents a theodicy in that it shows that what was not right in this life may at last be set right in the next (527de). It is also a final, once and for all,[39] judgment in that the soul will be judged once and never return to this life again.

---

[36]   *Gorg.* 523a-b. I say 'presumably' here, else why the phrases at *Gorg.* 525bc: "become better" by "paying the just penalty" and "profited from it" and "be released from injustice"?

[37]   *Gorg.* 526c. The other 'curables' presumably were first purged then admitted to the Isles of the Blest. This is only my inference since there are only two permanent afterlife alternatives in the *Gorgias*. However, Plato does not explicitly comment on this purging of the other curables. See the following note for more details.

[38]   E. R. Dodds points out that this concept of purgatory is unlike that of the Catholic one in that it "prepared its victims not for Heaven but for a return to Earth" (Dodds, *Plato: Gorgias*, 375, 381). I maintain that he is incorrect: the *Gorgias* did not prepare for a return to Earth, as there is no mention of reincarnation in the *Gorgias*. Dodds claimed that the doctrine of rebirth in the *Gorgias* is tacitly implied at 493c where "others, however, do profit from [the example of the suffering of the incurables] for all time…visible warnings to unjust men who are ever arriving," and 525c where "others [the curables] are benefited [presumably for rebirth] who see that for their faults they [incurables] are undergoing the greatest, most painful, and most fearful suffering…[as examples] for the unjust". However, this rebirth claim is rejected by both Annas and Irwin, and I would agree with them that there is no reincarnation in the *Gorgias*. Annas, "Plato's Myths of Judgment," 124; Irwin, *Plato: Gorgias*, 246. Indeed, I hold that not only is there no purging for a return to Earth, but that Plato gives only two alternatives: the Isles of the Blest and Tartarus.

[39]   In her excellent article, Julia Annas claims that the *Gorgias* myth is most like the Christian last judgment in that it is final and "justice, once done, stays done" (Annas, "Plato's Myths of Judgment," 123).

Conduct and behavior.[40] Just what, then, are these behaviors and conduct that are judged? In *Gorgias* 523ab, those who live justly (δικαίως)[41] and piously (ὁσίως) go to the Isles of the Blest (μακάρων νήσους) and those who live godlessly (ἀθέως) and unjustly (ἀδίκως) are stamped as curable or incurable and go to the prison in Hades or to Tartarus.

These adjectives are given concrete descriptions in 525a-525d for the godless and unjust where it is said: the soul is filled with scars from false oaths (ἐπιορκιῶν) and injustice (ἀδικίας); all things are crooked from lying (ψεύδους) and boasting (ἀλαζονείας); the soul is full of asymmetry (ἀσυμμετρίας) and ugliness (αἰσχρότητος) from arrogant power (ἐξουσίας), luxury (τρυφῆς), insolence (ὕβρεως) and incontinence (ἀκρατείας); those who are the greatest make the most impious (ἀνοσιώτατα) errors (ἁμαρτήματα ἁμαρτάνουσι).

Gorgias 526c-527d describes the just and pious: the soul that has lived piously (ὁσίως) and with truth (ἀληθείας); one who has done his own business (πράξαντος) and not been a busybody (πολυπραγμονήσαντος) in life; one who really is good (ἀγαθός) and noble (καλός), practicing virtue (ἀρετήν).

Earlier in the dialogue with Socrates, Callicles had made the claims that: the grasping for more that one's share (πλεονεκτεῖν) was not shameful (αἰσχρόν) or unjust (ἄδικον) (483c), and that only the uncourageous person (ἀνανδρία) praised self-control (σωφροσύνη) and justice (δικαιοσύνη) (492b). However, Plato's reason for writing this dialogue was to show that just the opposite was true and that one "will suffer nothing terrible, if you really are noble (καλός) and good (ἀγαθόj), practicing virtue (ἀρετήν) (527d). Since at 504d, Socrates had claimed that justice and self-control provide for the regular (τάξεσι) and orderly (κοσμήσεσιν) states of the soul and are called lawfulness (νόμιμον) and law (νόμος), we see that Plato had overcome Callicles' appeal to the law of nature (φύσις) with his appeal to the justice of νόμος.

Some of the above terms appear to be rather circular definitions that need defining themselves. This circularity was an ongoing problem in all of Socrates'

---

[40] Conduct and behavior terms for all of Plato's myths are summarized in Appendix E: "Tables of Conduct and Behavior Terms in Greek and English Translation."

[41] Greek terms are printed in the parts of speech as they appear in the Greek text of Plato for all <u>Conduct and Behavior</u> sections of this project. However, they will be stated in the nominative case in the comparison tables.

dialogues since his method of argument (<u>elenchus</u>) usually ended in aporia, an impasse, thus failing to arrive at any clear definitions.

The Phaedo

<u>Context</u>. This is the second of the eschatological myths of Plato. David Gallop allows that "the date of the composition is uncertain, but the work is usually assigned to Plato's 'middle period'...written more than a decade after the events it purports to depict."[42]

The story opens with Phaedo telling his friend Echecrates of the last day of Socrates. He says that:

> Although I was witnessing the death of one who was my friend, I had no feeling of pity, for the man appeared happy both in manner and words as he died nobly and without fear...it struck me that even in going down to the underworld he was going with the god's blessing and that he would fare well when he got there, if anyone ever does (58d-59a).[43]

This story tells the tale of immediate concern to one who is about to die; namely, just what is the nature of the soul and does it survive death. It takes place in the town of Phlius in the presence of a group of Pythagoreans[44], which leads us to suspect that the description of the soul and afterlife will contain a bit of Pythagorean theory.

---

[42]   David Gallop, *Plato: Phaedo* (Oxford: Clarendon Press, 1975), 74.

[43]   All translations of the *Phaedo* will be from G.M.A. Grube, "Phaedo," in *PCW*, 49-100.

[44]   Phlius was a Pythagorean enclave and Echecrates was an adherent, as were Cebes and Simmias the disciples of Philolaus, the leading Pythagorean at Thebes. Of course, one must wonder why Pythagoreans needed to be convinced of an afterlife, unless they were adherents only to their master's scientific theories by this time. Some scholars who have argued for a Pythagorean connection are David Ross, *Plato's Theory of Ideas*, 160-4; E.R. Dodds, *The Greeks and the Irrational* (Berkley: University of California Press, 1951), 209; Walter Burkert, *Lore and Science in Ancient Pythagoreanism*, trans. Edwin L. Milnar, Jr. (Cambridge: Harvard University Press, 1972), chapter 1 passim; idem, Greek Religion (Cambridge: Harvard University Press, 1985), 296-304. Other *Phaedo* commentators have also argued for the connection: Gallop, Plato: Phaedo, 74, 144, 148; Rowe, *Plato: Phaedo* (Cambridge: Cambridge University Press, 1993), 174; David Bostock, *Plato's Phaedo* (Oxford: Clarendon Press, 1986), 29.

Simmias and Cebes are the doubters whom Socrates must convince, not only of the pre-existence, but also of the durability of the soul though a number of future lives. Even with his proof of pre-existence and durability, the doubters still refuse to believe that the soul can last forever (95c). The doubters later acquiesce somewhat but hold private misgivings. Thus Socrates explains that, "if death were escape from everything, it would be a great boon to the wicked to get rid of the body and their wickedness together with their soul (107c)."[45] But, if the soul is really immortal, "there is no escape from evil or salvation for it except by being as good and wise as possible" in this life.[46] With that, Socrates launches the first part of the myth on the soul.

The myth (107c-108c, 112e-115a).

> We are told that when each person dies, the guardian spirit who was allotted to him in life proceeds to lead him to a certain place...after being judged, proceed to the underworld with the guide who has been appointed to lead them thither from here. Having there undergone what they must and stayed there the appointed time, they are led back here by another guide after long periods of time (107de).

The myth in the *Phaedo* is told in two parts: in part one (106e-108c)[47] Socrates says that "when death comes to man, the mortal part of him dies it seems, but the deathless part goes away safe and indestructible...and our souls will really dwell

---

45   See Gallop, *Plato: Phaedo*, 223.

46   Socrates is assuming that the soul is immortal in this passage, not trying to prove it to be so in a Kantian way. That is, the soul is not immortal in order that it may complete doing its duty or to be punished or rewarded for doing or not doing so. Rather, evil is intrinsically detrimental to the soul both now and after death. Still, immortality is only an assumption, since he later says, "it is fitting for a man to risk the belief...that this, or something like this, is true about our souls...since the soul is evidently immortal, and a man should repeat this to himself as if it were an incantation [χρὴ τὰ τοιαῦτα ὥσπερ ἐπᾴδειν ἑαυτῳ]" (114d). In other words, do this as though it were true. Two thousand years later Pascal would make the same wager. Cf. *Rep* 608a, *Phaedo* 77e-8a on singing charms.

47   Even before relating the main myth, Socrates says at 81de that some souls that have not been freed and purified never even make it to Hades but hang around in the visible world and again become imprisoned in the physical body. This is not mentioned again in the two parts of the main myth. Hanging around the tomb seems to reflect the pre-historic cults of the dead.

in the underworld" (106e-107a). The person is led by a guardian spirit assigned
to him or her in life to a place where the dead are gathered. There the person is
judged and goes to that other world where they spend a time until another guide
brings them back (107de). Furthermore the bad soul which is passionately
attached to the body hovers around the visible world for a long time, then is led
away by force to Hades.[48] "But the soul that has led a pure and moderate life
finds gods to guide it, and each of them dwells in a place suited for it (108bc)."

Some scholars see a problem here in that all souls are said to be brought back.[49]
The problem is, why are they brought back? To Julia Annas[50] it appears here that
all souls will be reincarnated appropriately to a judgment. She sees this as a
contradiction, that in this part of the story, literally all souls are reincarnated,
including the philosopher's, but this act of reincarnation had been previously
deemed a punishment, according to *Phaedo* 81c-82d[51] for a former bad life.

Additionally, it would seem that the souls have already suffered what is appropriate in the other world, thus a rebirth would then be a form of double jeopardy.

This idea of reincarnation as a punishment follows from the fact that Plato claims
that the excellence of the soul is its lack of attachment to the body. Good souls
separate easily at death but bad souls are too attached to the body to disengage
easily (108a).

---

[48]   This is contrary to 81c-82a for the bad soul, in that there the soul is never taken to
    Hades at all but wanders around until it is again imprisoned in a body (81e).

[49]   David Gallop rightly sees a conflict between the myth at 114c and 81a ("those who
    have purified themselves...live in the future altogether without a body" and "truly
    spend the rest of time with the gods") and the apparent claims of endless rebirths at
    77d. The purified are supposed to be immune from rebirth (i.e., not brought back as
    they also are in 107e). David Gallop, *Plato: Phaedo*, 224.

[50]   She says, "the myth begins by saying that souls are guided back when they have
    suffered what is appropriate (107de). This leads us to expect that reward and punish-
    ment after death will consist in appropriate reincarnations" (Julia Annas, "Plato's
    Myths of Judgment," 127).

[51]   "No one may join the company of the gods who has not practiced philosophy
    (82b)," and all others will be embodied again in some form of animal or human
    (81e-82b).

The identity of the judges is never divulged in this myth. All that is said is that we should be judged and go to that other world for a time. The details of that other world will be more fully explained in the second part of Socrates' myth but, as we shall see, the judges are not really identified there either.

Part two of the myth (112e-115a) comes after a treatise on cosmology and geography of "the true earth" (ἡ ὡς ἀληθῶς γῆ; 109c)[52] where Socrates increases the number of his afterlife destinations and is more explicit on what happens to the dead souls. They are now divided into five classes and most of the classes eventually go to the Acherusian lake to spend a time, then are reincarnated as living beings (113a). Those who have lived neither well nor ill go to the Acheron where they are purified, pay any penalty for wrongdoing and are then rewarded according to merit (113de). The "incurables" are cast eternally into Tartarus by appropriate destiny (113e).[53] Those who have committed great crimes, but are curable, are also cast into Tartarus but can eventually be brought to the Acherusian lake to be released if forgiven, not by the gods, but by those whom they wronged (113e-114b).[54] Those who excelled in holy living without benefit of philosophy are

---

[52] The 'true earth' is described as being very different from the earth of our common perception. On this 'true earth' we humans live in one of the 'hollows' yet believe it to be the entire earth. There are many other hollows, some deeper or less deep than ours. There is the surface where superhuman beings dwell and the subterranean depths, full of rivers and lakes, where the souls of most of the dead go for a time. Above the surface, in the pure ether beyond the stars, is the realm of the Forms.

[53] *Phaedo* 113e. This punishment, although harsh, lacks the sadistic quality of *Rep.* 615d-616a, where the souls of the incurables are taunted with freedom only to be denied at the last moment. This less severe punishment may reflect the heightened personal responsibility required by *Rep.* 617e, where one's daemon or guardian spirit was not assigned, but rather freely chosen. Whereas, here in the *Phaedo*, one has less personal responsibility since the daemon is simply allotted (107d).

[54] Here Plato has given two problems for the guilty. The first is that the victim must forgive the perpetrator. The gods do not have a say in this so it is up to the person one has harmed, which is a chancy proposition. The second problem is that the victim may not even be in the Lake when the guilty party comes by—another chancy prospect. The fifth century CE commentator, Damascius, made this second observation and asked how, then, is the guilty ever to be forgiven? His solution was that a 'justice phantom' resembling the victim is conjured up to do it. Damascius, *The Greek Commentaries on Plato's Phaedo*, ed. L.G. Westerink (Amsterdam: North-Holland Publishing Company, 1977), II.148, 364-6.

freed to dwell upon the surface of the true earth (114bc).[55] The philosophers will live without bodies forever in a still more beautiful abode (114c).

Thus we have five classes of the dead and four destinations: (1) most are reborn to the hollows (the average and the forgiven curables); (2) a very few go to the highest abode (the philosophers only); (3) a few more go to the surface of the true earth (the pious without philosophy); (4) a few are condemned eternally to Tartarus (the incurably evil).

Annas also sees a contradiction between parts one and two of the myth; she claims that: "now souls are judged and then rewarded or punished not in another life here but in the afterlife there, not by appropriate reincarnation but more traditionally, by torture in hell or bliss in heaven."[56] This is true of a few souls, but the myth clearly states that <u>most</u> of the souls will be reincarnated after a time at the Acherusian lake.

Still, another problem persists for those few as she further says: "if the philosophers' reward is final disembodiment, then the Isles of the Blest, the second-best reward of the non-philosophical good, will have to represent some kind of embodiment [a repulsive punishment]."[57] That last statement, I believe, does not necessarily follow with its implications of embodiments as a punishment. Just because there are two separate final reward locations for the purged and for the philosophically purified, there is no logical necessity that a disembodiment as a reward can not be available to both.[58] Therefore, although the two parts really

---

[55]   Cf. *Phaedo* 109b and 111b. "the earth itself is pure" and has "groves and temples dedicated to the gods, in which the gods really dwell."

[56]   Annas, "Plato's Myths of Judgment," 127. I disagree in that most are reincarnated from the Acherusian lake. The few others are placed in Tartarus, a supra-earth or even better realm. See my summary in the text above.

[57]   The Isles of the Blest are not mentioned in this myth, only the similar Elysion. The second best reward is the surface of the true earth, rather than the hollows of the normal earth on which we ordinary humans live (*Phaedo* 114c). White agrees with Annas that those humans and gods on the surface, although having far better bodies, nevertheless have bodies. Annas, "Plato's Myths of Judgment," 128. David White, *Myth and Metaphysics in Plato's Phaedo* (London: Associated University Presses, 1989), 248-9.

[58]   C. J. Rowe states that one group is distinguished from the other in that one does have bodies of a sort and refers to 111a-c, which describes the earth's surface above the hollows in which we live. But, Socrates, in a seeming contradiction, says at 76d

cannot be reconciled concerning whether all or just some souls are reincarnated, the force of Annas' thesis concerning the punishing embodiment of rewarded souls appears to be somewhat mitigated by the fact that the bodies under consideration are not of "our" kind.

Obviously the judgment in the *Phaedo* is no longer once-and-for-all as it was in the *Gorgias*. Now most of the souls of the dead are reincarnated to the normal earth as a punishment for a previous average or bad life. Even the pious on the true earth will die again. But, the reward or punishment for the philosophers and the incurably evil is eventually permanent and final.

If we take the two parts of the myth as a unity, we see that souls are judged, then given appropriate rewards on the true earth or even more beautiful abode, or punishments in Tartarus or 'purgatory'. This begs two questions: first, who are the judges and, second, where is 'the even more beautiful abode'? Could the judges be other souls or Destiny or even the gods? Other souls can forgive the curables, and Destiny is claimed only to put the incurables into Tartarus, but the gods are not mentioned as doing anything. So the answer to 'who are the judges?' is none of these three possibilities. Then, who are they?

Addressing my first question further, who would have the authority to allow philosophers to go immediately from the "hollows" to the even more beautiful abode?

---

that "the souls existed previously…apart from bodies, and they had intelligence" (Rowe, *Plato: Phaedo*, 289). So, which is it—bodies or no bodies in that other world? A possible solution to this dilemma can be found in the 15th century Neoplatonist, Marsilio Ficino's *Commentary* in chapter 8 where he postulates the existence of four types of bodies: earthly body composed of all four elements; sub-celestial body of air; celestial body of aither; and the ultimate union with the World-soul of the cosmic body (Michael J.B. Allen, *The Platonism of Marsilio Ficino* [Berkley: University of California Press, 1984], 97-8). Can these differentiations solve Annas' problem of the injustice of reincarnation into 'our' kind of body since the 'men' described at 111a-c [presumed to be the rewarded pious], are superior to us in every way? Therefore, the punishing type of reincarnation is to be refleshed in the 'hollows', not on the true earth. It is possible that Plato had something like this in mind since these concepts appear in the pre-Socratics such as Heraclitus and the popular ideas of ethereal or astral immortality, which we'll see in Chapters 3 and 4. Otherwise, we are stuck with the inconsistencies.

The unmentioned gods are not likely candidates since they apparently make their dwelling on the surface on the true earth.[59] Therefore, something higher than the gods must have the authority to allow philosophers to enter a higher realm than the gods' own. Plato does not explicitly address this issue but logically a judge of those higher than the gods must be assumed to be some mechanism equal to or exceeding the authority of the Forms.

What of my second question, 'Where is the even more beautiful abode'? Socrates had no time to describe it, probably because it was beside the point to his case, but modern scholars have attempted to identify the place. Annas[60] says that other scholars have suggested "the natal stars of the *Timaeus*."[61] What Plato might well have had in mind but did not specify is an alternate possibility that the 'even more beautiful abode' is, indeed, the very realm of the Forms themselves.[62]

Furthermore, in light of my first question of "who are the judges" and my proffered initial suggestion that the "who" is at least equal to the Forms, it follows logically therefore that the only authority that could possibly judge those souls who will reside in a higher place than the gods themselves do must be the Forms or even the Good itself.[63]

---

59   David White argues persuasively that the gods reside on the surface of the true earth. However, Rowe claims that the 'even more beautiful' place is, presumably, the habitations of the gods since at 82b it states: "No one may join the company of the gods who has not practiced philosophy." This is a direct contradiction of White's thesis that the Philosophers have no need of communion with the gods. David White, *Myth and Metaphysics in Plato's Phaedo*, 249, 265. Rowe, Plato: Phaedo, 289.

60   Annas mentions Burnet and Stewart as two of those scholars. See footnote following. Annas, "Plato's Myths of Judgment," 128.

61   Stewart, *The Myths of Plato*, 127. Agreeing with Stewart is John Burnet, *Plato's Phaedo* (1911; reprint, Oxford: Clarendon Press, 1959), 142. However, Rowe disagrees stating that, "These are presumably the habitations of the gods," citing 82bc as proof. Rowe, *Plato's Phaedo*, 289.

62   David White has addressed my second question in his commentary on the Phaedo, where he says, "it may be conjectured that the beautiful abodes to which the soul is attracted are the Forms" (White, *Myth and Metaphysics in Plato's Phaedo*, 265).

63   While locally logical, this idea conflicts with other parts of the Phaedo where the judges seem to be in Hades. Cf. 107de, 113d. What this analysis further points out is the inconsistency of the different parts of the myth. At 107de, the souls are judged before proceeding to the underworld. But, at 113d, the souls appear to be judged in the underworld then make their way to their rightful places.

Conduct and behavior. Upon death the soul will travel to that certain place in Hades along many potential routes for which the soul needs a guide. The soul that is called well-ordered and wise at 108a will follow one route while the soul that is polluted and impure (81b-e) will follow another way.[64] Those characteristics considered 'well-ordered and wise', Plato defines these with these terms: at 108a-c the soul is well ordered (κοσμία) and wise (φρόνιμος); it has led a pure (καθαρῶς) and moderate (μετρίως) life; at 114b-115a, led a pious (ὁσίως)life; have themselves purified (καθηράμενοι) by philosophy; make an effort to share in virtue (ἀρετῆς) and wisdom (φρονήσεως); has adorned his soul with moderation (σωφροσύνη), righteousness (δικαιοσύνη), courage (ἀνδρεία), freedom (ἐλευθερία) and truth (ἀλήθεια).

On the polluted and impure side he offers at 108a-b, passionately attached to the body (ἐπιθυμητικῶς); performed some impure deed (ἀκάθαρτον); involved in unjust (ἀδίκων) killings (φόνων); then at 113e-114e, committed great sacrileges (ἱεροσυλίας) or wicked (ἀδίκους) murders (φόνους); doing violence (βίαιον)to father or mother; the pleasures (ἡδονάς) of the body. Outside of and conflicting somewhat with the main myth, some vices are further defined: 81e-82a—gluttony (γαστριμαργίας), drunkenness (φιλοποσίας), tyranny (τυραννίδας)and plunder (ἁρπαγάς). Note that this list contains references to both self-absorption and infringement of others' rights type of behavior.

At *Phaedo* 69a-c Plato's Socrates ties together the primary good qualities that are all interchangeable with wisdom when he explains to Simmias: "with this we have real courage and moderation and justice and, in a word, true virtue, with wisdom...in truth, moderation and courage and justice are a purging away of all such things [pleasures and fears and other such feelings] and wisdom itself is a kind of cleansing or purification."

The Republic

Context. F.S. Halliwell notes that the *Republic* is usually dated between the 380's and 370's and that book 10 is thought to be later in the 360's.[65] Cross and

---

64   At 81b-e the polluted and impure soul actually wanders around the grave until its longing for the physical again imprisons it in a body. At 108b it wanders in the visible world for a long time, then is led away to Hades to be judged.

65   S. Halliwell, *Plato: Republic 10* (Wiltshire: Aris & Phillips, 1988), 194-5.

Woozey affirm that "many of the shorter dialogues" and "the longer dialogues *Gorgias, Meno, Symposium* and *Phaedo* precede the *Republic*."[66]

The *Republic* takes up the case of justice and the entire work is also known as 'On Justice'. The main thrust of Plato's argument is that justice is intrinsically valuable in itself to a person. If one takes the normal common English usage of the term 'justice', it is very difficult to see what Plato is attempting to prove. Sometimes he treats it as containing other virtues and sometimes it is on a par with the other virtues.

Many scholars have grappled with this dichotomy and several have expressed the fact that the Greek word δικαιοσύνη is simply not translated well by the English word 'justice'. Alasdair MacIntyre says that the term "has a flavor all its own and combines the notion of fairness in externals with that of personal integrity in a way that no English word does."[67]

Robin Waterfield, in his translation of the *Republic* ignores the usual translation and substitutes the word 'morality' because "to most people, 'justice' means roughly 'acting fairly and impartially towards others': this is a part, but not the whole, of *dikaiosune*."[68]

Gregory Vlastos, says that he "shall use 'justice' and 'just' merely as counters for δικαιοσύνη and δίκαιος, whose sense is so much broader: they could be used to cover all social conduct which is morally right."[69]

Aristotle would seem to seal the case for the above interpretations of dikaiosu/nh in his work on ethics (*N.E.* 5.1.1129b-1130a). He sees the term applying to two separate functions, as a general virtue better translated as righteousness, and secondly as a particular species of virtue concerned with one's deeds toward each other. When he refers to a person as just he means that that person possesses several attributes associated with goodness.[70] The phrase that 'justice is the whole

---

66   R.C. Cross and A.D. Woozley, *Plato's Republic* (London: MacMillan & Co., 1964), xi-xiii. Also, see my footnote number 22 for the scholarly consensus on the details of chronology.

67   Alasdair MacIntyre, *A Short History of Ethics* (New York: MacMillan Co., 1966), 11.

68   Robin Waterfield, *Plato: Republic* (Oxford: Oxford University Press, 1993), xii.

69   Gregory Vlastos, ed., *Platonic Studies* (Princeton: University Press, 1981), 111.

70   Aristide Tessitore, *Reading Aristotle's Ethics* (Albany: State University of New York Press, 1996), 53.

of virtue' (*N.E.* 5.1.1129b) expresses the general meaning, and this, I believe, is meant to be the theme of the *Republic*.

Some scholars have claimed that the Myth of Er in book 10 runs counter to the theme of the other books of the *Republic*. Julia Annas, for example, says that "the Myth of Er is a painful shock; its vulgarity seems to pull us right down…to offer us an entirely consequentialist reason for being just."[71] Nevertheless, other scholars have suggested that the myth is integral to the dialog.[72]

I would agree with the latter scholars in that Plato himself defends his thesis:

> Justice by itself is best for the soul itself (612b)[73] but "isn't it now, at last, unobjectionable, in addition, also to give back to justice and the rest of virtue the wages—in their quantity and in their quality—that they procure for the soul from human beings and gods, both while the human being is still alive, and when he's dead (612c)?

Therefore, if desirable consequences also follow, that is just so much the better.

In the *Republic*, the myth intensifies Plato's argument that the unjust (or unrighteous) become less fit to live in the ideal world and more fit to live in this world with their own kind of people. The total separation in the afterlife of the unrighteous from the righteous expresses a truth that mere dialectic cannot. Each will go to his own place; the better to the better and the worse to the worse.[74]

The myth (614b-621b).

> Once upon a time he [Er, son of Armenius] died in war; and…as he was lying on the pyre, he came back to life, and…told what he saw in the other world (614b).

---

71 Annas also calls this myth "lame and messy" (Julia Annas, *An Introduction to Plato's Republic* [Oxford: Clarendon Press, 1981], 349, 353).

72 For example: Stewart, Myths of Plato, 24-27; Edelstein, "Function of Myth in Plato," 463; Frutiger, *Les Mythes de Platon*, 4-5, 12-14.

73 All translations of the Republic are from Allan Bloom, *The Republic of Plato* (USA: Basic Books, 1991).

74 Cf. Rep. 442a, 472e, 519ab, 571b, 609e.

At *Republic* 10.614c, Plato's Er describes the site of the judgment. There are two openings side by side in the earth, and two openings in the heaven with judges sitting between them who judge the newly dead. The just are sent to the right and up through heaven and the unjust to the left and down (all wearing tokens, presumably to indicate their degree of goodness or badness).[75] The other two openings have souls coming back from a long stay in heaven or under the earth where they have been rewarded or punished ten-fold for their former behavior. This arrangement denies any once-for-all judgment since all those dead for a thousand years, except the incurably wicked, are brought back to be reborn.

The newly brought back are allowed to choose a new lot in life and are reincarnated. However, the choice is almost entirely based on one's previous existence here and there.[76] Reincarnation is now a continuous cycle (617d) and all good or curable people are reborn, including the philosopher. This raises the question: is reincarnation a further punishment after one has already paid the price, as in the *Phaedo*, or (worse yet) after one had already reaped the reward of one's past life only to have it taken away?[77]

Punishments in the afterlife are said by some to be purgatorial rather than vindictive[78], although the 'incurables' still remain forever in Tartarus. All other souls will continue to be reincarnated.

---

[75] *Rep.* 614cd. This differs from the Gorgias at 526bc in two major ways: the mark in Gorgias is only for those directed to Tartarus; and there the mark stands for curable or incurable. The tokens are reminiscent of the Orphic tablets and the Egyptian Book of the Dead texts that were buried with the corpse to mark their way through the underworld.

[76] *Rep.* 620a, 617e. Plato attempts to offer free will to the souls in order that the blame for any future failure not be on god since he insists "god is never in any way unrighteous" (Theatetus 176). His attempt fails because the choice is not really free. It is tied to the success or failure of a previous existence over which the 'new' person had no control and maybe even no memory.

[77] *Rep.* 619bc has one soul who had spent a thousand years in heaven now choosing a lot that will almost surely send it to Tartarus at its next death. Conversely, one who had been in Tartarus chooses a lot that will assist it to achieve heaven. Regardless, even the best souls of philosophers are condemned to the punishment of again being placed into a body. They can avoid future hells, but not future incarnations.

[78] *Rep.* 615a-616a. (cf. *Phaedo* 113e; *Gorg.* 525b-d; *Protagoras* 234b). Dodds says that it is either remedial or deterrent. Gallop and Waterfield seem to agree with Dodds that a deterrent works only if the doctrine of rebirth is assumed. Annas denies that the

In spite of the significant changes in afterlife beliefs from Homer to Plato, this myth appears to represent a regression back to Homer where all souls ended up alike in Hades whether they were good or bad.[79] Only now, it is not in Hades, but there in the 'other world', that all alike end up. Some may be treated better than others may be, but all are threatened with the same punishment: to be placed once more in a body.[80] The religions of India had by this time in history figured a way out of this continuous cycle of birth and rebirth,[81] but this possibility does not appear in the myth of Er, or indeed, anywhere in the rest of the *Republic*. What is needed is a way to accumulate wisdom throughout all reincarnations and then use that wisdom to finally break the cycle.[82]

---

doctrine of rebirth is required to justify the eternal punishment of the incurables in that Plato has said that punishment will cure wickedness. To many, eternal punishment for finite crimes seems quite vindictive (see my earlier note 36 on Olympiodorus). Gallop. *Plato: Phaedo*, 223; Dodds, *Plato: Gorgias*, 380-1. Annas, "Plato's Myths," 124; Robin Waterfield, *Plato: Gorgias* (Oxford: Oxford University Press, 1994), 453.

79 Homer will be discussed in chapter 2. For the time being, note that his main description of the undifferentiated dead is that of a 'strengthless head' (*Od.* 11.29, 476) in Hades having no true life at all (*Il.* 23.100 ff).

80 Scholars have noted this lack of individualism, e.g. Haliwell says that the myth of Er "is to provide an image of a universal and eternal world order which goes beyond justice for individual souls" (S. Halliwell, *Plato: Republic* 10, 20). I would disagree somewhat with his statement in that it is the individual incarnation only that is denied justice. It is possible for the eternal soul to achieve a never-ending series of heavenly blissful stays without ever going "underground" (619e). Even with this possibility, the soul's justice may still seem somewhat abrogated because it must also endure an endless series of incarnations, with a concomitant chance for failure to achieve the next scheduled bliss.

81 For a Hindu parallel compare *Bhagavad-Gita* 14.2 where it is stated "by becoming fixed in this knowledge, one can attain to the transcendental nature, like my own, and not be born at the time of creation or disturbed at the time of dissolution" (A.C. Bhaktivedanta Swami, *Bhagavad-Gita: As It Is* [Los Angeles: Bhativedanta Book Trust, 1977], 220). In his later myths, Plato would come to this same conclusion; that pre-natal knowledge (i.e., recollection) of the Forms would eventually allow cessation from the cycle of rebirth.

82 The Hindus, Buddhists, Empedocles and even the later Plato would solve this problem (for the individual). Heraclitus' dry souls (see reference in chapter 3) who have not drunk so deeply would solve it also, but neither that nor Plato's doctrine of recollection now help, because it is not explicitly noted in the Er myth nor in the entire Republic. Halliwell allows that Rep 6.498d may imply the needed continuity,

<u>Conduct and behavior</u>. The just are described at 615bc using the words: they had done good deeds (εὐεργεσίας) and proved just (δίκαιοι) and holy (ὅσιοι); for piety (εὐσεβείας) toward gods and parents; but the unjust are: those who were causes of death (θανάτων) by betraying (προδόντες) cities or armies and reducers to slavery (δουλείας); for impiety (ἀσεβείας) to gods or parents and for murder (αὐτόχειρος φόνου).

Earlier, at *Republic* 433b Plato defined his cardinal virtues[83] of moderation, courage, prudence and justice. Justice in the state is performing social functions in the city for which one's nature is best adapted (433a).[84] It "is the minding of one's own business and not being a busybody 433b)." For the remainder of book IV (435-445), Plato says that justice in the individual can be likened to that of the state; when all of its divisions are performing their functions, the entity is just. The just person is one who has integrity of the soul where each of its principle parts are in harmony with the rest which gives rise to health. But injustice is the warring of the principles in one's own soul and gives rise to "sickness, ugliness and weakness" (444de).

Whereas Plato, in the above dialectic, makes a great deal out of the above explanation of the three parts of the soul being analogous to the three parts of the just society, can it be said that he used the same definition of 'just' for the judgment of the soul in the myth? I do not think so.

---

and Waterfield says that Rep. 498c and 518c could imply recollection. These look doubtful. However, both of them have commented that Rep. 621a, concerning the measure of water drunk from the River of Forgetfulness, may have implications, a la Heraclitus, as to the soul's recollection in the next incarnation. Halliwell, Plato: Republic 10, 29n48; Waterfield, Plato: Republic, 425, 458.

83   "The actual phrase 'the cardinal virtues' seems to derive from St. Ambrose [Ambrose, *Lib V in Lucam*]; the doctrine emerged in Greece during the fifth and fourth centuries, and is presented for the first time in Plato's *Republic*" (John Ferguson, *Moral Values in the Ancient World* [New York: Barnes & Noble, 1959], 24). However, several other works discuss various combinations of other virtues (e.g., Laches has wisdom, justice and holiness). Agathon's speech in the Symposium contains all four virtues: "Now I have spoken about the god's justice [δικαιοσύνης], moderation [σωφροσύνης], and bravery [ανδρείας]; his wisdom [σοφίας] remains" (196d). *Phaedo* has all four virtues mentioned at 69c, so if the *Symposium* or *Phaedo* precedes the *Republic*, as is the consensus, the last part of Ferguson's quote is inaccurate.

84   Three of the cardinal virtues are tied to the three parts of the soul: wisdom—rational; courage—spirited; temperance—desirous or appetitive.

The tripartite soul is discussed frequently in the Platonic corpus,[85] but it is nowhere to be found in the myth of Er! Rather, as we have noted above, those who have paid the penalty for each injustice are defined by terms unrelated to the earlier dialog's definition of the tripartite soul. Here, the myth in *Rep.* 10 relies on one's conduct to define injustice such as: causing deaths; betraying armies or cities; reducing to slavery; committing impiety or murder, while the just receive rewards for having done good deeds, become just or holy.

The description of the wrongdoer seems to have little to do with the ordering of a complex soul. Nor does the description of their 'good' opposites stress an order of a composite soul, but neither does it negate such a concept. What this lack of tripartitness means is not discussed in the myth but it could mean that Plato believes that the soul no longer consists of three parts after death.[86]

Outside of the Myth proper, at *Rep.* 402c, soberness, courage, liberality (ἐλευθεριότητος) and high-mindedness (μεγαλοπρεπείας)are included as virtuous conduct and at 443a sacrilege, theft (κλοπῶν), betrayal, not keeping oaths, adultery (μοιχεῖαι), sacrilege and neglect (ἀμέλειαι,ἀθεραπευσίαι) of parents and the gods are vicious conduct. However, honoring such are included in the myths as virtues. At 560e, some additional vices are defined as insolence, anarchy (ἀναρχίαν), prodigality (ἀσωτίαν) and shamelessness. The words here underlined and translated are some terms left out of all of the myths. Is there any good reason why this is so? There does not appear to be any difference in internal character traits (i.e., soberness vs. liberality) or infringement of others' rights (betrayal vs. theft). These terms could all be considered detrimental to orderly living, hence there is no apparent motivation for their absence in the myths just on that basis.

However, I believe that Plato was attempting to emphasize only the most serious virtues and vices in order to press his case for the truly important conventions (νόμος) being more like the laws of nature (φύσις). Telling a Thrasymachus, who believed that it was better to inflict that to suffer wrong, that just any social custom was equivalent to natural law would have been counterproductive.

---

85 See Table 1 in Appendix C for more information concerning the attributes of the soul in the Platonic corpus.

86 However, the non-incarnated soul in the later *Phaedrus* is tripartite.

The Phaedrus

Context. This is the last of the otherworldly myths. Rowe, against the consensus, places the *Phaedrus* near the end of Plato's life. He says it "is certainly later than the *Republic*...certainly later than the *Timaeus*...probably earlier than the *Philebus*."[87] DeVries says that it was likely written after the *Republic* and around the time of the *Parmenides*, or approximately 367 BCE.[88] Regardless of these disagreements, it is the last of the myths.

As in the *Republic*, the dogma of the tripartite soul is expressed. In line with the method of appealing to both the rational and irrational parts of the soul, Socrates again uses both dialectic and myth.

In the case of *Phaedrus*, the myth will not only appeal to all parts of the soul, but it further describes those parts as being in continuous conflict.[89]

The myth (245c-249c, 253c-e). The myth is introduced by Plato's claim that every soul is immortal. Then, because explaining the actual soul would take a godlike power, Plato's summary will describe it in a simile (246a). The *Phaedrus* describes the soul as it exists in the real world of the true heaven. There, the soul is pictured as a winged chariot that follows in the train of the gods and, while flying to the upper-most super-celestial regions, many behold the true forms of justice, temperance and knowledge. The chariot of the non-divine souls consists of a charioteer and two steeds, one of which is noble and good and the other unruly.

Souls that have lost their wings fall to earth and take earthly bodies and are called 'living being' and 'mortal'. Of the 'immortals', Plato says that they are deathless living beings and emphatically denies that they have a soul and a body joined together forevermore (246cd).[90] Those non-divine souls who best follow after the

---

87 See my footnote 22 for consensus dating of the Platonic corpus. C.J. Rowe, *Plato: Phaedrus* (Wiltshire: Aris & Phillips, 1986), 14.

88 G.J. DeVries, *A Commentary on the Phaedrus of Plato* (Amsterdam: Adolf M. Hakkert, 1969), 7-11.

89 "We require the cooperative engagement of our non-intellectual elements in order to get where our intellect wants us to go" (Martha C. Nussbaum, *The Fragility of Goodness* [Cambridge: Cambridge University Press, 1986], 214).

90 Nichol's translation is followed for the *Phaedrus* except as noted. James H. Nichols, Jr., *Plato: Phaedrus* (Ithica: Cornell University Press, 1998), 50.

gods[91] get to glimpse the true Forms but eventually they are distracted and fall to earth to be born. Some souls have pre-natally seen more of the true Forms than others and so are concomitantly born into nine varying types of people ranging from seekers of wisdom down to tyrants (248de). Most souls never even get a glimpse of the Forms and lose their wings. Failing to see reality, they feed upon opinion (apparently as fallen humans).

After their fallen first life on earth, upon death they will be judged, the just obtaining a better lot and the unjust a worse one. As in the earlier myths, the unrighteous will receive chastisement beneath the earth for one thousand years and the righteous will be borne aloft by Justice to be rewarded for past merit in a heavenly place (249ab). Most souls will go through ten incarnations (10,000 years) before returning to the realm of the Forms; however, philosophers will achieve this salvation in three incarnations.[92]

The *Phaedrus* solves the problem of the salvation of the individual that the *Republic* failed to do. Now, the doctrine of recollection assists the most wise to remember the true Forms and to make their way back to the highest regions.

As I stated earlier, the *Phaedrus* is neither a <u>nekyia</u> nor an eschatological myth. It deals not at all with an underworld,[93] nor can it be said to deal with last things, for, in this story, there is no last thing in the eternal cycle of being and becoming in the cosmos.[94] The *Gorgias, Phaedo* and *Republic* all contain a 'hell' and a

---

91   *Phaedrus* 248a, 249c. Cf. *Phaedo* 109d-110a, where it is a strong human who might, if he were able, lift himself from the hollows to the upper limit and see the true earth.

92   There are 10 small cycles of 1000 years each before the non-philosopher can again return to the great cycle of 10,000 years. Unanswered here is whether the great cycle continues over again, as it does the later Stoic belief, or is there only the one with 10 small cycles?

93   Although neither dealt with nor described, the underworld is mentioned in that the less-than-perfect will pay the penalty under the earth, but only for the small cycle, and the exalted will stay in the heavens (249ab). Eventually, everyone returns to the heavens at the end of the great cycle after 10,000 years.

94   Recall that the earlier myths all had a non-cyclic terminus: eternal damnation for the incurable or eternal bliss for the philosopher.

'purgatory'[95] along with a 'heaven', whereas the *Phaedrus* deals with only a 'heaven'[96] since all the post-mortem action takes place in the celestial or super-celestial realm. Nevertheless, the common thread among all these myths is a judgment, and that is the primary focus of this inquiry.

<u>Conduct and behavior</u>. At 248e, Plato says, "whoever passes his life justly (δικαίως) receives a better allotment afterwards, and whoever unjustly (ἀδίκως) a worse," and justly and unjustly are expressed in more detail in 246b-249b where: the just are noble (καλός), good (ἀγαθός), wise (σοφόν) and do their own thing (χπράττων) and observe Justice (δικαιοσύνης) and moderation (σωφροσύνην), is a philosopher (φιλοσόφου), a lover of the beautiful (φιλοκάλου), passes his life justly (δικαίως) and sees the truth (ἀλήθειαν). But the unjust are ugly (αἰσχρῶ), bad (κακῶ), filled with envy (φθόνος), forgetfulness (λήθησ), badness (κακία) and pass their life unjustly (ἀδίκως). The virtues and vices of the individual are thus expressed and furthermore, when Plato describes the horses, he has the badness (κακία) of the bad (κακοῦ) horse as being crooked (σκολιός), a comrade of wantonness (ὕβρεως) and boasting (ἀλαζονείας). The virtue (ἀρετή) of the good (ἀγαθοῦ) horse is described as being straight (ὀρθός) in form (εἶδος), a lover of honor (τιμῆς) with moderation (σωφροσύνης) and with a sense of shame (αἰδοῦς), and a comrade of truthful (ἀληθινῆς) opinion (253de).[97]

A Summary of the Four Myths

It is clear that Plato's myths evolve over time and that many of his concepts change markedly. This summary will analyze some of those differences, but we must bear in mind that our real goal is a synoptic approach that will look at the core similarities. This core will then be compared to the thinking of the pre-Platonic Greeks and the ancient Egyptians.

---

[95] These terms are medieval and are not in Plato. For Plato, Hell and Purgatory are in Tartarus and Hades, but Heaven is in the Isles of the Blest, the true earth or the celestial regions. However, there is a leap from the underworld and earth-bound regions to the celestial in the Phaedrus. Could the case be made that Plato had at last fully incorporated the Pythagorean/Orphic view into his myths and finally left the Homeric tradition behind? It would seem so.

[96] The ten thousand year great cycle is always from the celestial to earth back to the celestial (248e-249a).

[97] Translation by Rowe, *Plato: Phaedrus*, 75.

The first difference one notices is that of the judges and the judgment. It is only in the *Gorgias* that we have them named, although even there the judgment appears to be automatic based on the severity of one's life acquired scars. However, in the later myths, the judges are not named and an even more automatic judgment takes place.

Whereas in the *Gorgias*, the judgment was final, in the others a cyclic re-birth for all but the 'incurables' has been posited. In the early myths, the punishment for the incurables is to spend an eternity in Tartarus, but there are no incurables in the *Phaedrus*, where all persons eventually get back to the heavenly sphere. The *Phaedrus* allows punishment between incarnations in order to have a remedial effect on the person, whereas the other myths allow punishment for revengeful reasons in addition to its remedial effect.

The concept of the soul changed radically from the *Gorgias* to the *Phaedrus*. In the former and the *Phaedo*, the soul was a simple unity in dualistic opposition to the body. With the *Republic*, the soul had become compounded of parts to match the three parts of the perfect state. This tripartite soul is continued with the *Phaedrus*.

Plato's signature concept of the Forms is not introduced until the *Phaedo* where he also explains his theory of learning by a remembering of the Forms from one's pre-natal existence. Unfortunately, Plato leaves out this concept in the *Republic*, and there he has no good explanation of how one can successively improve one's virtue through accumulation of knowledge throughout multiple rebirths. The 'remembrance of the Forms' solves this problem in the *Phaedrus*.

A final major difference between the myths is that of the location of the afterlife. In the *Gorgias*, the Homeric and Hesiodic concepts of Tartarus and the Isles of the Blest suffice. Tartarus disappears only with the lofty ideas of the *Phaedrus* where those who are temporarily punished dwell in prisons under the earth. The earth-bound Isles of the Blest in the *Gorgias* are elevated in the *Phaedo* to the "true earth" which lies above our present existence in the earth's "hollows". Then, in the *Republic*, Plato has the place of reward located in the heavens. Finally, in the *Phaedrus*, the place of the Blessed is either in the celestial realm or even higher in the super-celestial realm above the dwelling place even of the gods.

All of these differences aside, Plato has some concepts, which are consistent throughout all of his eschatological myths: there is always an immortal soul that is judged after the individual's death. This judgment is based on the individual's conduct and behavior while living a bodily existence. Although the detailed content of the myths may change over time, Plato has certain modes of conduct that remain fairly consistent throughout.

There are rewards for those who are just (righteous), pious, well-ordered, wise, and good, while those who are godless, unjust, polluted, impure and bad receive punishments in the afterlife.

Except for the early *Gorgias,* all of the myths posit a reincarnation and a theory of the Forms.

Our task in this project is to compare these synoptic views of Plato with those of his predecessors who are of interest to us. This is especially true of his views on the modes of conduct and behavior as they affect the afterlife. Therefore, the following overview highlights those positive or negative modes of conduct that appear in the eschatological myths.

Modes that appear in two or more eschatological myths:
> justice, piety/godliness, truth, goodness, virtue, orderliness, wisdom, moderation/temperance/continence, shamefulness, care of gods—parents—strangers (i.e., as concerning oath keeping, insolence, killing, sacrileges, violence, betrayal, enslavement).

Modes that appear in the *Gorgias* myth only:
> luxury, mind own business, not busybody.

Modes in the *Phaedo* myth only:
> bodily attachment, purity, pleasures, courageousness

Modes in *Phaedrus* myth only:
> honor.

These terms from the four eschatological myths of Plato are summarized in tabular format in Appendix E: "Tables of Conduct and Behavior Words in Greek and English Translation, Tables 3 and 4."

CHAPTER 2

The Development of the Afterlife Concepts in Pre-Platonic Greece: Homer

The Pre-Platonic Greek Authors

Having looked at the judgment of the dead, behavior and conduct in this life and the concept of soul in Plato, we will now investigate earlier Greek literature in order to explore how these concepts developed from the earliest Greek writers to the time of Plato.

The chart following is a chronological summary of authors or other works of interest that appear in the three chapters covering the Greek considerations on the afterlife.

CHRONOLOGICAL CHART Of

The Key Greek Authors and Works Referenced for
Conduct, Behavior and the Judgment of the Dead

Author	Classification	Dates	Approximate Mid-point of Works
Homer	Epic poet	Early 8th cent	750 BCE
Hesiod	Poet	Late 8th cent	700
"Homeric Hymn to Demeter"		650-550	600
Solon	Didactic poet	640-559	575
Pythagoras	Philosopher	582-507	540
Theognis	Didactic poet	Sixth cent	525
"Orphic poetry"		Late sixth cent	-
Xenophanes	Philosopher	560-470	515
Simonides	Lyric poet	556-468	515
Heraclitus	Philosopher	535-475	490

Aeschylus	Tragic dram.	525-456	475
Pindar	Lyric poet	522-438	465
Parmenides	Philosopher	515-450?	465
Bacchylides	Lyric poet	510-450?	460
Empedocles	Phil. poet	495-435	450
Protagoras	Philosopher	481-411	450
"Orphic bone tablets"		Late fifth cent.	440
Sophocles	Tragic dram.	496-406	435
Herodotus	Historian	484-424	435
Euripides	Tragic dram.	480-406	430
Socrates	Philosopher	470-399	425
Democritus	Philosopher	460-370	420
Aristophanes	Comic dram.	448-380	415
Xenophon	Historian	428-354	375
Plato	Philosopher	428-347	365
Isocrates	Orator	436-338	365
"Orphic gold leaves"		325	325
Aristotle	Philosopher	384-322	335
Demosthenes	Orator	384-322	335

The Iliad and the Odyssey

> Even in the house of Hades there is left something, a soul and an image, but there is no real heart of life in it (*Il.* 23.102-4).[98]

> Father Zeus…and you who under the earth take vengeance on dead men, whoever among them has sworn to falsehood, you shall be witnesses, to guard the oaths of fidelity (*Il.* 3.276-80).[99]

We are looking for three issues in each of the writers that follow. First, was there a belief in an afterlife? Second, did conduct and behavior figure in this afterlife and,

---

[98] There is no period of Greek history when a belief in some sort of an afterlife was totally absent. Some post-Homeric writers deny an afterlife but most people appear to follow Homer's main line of thought; that of a "strengthless or senseless heads" (*Od.* 11.29, 476) existing without their mind in Hades.

[99] All Homer translations, unless otherwise stated, are from Richmond Lattimore, *The Iliad of Homer* (Chicago: University of Chicago Press, 1951); idem, The Odyssey of Homer (New York: Harper & Row, 1967).

if so, what conduct and behavior contributed to posthumous reward or punishment? Finally, what was their concept of the entity being judged and how did it compare to Plato's mature concept of the soul? Not all of the writers we will investigate will provide positive answers to these questions, but they are nevertheless looked at for purposes of comparison.

In Homer we find all these issues are raised. There is an afterlife belief.[100] There is conduct and behavior that figures into that afterlife, and there is a concept of something that continued to exist in the afterlife. After all, as stated in the opening quotations above, dead men went to Hades as "something" and the gods punished them for breaking oaths. However, these ideas bore little resemblance to what was to develop over the next three or four hundred years. Nor are they consistent among themselves, for surely the two tales of the *Iliad* and the *Odyssey* developed over a long period of time and incorporated many different and competing eschatological ideas.[101]

"Un-Homeric" Passages in the Odyssey

The variation is so extensive that many scholars have questioned the authenticity of certain Homeric passages, especially those in *Odyssey* books 11 and 24.

There are two major scenes where 'Homer' takes us into the underworld and shows us the activities of the dead. The first is the *Nekyia* of *Odyssey* 11 and the second is *Odyssey* book 24.[102] If we could be sure of the authorship of these two sources, we would have fewer problems discussing the types of conduct and behavior that would allow for an afterlife judgment. Unfortunately, these are

---

[100] In his *Psyche*, Rohde argues that there was never a popular belief in afterlife rewards and punishments for centuries after Homer. He uses the famous painting by Polynotos (as described by Pausanias) to prove that there was even at that later time "no reward of virtue [nor] punishment of wickedness." As to Homer himself, Rohde says there is no support for the opinion that "Homeric poetry knew of a belief in retribution hereafter" (Erwin Rohde, *Psyche*, trans. W.B. Hillis [New York: Harcourt, Brace & Company, 1925], 238, 242).

[101] Many scholars see layers of religious beliefs in the Homeric corpus. See Alfred Heubeck and Arie Hoekstra, *A Commentary on Homer's Odyssey*, vol. 2 (Oxford: Clarendon Press, 1989), 75.

[102] The passages in dispute are lines 568-627 in book 11 (the Nekyia), and starting at line 297 in book 23 through the entire book 24 (sometimes referred to as the second Nekyia).

precisely the two passages that have been disputed since antiquity and continue to be disputed by contemporary scholars.

This question is important if we are to discover the beliefs concerning the afterlife in the 'Homeric age'. Was Homer the final redactor of the poems or were there other redactors? If there were others, why would any one redaction be any more Homeric than another redaction? If there was a real Homer, then anything added to his works is inauthentic. If there was no single Homer, then we have the problem of just when to canonize the text. Should it be 800 BCE, 750, 700 or later? That is difficult to say, but it is clear that we should, at the very least, be able to say that if the Homeric canon had been considered closed by the 8th century, it would not do to have the religious ideas of the 5th century grafted onto them.

Since these passages are potentially so important to our conclusions concerning the afterlife as it appears in Homer, we must investigate the history and current state of scholarship on the matter. However, due to its length, further investigation will be placed in the appendix[103] for those readers who are interested and I will carry on as though the disputed passages were an integral part of the *Odyssey*.[104]

Even assuming that there are interpolations, these passages still contain a very old conception of the afterlife. Therefore, let us use it for the pre-sixth century time period with appropriate recognition that it may not actually represent the eighth-century Homeric mainstream view.

---

[103] See Appendix F: "The Question of Interpolation in Homer," where I argue for interpolation.

[104] I would accept the theory that the 'innovations' of the disputed passages in books 11 & 23/24 may also be archaisms that reflect forgotten Minoan or Mycenaean, or even Egyptian, beliefs. See scholarly support for this idea: Martin P. Nilsson, *The Minoan-Mycenaean Religion and its Survival in Greek Religion* (Lind: C.W.K. Gleerup, 1950), passim; Burkert, *Greek Religion*, 198, 294; J. Gwyn Griffiths, *The Divine Verdict* (New York: E.J. Brill, 1991), 295, 297; J.A.K. Thompson, *Studies in the Odyssey* (Oxford: Clarendon Press, 1966), 155; Emily Vermeule, *Aspects of Death in Early Greek Art and Poetry* (Berkeley: University of California Press, 1979), 62ff, 160f; Alfred Heubeck, Stephanie West, J.B. Hainsworth, *A Commentary on Homer's Odyssey*, vol. 1 (Oxford: Clarendon Press, 1988), 227. Cf. B.C. Dietrich, *The Origins of Greek Religion* (Berlin: Walter De Gruyter, 1974), 160ff; J.C. Griffiths, *Apuleius of Madauros: Isis Book* (Leiden: E.J. Brill, 1975), 113ff.

The Soul[105]

Let us look at the Homeric 'soul' first. A person is a physical body that contains at least two different types of souls, "the body-soul or souls (θυμός, νόος, μενός), active when a person is awake, and the free soul (ψυχή), active only when the person loses consciousness or dies."[106] So, in Homer we have multiple entities that make up the human personality: the body, the psyche and the thymos.[107] The thymos was the spirit that is located in the midriff and is responsible for passion and feeling. These functions would later be assumed by the psyche.[108] However, at the time of Homer, the psyche, in popular thought, was simply the breath of life that would escape from a dying person and generally go to Hades to continue as a shade (εἴδολον) without feelings or thought or much in the way of an existence at all.[109] In the religious strata of the Homeric poems, however, the substantiality of the psyche ranges widely from being just one's breath of life[110] to that which is still aware and retains its mental capacities.[111]

---

[105] See the summary table comparing Platonic and Homeric views of the soul in Appendix G: "Attributes and Features of the Homeric Soul, Table 5."

[106] deStrycker, *Plato's Apology of Socrates*, 218; Jan Bremmer, *The Early Greek Concept of the Soul* (Princeton: Princeton University Press, 1983), 66-7.

[107] Along with the other 'body souls,' i.e., the mind (νόος) and the spirit (μένος). See Bremmer, *The Early Greek Concept of the Soul*, passim. All of these might be compared to Plato's multi-part soul and Egypt's many souls.

[108] By the time of Heraclitus the ψυχήhad usurped "many of the functions of the Homeric θυμόςΠτηε ψυχήhas become the seat of feeling, and the entity of which moral and intellectual qualities are predicated" (M.L. West, *Early Greek Philosophy and the Orient* [Oxford: Clarendon Press, 1971], 149).

[109] *Eidolon* is equated to psyche at *Od.* 11.81-3. At *Od.* 51, "But first came the soul (ψυχή) of my companion, Elpenor." Then at *Od.* 83, while still talking to Elpenor, Odysseus says, "while opposite me the phantom (εἴδωλον) of my companion talked long with me."

[110] The psyche, which is a material substance of the nature of breath or air separates from the body at death, either through the mouth or a wound as in, "a man's life breath cannot come back again—once it slips through a man's clenched teeth (Il. 9.409)," and "his life, gushing forth through the raw, yawning wound, went pulsing fast and the dark came swirling down across his eyes" (*Il.* 14.518). Here death is equated to the loss of breath or fluid. And, the only immortality was through fame. Cf. *Il.* 9.408-9 and *Il.* 12.322-8.

[111] As Teiresias does at *Od.* 11.90ff and as the suitors do at *Od.* book 24. The 'seer' Teiresias is a rare exception to the more general rule in Homer. The Teiresias incident

The Afterlife

We find that although the *Iliad* does not give much hope for any kind of a pleasant afterlife existence, the *Odyssey*, although contradictory, does do so.[112] There the psyche can exist after death as gibbering spirits (*Od.* 24.5f) or indeed as articulate entities (*Od.* 11.601ff, 24.19ff). However, even the *Iliad* allows that "in Death's strong house there is something left, a ghost, a phantom—true, but no real breath of life" (*Il.* 23.100-4). Thus, the Homeric poets had "disentangled the ghost from the corpse," with the novel concepts of *Il.* 23.103 and *Od.* 11.216-224.[113]

Nevertheless, the bedrock statement of the general belief in the Homeric corpus concerning the common lot in the afterlife can be succinctly summed up in Sarpedon's speech to Glaucus and the story of his death.

> Man, supposing you and I, escaping this battle, would be able to live on forever, ageless, immortal, so neither would I myself go on fighting in the foremost nor would I urge you into the fighting where men win glory. But now, seeing that the spirits of death stand close about us in their thousands, no man can turn aside nor escape them, let us go on and win glory for ourselves, or yield it to others (*Il.* 12.322-28).

Sarpedon would avoid the fight and the attendant glory if only he were immortal. Since he is not, he must gain some portion of immortality the only way the Homeric Hero can, by glorious remembrance.

---

might usefully be compared to the one in I Samuel 28 where Saul has a medium summon Samuel's shade. In both cases this occurs in order to obtain information from the dead even though the Israelite Sheol, like the Greek Hades, is usually thought of as a place of no consciousness.

[112] But note that Rohde claims that speaking of the soul as though it were involved in a future life in Homer would be wrong since "it is only a little more life than that of our image in a glass" (Rohde, *Psyche*, 10). And the souls of the dead are spoken of the unheeding dead and as "strengthless heads," (ἀμενηνὰ κάρηνα) without diaphragm (φρένες), which is the Homeric man's locus of intelligence. See *Od.* 11.29, 476, *Il.* 23.104.

[113] For example, the ghost of Patroclus and the ghost of Achilles' mother. Dodds, *The Greeks and the Irrational*, 136-7, 157 n. 7.

Later Sarpedon is faced with imminent death at the hands of Patroclus. His father, Zeus, wants to save him from death, but he is dissuaded from doing so by the goddess Hera who claims that if Zeus saves his son, all of the other gods would want to do likewise. Rather "bury [him] with a grave and a marker. This is the lot of mortals" (*Il.* 16.430-65). Here, Homer is saying that even the son of a god is mortal. Even Sarpedon must accept the fate of all lesser mortals, which is the finality of death where the immortal fame of the dead survives only in the memory of future generations. Sarpedon and, in these passages presumably Homer, accept the belief that without the immortal fame acquired by heroic deeds, the person at the end of his life is truly dead.

If this is the main afterlife belief in Homer, there are variations nonetheless.[114] In some beliefs the psyche escapes to dwell as a mindless phantom in a common Hades. Sometimes the dead dwell in a common Hades where more of the articulate qualities of the thymos now attend the psyche.[115] Sometimes heroes are given immortality in a paradisiacal Elysium,[116] and some wicked men are eternally punished in Tartaros.[117] Even in the *Iliad*, Hades may be seen to be a place of punishment for wrongdoing for all people.[118]

Those who would agree that *Od.* 11 is an integral part of Homer would also have to agree that the concept of a post-mortem punishment appears in Homer.[119] Nevertheless, as we will see, that concept is still doubted by many scholars who accept *Od.* 11.

Arthur Adkins proposes: "if a man can be unjust and prosper in this life…[and] since the Greeks already in Homer believed in some kind of life after death, it might seem natural to believe that the misdeeds of this life are punished in

---

[114] The references to a common Hades for mindless phantoms and Elysium for certain heroes are in passages that are not disputed. The articulate spirits and those in Tartarus are referenced in the allegedly 'interpolated' passages.

[115] See *Od.* 24.5ff where Hermes rouses the ghosts and they follow gibbering; 24.19ff where Achilles and Agamemnon converse.

[116] Rhadamanthus and Menelaus are 'rewarded' with eternal life. *Od.* 4.561-9.

[117] There is eternal punishment for the extremely wicked. *Od.* 11.576-600.

[118] *Iliad* 3.278ff, 19.256ff.

[119] See Appendix F: "Interpolation in Homer." For example, Dodds believes in "the plain meaning of [the] words." Dodds, *The Greeks and the Irrational*, 158.

Hades." He goes on to say that it is "not merely not natural but impossible to suppose this." The souls of men only gibber, Minos does not judge the dead for earthly wrongs and the great sinners are not paradigms for judgment since "ordinary men and women cannot hope to do wrong on this scale, and may be left to gibber." In his note, Adkins also states regarding colossal sinners that "these crimes are not viewed as instances of immorality: they are insults to the *time* of the gods on an unparalleled scale, and provoke an unparalleled revenge."[120]

J. Gwyn Griffiths agrees with Adkins and says that "nowhere else [other than book 11] does he [Homer] suggest a doctrine of posthumous punishment."[121]

I would disagree with Adkins' claim that it is 'impossible to suppose' that 'misdeeds of this life are punished in Hades'. Men and women can, and indeed do, commit great hubris against the gods and the great sinners could therefore very well be paradigmatic of other mortals. In fact, by the sixth century, other writers were developing theodocies to address just these very issues of seemingly unpunished wrongdoing.[122] These considerations lead me to conclude that, by the time of Homer, the gods were believed to exact divine retribution in the next world. Moreover, even the undisputed Homeric lines at *Iliad* 3.278, as Adkins himself admits, claim that ordinary sinners are punished beneath the earth.

> Father Zeus…and Helios…and you who under the earth take vengeance on dead men [καμόντας ἀνθρώπους], whoever among them has sworn to falsehood, you shall be witnesses, to guard the oaths of fidelity (*Il.* 3.276-80).

---

[120] Adkins, *Merit and Responsibility*, 67, 81 n. 14. E.R. Dodds had earlier made the claim that he had found "no indication in the narrative of the *Iliad* that Zeus is concerned with justice as such." Furthermore, he stated "those who argue otherwise seem to me to confuse the punishment of perjury as an offence against the divine τιμή(4.158 ff.), and the punishment of offences against hospitality by Zeus Xeinios (13.623 ff.), with a concern for justice as such." Later, in the same work, Dodds also allows that there is a "post-mortem punishment of certain offences against the gods," and that "the oath-formulae of the *Iliad* preserve a belief which was older than Homer's neutral Hades" (Dodds, *The Greeks and the Irrational*, 32, 52 n. 18, 137, 158 n. 10).

[121] Griffiths, *The Divine Verdict*, 294.

[122] See the next section, From Hesiod to the Orphic Tablets, for examples on wrongdoing being punished now or later.

Also, later in book 19:

> Let Zeus first be my witness…and Earth, and Helios the Sun, and the Furies,
> who underground [ὑπὸ γαῖαν] avenge dead men, when any man has sworn to
> falsehood (*Il.* 19.257-260).[123]

Iliad 3.279 and 19.258 would seem to be a clear attestation of a conduct-based judgment of the dead. However, the meaning of this passage has been regularly disputed.

Adkins says of this passage:

> Admittedly, *Iliad* iii 278, perjurers are said, in the invocation of an oath, to be
> punished below the earth; here by two gods…presumably Zeus of the lower
> world and Persephone, mentioned in *Iliad* ix. 457; but we see no sign of this
> either in the Nekyia of *Odyssey* xi or in that of *Odyssey* xxiv. Accordingly, it
> seems not to have been assimilated by the Homeric Hades, but to have existed
> illogically, though serving a very definite function, as do so many Homeric
> beliefs about the supernatural.[124]

So, Adkins disallows that this passage is representative of Homeric doctrine, thus denying a concept of post-mortem retribution to the Homeric Greeks.

Also arguing against the judgment in Homer, Thomas Day Seymour says that "the duties of men to the gods were ritualistic rather that ethical," thus eliminating ethical conduct and behavior from consideration at all for the afterlife. Then he goes on to claim that in the case of *Il.* 19.259 where Agamemnon "swears by 'the Erinyes beneath the earth' punish perjury (T 259),—where 'beneath the earth' cannot be equivalent to 'after death,' as is indicated clearly by the order of words as well as by the other offices of these divinities." Therefore, for him, these lines do not speak of post-mortem punishment. Rather, I would presume, they speak of the divinities who live beneath the earth and who punish living men. Seymour further says that "the Erinyes [Furies] are not to be understood as ministers of

---

[123] All Homer translations are by Richmond Lattimore, *The Iliad of Homer* (Chicago: University of Chicago Press, 1951); The Odyssey of Homer (New York: Harper & Row, 1965).

[124] Adkins, *Merit and Responsibility* (Oxford: Clarendon Press, 1960), 81 n.14.

suffering to the souls of the dead," since "the Homeric Greeks knew of no evil-minded or unkindly divinities."[125]

In *Psyche*, Rohde looks at the evidence for belief in afterlife recompense in *Odyssey* 11 and says that "Even the sinners and their punishment which later imitation added to the story of Odysseus' Journey to Hades, considered without prejudice, do not support the opinion that Homeric poetry knew of a belief in retribution hereafter."[126] He admits that "Homer makes hardly the most distant allusion to such a belief. The perjurer alone suffers in Homer the punishment at the hands of the gods of the underworld." Nevertheless, Rohde concludes that "all this [*Od.* 11 and *Il.* 3, 19] does not, even in the slightest degree, suggest a general belief in future rewards and punishments" in Homer.[127]

More recent scholars also deny such beliefs in Homer. Alfred Heubeck denies that the oath-breakers of *Il.* 19.259 are actually punished beneath the earth. Rather, he holds that the Erinyes punish the guilty man while alive and kills him and so sends him beneath the earth.[128]

Mark Edwards says, "the Erinues act against those who break an oath. ὑπὸ γαῖαν [under the earth] is the Erinues' home, and does not necessarily mean that they punish *dead* men there."[129]

The afterlife punishment concept may have been embryonic, undeveloped, lacking a general assimilation into the Homeric poems and even illogical when compared with the rest of Homer. Nevertheless, despite the objections of some scholars, the

---

[125] Thomas Day Seymour, *Life in the Homeric Age* (New York: Macmillan Company, 1907), 469-470.

[126] Indeed, he questioned that there was even a real concept of an afterlife in Homer at all: The soul in Homer is not involved in an afterlife since, "it is only a little more life than that of our image in a glass" (Rohde, *Psyche* [New York: Harcourt, Brace & Company, 1925], 10). This is, of course, true in most of Homer, but not all.

[127] Rohde *Psyche*, 238.

[128] Es ist vielmehr so, daß die Erinyen—geradezu im Namen von Zeus, Gaia und Helios—die Meineidigen "unter die Erde (ὑπὸ γαῖαν!) strafen"; d.h. "sie schicken sie strafend unter die Erde, strafen sie mit dem Tod. A. Heubeck, "ἐρινύς in der archaischen Epik," Glotta 64 (1986): 147.

[129] Mark W. Edwards, *The Iliad: A Commentary* (Cambridge: Cambridge University Press, 1991), 265-6.

punishment of humans-when-dead was already indicated as early as the *Iliad*, so there should be no difficulty in accepting that such eschatology would show up in the later *Odyssey*.

Two final views of possible Homeric immortality will be looked at before moving on to the consideration of conduct and behavior.

The Dioscuri. "Kastor, breaker of horses, and the strong boxer, Polydeukes. The life-giving earth holds both of them, yet they are still living, and, even underneath the earth, enjoying the honor of Zeus, they live still every other day; on the next day they are dead, but they are given honor even as the gods are (*Od* 11.300-4)."

Odysseus. "Kalypso who detained him [Odysseus] with her, desiring that he should be her husband, in her hollow caverns, and she took care of him and told him that she would make him ageless all his days, and immortal" (*Od* 23.333-6).

In the *Iliad* 3.235ff, Helen looks in vain for her brothers and we find that they "now were fast holden of the life-giving earth there in Lacedaemon, in their dear native land;" quite dead. But the *Odyssey* in the *Nekyia* relates the story in brief about how the brothers each live on alternate days in turn and are dead on the other days. We will find out in Pindar's *Nemean* 10.54ff why this is so. The one brother, Polydeuces, was the son of Zeus and for the love of his brother, Castor, he gave up half of his immortality. Hence, we can say that Castor won partial immortality after death because of his in-law relationship, much like that of Menelaus, to Zeus. Nevertheless, in the first case we clearly have a beneficent afterlife for two brothers.[130]

In the second case, of Odysseus and Calypso, immortality was only promised and we do not know if Calypso could have actually performed the deed if Odysseus had accepted her offer. Even if she could have done so, this has nothing to do with an immortal soul or even an afterlife. Odysseus was to have remained quite alive and forever with Calypso.

---

[130] Since the two versions of the story are so different, this could be taken as a further indication that the Nekyia is not from the same hand as most of the rest of Homer.

Conduct and Behavior

Conduct and behavior play a great part in the ethos of Homer. However, very little of it applies to an afterlife judgment. Here, we will examine only that conduct and behavior that occurs in the passages related to the afterlife, even though there obviously is other behavior that is important for Homer's characters. Most of that behavior would eventually come to figure in an afterlife judgment only in later authors.

In writing of Homeric morality early in the twentieth century, James Adam said:

> The mainspring of Homeric morality is not the *imitatio Dei*, but that which Homer calls αἰδώς, a word which combines the meanings of 'noble shame' or *pudor* with regard for the opinion of one's fellow-men, and possibly also fear of the divine vengeance.[131]

The conscience, if one can so call it, of the Homeric person was the external voice of 'shame' he heard as a result of being concerned with 'what will people say about me', as opposed to the internalized voice of 'guilt' so prevalent in later cultures. The difference was that one feels shame for looking bad to one's fellows whereas one feels guilt for failing to live up one's inner convictions.[132]

Dodds' classifying the ancient Greeks as a shame, and not a guilt, culture may have contributed to the idea that they do not posses a conscience, feel no sense of sin and are therefore devoid of what we moderns would consider an ethical basis for conduct and behavior. I believe this to be a cause of error and that such a basis to Greek morality is to be found much earlier than this division would allow.

---

[131] James Adam, *The Religious Teachers of Greece* (Clifton: Reference Books Publishers, 1965), 65. Originally published in 1908. E.R. Dodds was later to make the shame vs. guilt culture a part of the academic terminology.

[132] Dodd's bifurcation between "shame" and "guilt" has stood for decades. Recently Douglas Cairns has argued that there are so many variables involved that the shame vs. guilt culture holds no useful meaning. He argues well and at a complex level that the dichotomy may well be a simplistic means to categorize. He says that: "such a conception of shame and guilt is untenable, since at all stages both shame and guilt possess an internalized component, and neither are differentiated from the other by the fact that it may occur before a real audience, before a fantasy audience, or before oneself" (Douglas L. Cairns, *Aidos* [Oxford: Clarendon Press, 1993], 15, 27, 47).

Indeed, because of this way of thinking, many scholars claim that duties to the gods appear to be mostly ritual rather than ethical. One can be in the favor of the gods simply if one offers sacrifices to them, commits no perjury which offends the god's honor, and respects certain other people who are under the gods' protection.[133] What our modern culture would claim as serious transgressions, such as adultery and murder, are punished in the Homeric society, but <u>not</u> by the gods (*Od.* 1.37). However, Homer has Eumaeus the swineherd ironically suggest, "That would be virtuous of me...if first I led you into my shelter, there entertained you as guest, then murderer you...Then cheerfully I could go and pray to Zeus" (*Od.* 14.406). Still, this passage could be more a caveat against guest violations than against murder.

The gods do not seem to be the paragons of what we would call virtue, but "Homer nevertheless regards them as the appointed guardians of morality in general and of justice in particular: "no virtue in bad dealings"; for the Gods "reward justice and what men do that is lawful" [*Od.* 8.329. 14.84].[134] To show the strength of the Homeric belief that the gods protect strangers, we have only to look at the scene where Antinous has just struck the disguised Odysseus:

> A curse on you, if he turns out to be some god from heaven. For the gods do take on all sorts of transformations, appearing as strangers from elsewhere, and thus they range at large through the cities, watching to see which men keep the laws (εὐνομίην), and which are violent (ὕβριν).[135] (*Od.* 17.484-7).

---

133 One could certainly make a case for an ethical content here as concerning perjury and respect for others. However, many scholars have claimed that these 'ethical' activities were done only to enhance and protect the god's τιμή, and not as being the right thing to do for the sake of one's fellow man. For an example of such a scholar, see Seymour, *Life in the Homeric Age*, 445. However, on this very important question I would come down on the side of these things as being ethical and therefore in line with justice as it will appear in Plato's myths.

134 Adam, *The Religious Teachers of Greece*, 41.

135 Although Plato's δικαιοσύνη did not appear as a term in Homer, the concept was already there. Also the term δίκην at Od 14.84 is "already 'justice', or coming quite close to it" (Heubeck and Hoekstra, *A Commentary on Homer's Odyssey*, 198).

Summary

Homer never denies an existence after death for anyone. As we have seen above, this afterlife can range from that of a gibbering shadow to that of an articulate ghost and even to that of a very few heroic personalities being rewarded or punished.

Although there are several passages in the Homeric corpus that speak of an afterlife, the following are the only ones that indicate any sort of a punishment or reward in that afterlife. Even then, only the first three associate the afterlife fate with one's living conduct and behavior.[136]

Iliad

3.278   An you who under the earth (ὑπένερθε) take vengeance on dead men (καμόντας ἀνθρώπους), whoever among them has sworn to falsehood (ἐπίορκον ὀμόσση?).[137]

19.259   Furies, who underground (ὑπο γαῖαν) avenge dead men (ἀνθρώπους), when any man has sworn to a falsehood (ἐπίορκον ὀμόσση?).

Odyssey

11.576   eternal punishment for extremely wicked in afterlife.

4.561   reward of eternal life for Menalaus.

11.300   reward of eternal life for Castor and Polydeuces.

23.333   promise of eternal life for Odysseus.

---

[136] For a sampling of instances of conduct and behavior in Homer that does not involve an afterlife scenario, see Appendix I: "Instances in Homer of Important Conduct and Behavior not Associated with an Afterlife, Table 6."

[137] These two passages are so important that they are stated here in the Greek for amplification: *Il.* 3.278—τοῖσιν δ᾿ Ἀτρείδης μεγάλ᾿ εὔχετο χεῖρας ἀνασχών·/Ζεῦ πάτερ᾿Ιδηθεν μεδέων κύδιστε μέγιστε,/)Ἡέλιός θ᾿, ὅς πάντ᾿ ἐφορᾷς καὶ πάντ᾿ ἐπακούεις,/καὶ ποταμοὶ καὶ γαῖα, καὶ **οἳ ὑπένερθε καμόντας/ἀνθρώπους τίνυσθον ὅτις κ᾿ ἐπίορκον ὀμόσση,**/ὑμεῖς μάρτυροι ἔστε, φυλάσσετε δ᾿ ὅρκια πιστά. And *Il.* 19.258—ἴστω νῦν Ζεὺς πρῶτα θεῶν ὕπατος καὶ ἄριστος Γῆ τε καὶἩέλιος καὶἘρινύες, αἵθ᾿ ὑπὸ γαῖαν ἀνθρώπους τίνυνται, ὅτις κ᾿ ἐπίορκον ὀμόσση.

Thus we see that Homer has only a few instances to offer for our inquiry into conduct and behavior[138] as it affects the judgment of the dead. Nevertheless, the real significance of our investigation of Homer is that these concepts, indeed, do already appear at this early date.

---

[138] For a summary on conduct of Homer and other Greek writers, see Appendix K: "Conduct and Behavior that Influences the Afterlife: Greek Authors Inverse Index, Table 7."

CHAPTER 3

The Development of the Afterlife Concepts in Pre-Platonic Greece: From Hesiod to the Orphic Tablets

Pindar—Prelude to Plato

> But those with the courage to have lived three times in either realm while keeping their souls free from all unjust deeds, travel the road of Zeus to the tower of Kronos, where ocean breezes blow around the Isle of the Blessed (*Olympian* 2.68ff).[139]

Pindar was born at Cynoscephalia, close to Thebes around 518 BCE. He wrote his first victory ode, *Pythian* 10, in 498 BCE and his last, *Pythian* 8, in 446 BCE. In between those two dates he wrote the victory ode that is most significant to our inquiry: the second *Olympian* for the chariot victor of the 476 BCE games, Theron of Acragas.[140] According to Frank Nisetich, the "*Olympian* 2 contains the first passage in western literature to make reward after death depend on the observance of justice."[141] This is, of course, the very thesis I am examining in this project.

---

[139] All Pindar translations are by William H. Race, *Pindar*, 2 vols. (Cambridge: Harvard University Press, 1997), 1:71. This is the first extant Greek reference to metempsychosis after the saying of Xenophanes about Pythagoras (B7 DK).

[140] This chronology is from M.M. Willcock, ed., *Pindar: Victory Odes* (Cambridge: University Press, 1995), 1-4.

[141] This might also be claimed for Aeschylus. See *Eumenides* 267-75 and *Suppliants* 225-31, where punishment is the post-mortem reward for bad conduct. Norwood originally said that, "Of the judgment after death…an august picture is given by the Second Olympian, where for the first time in European literature we hear the tremendous doctrine that reward and punishment for the deeds of earthly life are meted out in another, on a principle moral and moral only" (Gilbert Norwood, *Pindar* [Berkeley: University of California Press, 1945], 60). This citation is referenced by Nisetich, *Pindar and Homer*, 27.

In the three hundred years between the flourishing of Homer and that of Pindar, it would appear from reading *Olympian 2* that much had changed in the beliefs concerning the human soul and its punishment or reward for its conduct and behavior during a person's lifetime. But, how did these changes come about? And, what were they?

Around the mid-sixth century BCE, one hundred years before Pindar, there appeared on the scene a man with a vastly different view of these beliefs than had ever appeared in the greater Greek world heretofore. Pythagoras originally came from Ionia, but at around the age of forty (c. 540 BCE), he moved to the region of Southern Italy and Sicily where Pindar was later to write much of his poetry.

Pythagoras held that a person consisted of a body and a soul, and that, although the body died, the soul was an eternal being that lived through many lifetimes.[142] It is believed by several modern scholars that Pythagoras derived these ideas from central Asian shamanism, where the soul of the shaman could descend into the world of the dead and return with "health for the sick...and to conduct the souls of the dead to their new home."[143] Homer's *Nekyia* and second *Nekyia* show similar functions being performed by Odysseus (getting information) and Hermes (conducting souls).

Many scholars believe that Pindar, in turn, received his beliefs concerning the afterlife from Pythagoras via Theron, the aforementioned tyrant in Sicily, for whom he wrote the victory ode for his Olympic victory of 476 BCE.[144] This is a

---

[142] For general information on Pythagoras, see G.S Kirk, J.E. Raven and M. Schofield, *The Presocratic Philosophers* (Cambridge: Cambridge University Press, 1983), 214-38; also see *Iamblicus: On the Pythagorean Life*, trans. Gillian Clark (Liverpool: Liverpool University Press, 1989), passim.

[143] Dodds thinks that both Greek and Indian metempsychosis have roots in shamanism. But Burkert suggests that the Greek theory may derive directly from India. Dodds, *Greeks and the Irrational*, 172n97. Burkert, *Lore and Science in Ancient Pythagoreanism*, 162ff.

[144] Woodbury argues for a Pythagorean connection in Pindar. But Nisetich says that "it has been all too easy to assume that he [Pindar] wrote Olympian 2 under the influence of an alien persuasion, that he was following a source," and cites H.S. Long and M. Nilsson as crediting Pythagoras or the Orphics as that source. Nisetich wants to show that it was Pindar himself that deserves the credit for the ideas in the poem. Leonard Woodbury, "Equinox in Acragas: Pindar, 01.2.61-2," *TAPA*, 97 (1966): 597-616; Nisetich, *Pindar and Homer*, 27f.

probable scenario, but it is by no means a definite one.[145] After all, two hundred and fifty to 300 years earlier, Homer and Hesiod had already defined many of the key religious concepts that were to go into Pindar's Olympic ode. So, we must question, why should Pindar's religious thinking require the ideas of Pythagoras?

We have already seen the evidence for an afterlife judgment in Homer. Moreover, his immediate successor, Hesiod, had claimed that there were five separate periods of generally devolving mankind, starting with an era of a 'golden' race on down to the time immediately prior to ours, which was the time of the Heroes. These Heroes were rewarded for their heroic conduct in a glorious place called the Isles of the Blest, which appears to be very similar to Homer's sparsely populated paradise of Elysium. However, in neither Homer's nor Hesiod's case were the inhabitants of the Isles to have died first but were, rather, translated alive to this place of eternal reward.

So, what specifically did Pindar add to Homer and Hesiod's picture of the afterlife? In the first place, in addition to the punishments found in Homer, there is now also a reward[146] that is to come and not just for a few people and, unlike Homer's and Hesiod's Heroes, it comes only after one's death. Secondly, this afterlife reward was not to be permanent; the soul must once more descend into a new body to live all over again. There was a way out of this return for those very few who persevered in justice over the period of three lifetimes, as cited in this chapter's opening quotation, when they could receive their permanent reward. The others presumably were doomed to repeat the cycle of birth and death, or to bear "pain too terrible to behold," eternally.[147]

---

[145] Roland Hampe denied a Pythagorean connection with the ode as does Nisetich. Roland Hampe, "Zur Eschatologie in Pindar's zweiter olympischer Ode," in *Hermenia-Festschrift fuer Otto Regenbogen*, 46-65; Frank J. Nisetich, "Immortality in Acragas," *Classical Philology* 83 no. 1 (Jan 1988): 6-12. See also, Fitzgerald who says that the poem is often read "in the light of certain esoteric beliefs [Pythagorean/Orphic] that the passage is supposed to reflect" (William Fitzgerald, "Pindar's Second Olympian," *Helios* 10 n. 1 [spring 1983], 50). He makes no claim for or against that supposition. Also Zuntz who says, there was a connection and that Pindar had deep convictions about it. Gunter Zuntz, *Persephone* (Oxford: Clarendon Press, 1971), 87-9.

[146] Homer had only punishment after death or a living translation to the Isles of the Blest.

[147] Pindar *Ol.* 2.67. There seem to be three classes of people in the afterlife: the good, the evil and the enduring good. This compares closely to Plato's reincarnatable curables, incurables and philosophers in the Phaedo.

Since neither of these two ideas, post-mortem reward and reincarnation, were in Homer or Hesiod, it therefore seems more likely that Pindar had gotten these additions from a 'Pythagorean/Orphic' source. After all, Pythagoras had lived and taught in Sicily, his followers continued his traditions in that region and Pindar's patron/client Theron was a Sicilian who most likely held Pythagorean beliefs.[148]

Pindar had written two odes, *Pythian 6* and *Isthmian 2*, for Theron's brother, Xenocrates, in which is found not a hint of the afterlife scene of Theron's *Olympian 2*. If the brother shared Theron's 'Pythagorean' beliefs, Xenocrates did not influence Pindar to include them in the odes for himself. So, it follows that Theron's family may not have believed in the odes' afterlife, but Theron himself still could have.

In assessing Pindar's real views it is most significant to look at the poem considered to have been written toward the end of his life. In *Pythian* 8, although it does not explicitly deny an afterlife, Pindar seems to express a diametrically opposite feeling from that of his earlier *Olympian* 2 poem for Theron:

> In a short time the delight of mortals burgeons,
> but so too does it fall to the ground,
> when shaken by a hostile purpose.
>
> Creatures of a day! What is some one? What is no one?
> A dream of a shadow is man.
> But whenever Zeus-given brightness comes,
> a shining light rests upon men, and a gentle life.[149]

This is a beautiful and optimistic verse, but it makes no mention of a beneficent afterlife. Consequently, from this we can say that Pindar himself may not have, or

---

148 Are we really sure of what Theron believed? We might determine this by looking at other poetry about Theron or his family—did it also include an afterlife scenario? If such poetry about Theron written by another poet were to express the afterlife concepts of *Olympian* 2, then we could say that Theron actually held them. I have, as yet, found no such poetry in other Sicilian poets.

149 *Pythian* 8.93-97 (Trans., Race, Pindar, 337). Nemean 11.13ff is even gloomier where in the midst of riches, beauty and winning contests one must "remember that mortal are the limbs he clothes and that the earth is the last garment of all he will wear" (trans., Race, *Pindar*, 127).

no longer, believed in his earlier odes' afterlife.[150] Even if that is the case, whether he personally believed or not, his one victory ode is evidence for new details in the concept of an afterlife.

Other Sicilian Poets

Whatever Pindar himself may have personally believed, did he get the religious beliefs for his second *Olympian* ode via Theron?[151] Possibly, since Pindar's other odes contradict and deny the afterlife beliefs found only in Theron's ode (and a few fragmentary dirges), so indeed, it looks like Pindar might simply have been using his patron's belief system when writing about him.[152]

Nevertheless, a reasonable method to further pursue a more definitive answer to this question might be to see if Sicily's other lyric poets had also written of similar afterlife beliefs. That is, are those afterlife beliefs found in any other poets' writings dedicated to Theron's family or his fellow Sicilian tyrant, Hieron? As it happens, we do have two other lyric poets from the same time period who competed with Pindar for the commissions of Theron and Hieron, namely, Simonides and Bacchylides.

Did their poetry contain a 'Pythagorean' or any other vision of the afterlife? If it did, the ideas were likely 'in the air' for all to use. If not, we could reasonably claim that the new afterlife ideas in <u>Olympian</u> 2 may have originated with Theron and/or Pindar.

---

[150] Indeed, Pindar echoes Sarpedon in Homer *Il.* 12.322-28 where he says, "But since men must die, why would anyone sit in darkness and coddle a nameless old age to no use, deprived of all noble deeds? No! that contest shall be mine to undertake; you [the god] grant the success I desire" (*Ol.* 1.82-5).

[151] Note that C.M. Bowra, *Pindar* (Oxford: Clarendon Press, 1964), 121 claimed that in his account of life after death, Pindar "turns into high poetry Theron's own views," and "Theron must have instructed Pindar in his own esoteric beliefs." Conversely, Rohde, *Psyche*, 416 had said that Pindar's 'subservience to another man's belief—that is quite unthinkable."

[152] M.M. Willcock shows that earlier scholars (i.e., Wilamowitz and Bowra) have seen in Pindar's work a key to the poet's own beliefs, whereas Bundy in 1962, "set his face firmly against the discovery in them of private opinions or beliefs of the poet…What appears to be personal views are not those of Pindar the citizen of Thebes, but of Pindar the poet." Since then other scholars, "such as Kohnken are not quite persuaded that absolutely everything is for praise and no personal references are made." For this brief discussion on Pindar's personal beliefs see Willcock, *Pindar: Victory Odes*, 19-20. Thus, the question remains open.

My thesis here is that there were <u>no</u> advanced [toward Pindar's] afterlife ideas in Simonides or Bacchylides reflecting the advanced beliefs of the Sicilians—thus they are not Hieron's, Xenocrates' or their own. The ideas must come from either Theron and/or Pindar originally or from another Sicilian connection. We will investigate this thesis in the following texts.

Simonides of Ceos.

There are only negative allusions to the afterlife in Simonides's poetry:

> Man's strength is little, and futile his concerns, his lifespan is short, filled with trouble on trouble; and over it death, inescapable, uniform, looms, to be dispensed in equal shares to high and low alike (*Dirges* 520).[153]

These words harken back to the common post-mortem fate of all men as found in the *Iliad*, thus Simonides did not believe in a beneficent afterlife.

Bacchylides.

His poetry shows a more positive outlook on the afterlife as found in his third and fifth Olympian Odes for Hieron where, in the story of Croesus, he shows two concepts of immortality, a translation and a *katabasis*:

> "Apollo the Delian whisked old Croesus away to Hyperborea, and nestled him down with his dainty girls—for piety: he sent up most to holy Pytho" (*Ol.* 3).

And, he has Heracles' and Meleager's shades meet and converse in Hades.

> "He [Heracles] glimpsed the shades of the sorry men—flitting like leaves that rustle to breezes…knowing the man, Meleager's shadow" (*Ol.* 5).[154]

---

[153] Translated by M.L. West, *Greek Lyric Poetry* (Oxford: Clarendon Press, 1993), 162. Simonides also wrote an ode on the Spartans at Plataea: "They died but are not dead: there is that which raises men above Hades' call" (William J. Philbin, trans. *To You Simonides* [Dublin: Dolmen Editions, 1977], 42). This does not mean an afterlife, only immortal fame.

[154] Translated by Robert Fagles, *Bacchylides: Complete Poems* (New Haven: Yale University Press, 1961), 9, 14-15. The *katabasis*, or descent into the underworld, pre-dates Homer as shown by the story of Eurystheus' labors (fetching the hound of Hades) at *Od.* 8.360ff.

Here, in the third ode, we have an old story that does offer a reward for piety, but it is of the same type as found in Homer's and Hesiod's bodily translations to Elysium and the Isles of the Blest, and therefore should not be considered an advance over these poets' religious thought. The fifth ode has a familiar *katabasis* theme that was widespread throughout the Greek world and offers no advance toward what we find in Pindar.

Therefore, one can see that we might reasonably claim that Pindar's contemporary Sicilian poets did not write about the afterlife themes found in Pindar.

The reason the other poets did not make use of the more progressive afterlife themes could be because their patrons did not demand it since those patrons did not hold the ideas themselves. They are then either Pindar's ideas or they came to him from a Pythagorean source ignored by the other poets. Theron may have held these ideas but his brother Xenocrates might not have done so. Thus, there would be no need for Simonides to write of them, and if Hieron did not believe them, there is no reason for either Simonides or Bacchylides to write of them. The question still remains open as to who, if anyone, influenced Pindar. We must look yet further.

Geographical Considerations—East and West

Another direction for our inquiry into possible external influence on Pindar would be to examine what was taking place in religious thought from the time of Homer until that of Pindar in the non-Italian part of Greater Greece. How did the ideas we find in Homer resonate with his mainland Greek successors? Did his mainland successors advance his afterlife concepts such that we would expect the development we see in Pindar? If not, we could reasonably expect that the development took place elsewhere.

In order to look into these possibilities, we will look at or go back and revisit some of the writings of Hesiod, Solon and Theognis on the Greek mainland, and then at Simonides, Bacchylides and Empedocles in the Italian/Sicilian region, along with Heraclitus from Ionia. The usefulness of performing this type of investigation, besides searching for Pindar's influencer, if one may be found, is that it also provides us a framework in which to examine the afterlife beliefs of these other authors.

Hesiod (c. 750).

It would be fair to say that there is no claim to an afterlife for a contemporary person in the poems of Hesiod. On the contrary, although he is constantly extolling the value of justice and oath-keeping, nowhere does he suggest that there is an afterlife reward for excelling at these conducts.[155] Condemning vice in the harshest way, Hesiod says:

> But whoever deliberately lies in his sworn testimony, therein, by injuring
> Right, he is blighted past healing; his family remains more obscure thereafter,
> while the true-sworn man's line gains in worth (*Works* 280ff).[156]

Clearly, for Hesiod, the penalty for sins and the reward for virtues are visited on the future generations, and not in a future life.

There is, nevertheless, an afterlife in Hesiod where the 'golden' race "in the time of Kronos...[after they died] they have been divine spirits...watchers over mortal men" (*Works* 110ff). The next race of silver, when they had died "have been called the mortal blessed below" (*Works* 142f). These races did nothing in the way of conduct or behavior to deserve their reward. Indeed, those of the silver race were witless, committed crimes and dishonored the gods but still they had a blessed afterlife.

The next race, that of the bronze, deserved punishment for their crimes and did suffer the more traditional Homeric non-*Nekyia* common fate of going down "to chill Hades' house of decay leaving no names" (*Works* 153f). As we saw earlier, the members of the fourth race of the Heroes were the first to be rewarded for their conduct. Although some of them died and suffered the traditional fate,

---

155 However, West's commentary on Works and Days has line 218 look like a theodicy, were he says, "as bad men often appear to prosper, morality has to say that they will be worse off in the end, whether the punishment falls later in life, <u>in the afterlife</u>, or upon their children and descendants" (M.L. West, *Hesiod: Works and Days* [Oxford: Clarendon Press, 1978], 210-11; emphasis mine). I cannot agree with West's full statement since punishment in an afterlife for the current race is not attested anywhere in Hesiod.

156 All Hesiod translations, unless noted, are in M.L. West, *Hesiod: Theogony and Works and Days* (Oxford: Oxford University Press, 1988), 45.

Zeus allowed some to be rewarded for their heroism and be sent alive to the Isles of the Blest (*Works* 166f).[157]

Hesiod, and we, belong to his fifth race and can be rewarded by the gods for conduct and behavior, but never in a personal afterlife. In fact, a final cataclysm will eventually descend on this race and even the gods will abandon mortals to defenselessness against evil (*Works* 175ff).

The Peasant Bard, Hesiod, seems to have no conception of a blessed afterlife for the people of his and our race. If Hesiod, did not know of such an afterlife could the earlier Homer have known? Could the foregoing observation be cited as an indication that the afterlife sections of the even earlier Homer are actually later non-Homeric interpolations? Perhaps it could, but this small observation will not resolve that great scholarly question. For, it is just as likely that it could also simply show that the non-aristocratic Hesiod reflected the more popularly accepted belief of the common lot for all in Hades, that of being a mindless shadow of the person that is hardly a life at all.[158]

Solon (c. 575).

Even 150 years later, Solon was still holding out no hope for a blessed afterlife. He, just like Hesiod, stressed a high degree of virtue[159] for the living but offered no concomitant post-mortem reward. He does say that Zeus will address all insults:

> "Such is the punishment of Zeus...one pays at once, another later; and if some escape the gods' pursuing fate themselves, it comes sometime for sure,"

But, like Hesiod, he too claimed only that those who displayed wicked conduct would eventually pay the price, either—

---

[157] The heroes in Homer were translated to Elysium due to some relationship with the gods but in Hesiod Works (156ff) it is justice and nobility that wins a reward for the fourth race of humans in the Isles of the Blest.

[158] We should also consider that just because a belief appears at any given time (Homer), it is not necessary that subsequent people (Hesiod) have to continue adherence to it.

[159] Solon's desire for good order (eu)nomi/h) led him to condemn disorder, wickedness, roughness, pride, outrage, mad folly, crooked judgments, proud deeds, and deadly strife (frag 3.30-389). See C. M. Bowra, *Early Greek Elegists* (Cambridge: Harvard University Press, 1938), 85.

"their children, or their later family" (frag 2.15).[160]

Solon was an aristocrat as was the earlier Homer, and he still held to the traditional Greek view of a common lot in Hades for all of the dead, bereft of any reward or punishment for their conduct and behavior while alive. So, perhaps it was not just the societal class that affected these beliefs but rather it was the geographical location; that of western vs. eastern Greece.[161]

Theognis (c. 525).

What of the aristocratic Theognis just a few years later? He also held fast to the traditional beliefs of having no afterlife in which to receive either reward or punishment. Even though he was an aristocrat, he is supposed to have said that "the whole of a)reth/is summed up in δικαιοσύνη, and every man may be ἀγαθός if he is δίκαιος" (147f).[162] This seems to contradict his other writings' attitude toward anyone but the elite, where a person is agathos by birth only (57f, 131f). Again, like Hesiod and Solon, even with his emphasis on righteous conduct, the most he would grant even to his friend Cyrnus was the fact that "not even in death will your fame fade, but men will always cherish your immortal name" (237ff).[163] He also said: the wicked prosper and righteousness is forsaken

---

[160] Translated as 13.25-32 in M.L. West, *Greek Lyric Poetry*, 77. This was the same conception of the sins of the fathers being visited on the future generations that was held by Homer *Il.* 4.160.

[161] There were the mysteries at Eleusis at this same time, but they allowed only for a better fate after death. There was no Pythagorean metempsychosis type of belief as would later appear in Sicily in the west.

[162] Theogonidae writings are inconsistent. The traditional agathos were aristocrats—a common person could not be agathos in Homer—and not usually in Theognis, except here.

[163] Translated by West, *Greek Lyric Poetry*, 68-9. But, Bowra has 37ff translated: "Ne're even in death shalt thou thy fame forego, but men will keep in memory unchanging the name of Cyrnus…world without end, shalt live a song to men [πᾶσι δ᾽, ὅσοισι μέμηλε, καὶ ἐσσομένοισιν ἀοιδὴ ἔσσηι ὁμῶς, ὄφρ᾽ ἂν γῆ τε καὶ ἠέλιος]" (C. M. Bowra, *Early Greek Elegists*, 164-6). Using these words Bowra makes an excellent case for the "belief that song and memory literally give life to the dead," and not just figuratively. Some may have believed that, but to me it seems more likely that song was simply a way to 'immortalize' the name and fame of a person; ἀοιδήshould thus be taken as "celebrated in song" as long as earth and sun are possible and not "live a song to men".

(743ff), and all alike pass to Hades (708ff), where all earthly pleasures are over (973ff).

One did have to pay for wickedness, but as with his other mainland predecessors, for Theognis, it was either in the present or in future generations (731-52), the latter of which he thought unjust.

None of our eastern Greek writers that we reviewed so far seemed to be influenced by either the mysteries or by Pythagorean/Orphic type of religious thinking.[164]

Heraclitus (c. 490).

However, just a generation later the afterlife beliefs blossomed significantly. Around 490 BCE in Ionia, Heraclitus was expounding on radically different themes concerning an elaborate set of afterlife concepts.[165] Now, the gods honor dead warriors who "win <for themselves> greater (better) destinies" (frag 24-5).[166] "Justice will catch up with fabricators of falsehoods and those who bear witness to them" (frag 28b). and "There await people when they die things they neither expect nor <even> imagine" (frag 27). There is even a final judgment and conflagration (frag 66).

The living and the dead are the same (frag 88), and the soul of the living comes from the dead (frag 62). The dead will rise and become the guardians of the living (frag 63).[167] He claims that the dead are awake and the living sleep (frag 21),

---

[164] Furthermore, a hundred years later, the mainland Democritus was still condemning the idea of an afterlife and its punishments as something that could be used to threaten people. At least, the mainland intellectuals had not accepted the afterlife concept as yet.

[165] There is a scholarly debate over whom Heraclitus was following. Since in fragments 40 and 120, he reproaches Pythagoras (and Hesiod), it is believed that he gave the Orphics priority and said that Pythagoras used them as a source. Rohde, *Psyche*, 336 claimed that Pythagoras got his theory of metempsychosis from Orphism. Walter Burkert says, "it is the Pythagorean variant of Orphism that is manifest in Pindar, Empedocles, Herodotus, and Plato" (Burkert, *Lore and Science in Ancient Pythagoreanism*, 128-33).

[166] All Heraclitus translations by T.M. Robinson, *Heraclitus* (Toronto: University of Toronto Press, 1987), 23-69.

[167] Compare Hesiod's guardians.

then at frag 89, the awake see a holistic universe but the sleeping see their own individual universe.[168]

In fragment 118, Heraclitus makes the strange claim that dry souls are wisest and best. This enigmatic statement may have to do with the water of forgetfulness. If a soul drank too much of the water, it would forget all of its previous life, whereas the wise soul would drink a little and retain his or her pre-natal memories. Did Heraclitus himself believe this interpretation, or were his words usurped inappropriately by later writers to describe the mechanics of reincarnation? Regardless of Heraclitus' intent, Plato will use it in the Myth of Er to explain our apparent natal forgetfulness.

Heraclitus' time frame is approximately the same as Theognis,[169] so why the wide difference in their afterlife beliefs? I would argue that most significantly, Theognis comes from a long line of mainland Greek tradition but Heraclitus comes from the eastern Ionian area. There and in the western Italian, the beliefs concerning the afterlife had taken a major turn away from the undifferentiated Hades of the *Iliad* and now look more like the so-called 'interpolation' of book 11 in the *Odyssey*. Indeed, it looked even more like the thinking attributed to Pythagoras, originally Ionian now Italian, and to the Orphics.

Pindar resumed. After our excursion through his predecessors and contemporaries, here we return to Pindar in order to complete the deliberation on his personal beliefs.

He is moving in the same Italian circles in which we find Pythagoras and the Sicilian tyrants, so the logical conclusion would be that he got his ideas from what was in circulation at that place and time. But, what of Simonides and Bacchylides? Did they share in this religious thinking of their time and place? According to their extant works on behalf of the same patrons/clientele of Pindar, we have seen that they did not.[170]

So, on the one hand, we have the evidence from mainland Greece denying a pleasant afterlife in the sixth century, which would indicate that the 'witless

---

[168] Also, compare Plato's awake pre-natal souls that see the reality of the Forms but the sleeping (enfleshed souls) perceive only shadows.

[169] Perhaps 20 to 30 years different.

[170] See argument on Simonides and Bacchylides above.

shades in Hades' concept was <u>the</u> dominant and traditional belief. On the other hand, where we would expect to see the new belief becoming dominant with the poets of the Sicilian tyrants, we find that it is not. Most surprisingly, they are not dominant even with Pindar himself except for the one victory ode to Theron. The conclusion that seems most reasonable, although Pindar certainly could have 'invented' the concepts himself, is that it is nevertheless much more likely that he acquired them from and used them for the benefit of his client. And, for the next fifty years of his life, he never used them in an extant poem again. These religious ideas came to him neither from the mainland nor from his contemporary poets and they even contradict his own otherwise stated beliefs as spelled out above. Therefore, they are not his invention and most likely do derive from Pythagorean sources, probably at Theron's urging.

Empedocles (c. 450).

Another near contemporary Sicilian was Empedocles, in whom we find no such Pindaric contradictions concerning an afterlife belief. In his *Physics* he claims the preexistence of the person in a unity: all is a single whole and complete (frag 14), and people exist before and after this life (frag 15), and one is from all and all is from one (frag 17).

In his *Purifications*, he proclaims the truth of and the reason for his belief in reincarnation : people are exiled from the gods for error and breaking oaths (frag 115), and separated from honor and great happiness (frag 119), and reincarnated in many forms (frag 117). We are now in a joyless place (frag 121), and clothed in an unfamiliar garment of flesh (frag 126). However, "at the end they come among men on earth as prophets, minstrels, physicians, and leaders, and from these they arise as gods, highest in honor" (frag 146), where "they are mortals no longer" (frag 112).[171]

Empedocles has no explicit conception of a judgment in the afterlife, but there must be an implicit judgment that caused one's exile from the realm of the gods to this realm of flesh; however, he does not seem to indicate who or what has judged one guilty of error.[172] The reincarnation espoused by Empedocles will

---

[171] Translated by M.R. Wright, *Empedocles: the Extant Fragments* (New Haven: Yale University Press, 1981), 166-291.

[172] We have seen this same kind of implicit judgment in all of Plato's myths, especially in the *Phaedrus*, and will see it in the Egyptian texts.

figure heavily in Plato who will integrate it with an afterlife judgment. Thus, we see here a part of the entire scenario of rewards and punishments in the afterlife that will fully flourish with Plato.

Orphic Gold Tablets (c. 325-275).

On the famous gold tablets found in Petelia and Thurii in southern Italy we find some very interesting inscriptions that have usually been considered as reflecting Orphic beliefs in the afterlife. Two of these tables, from Petelia and Thurii respectively, are partially cited here:[173]

> I am a child of Earth and starry Heaven;
> But my race is of Heaven alone.
> This ye know yourselves.
> But I am parched with thirst and I perish.
> Give me quickly the cold water flowing
> <u>forth from the Lake of Memory</u>.[174]

Also

> I come from the pure, pure Queen of those
> below...For I also vow that I am of
> your blessed race.
> And I have paid the penalty for deeds
> unrighteous...I have flown out of the sorrowful, weary circle...
> And now I come as a suppliant
> To holy Persephoneia...Happy and blessed one, thou shalt be a god instead of
> mortal.[175]

---

[173] Both translated by W.K.C. Guthrie, *Orpheus and Greek Religion* (London: Methuen, 1935), 171-5.

[174] The <u>Petelia</u> tablet reflects the belief that humans are fallen gods who return to their heavenly home after a sojourn in the flesh on earth. This mirrors the inscription on the fifth century bone tablet of Olbia on which we find the words, 'life-death-life;' a reference to one's multiple existences. One lives in the divine world, suffers death in the flesh, then returns to the divine world.

[175] The <u>Thurii</u> tablet expresses essentially the same thing as the <u>Petelia</u> tablet, but adds two issues: a judgment penalty for unrighteous deeds; and an allusion to a cycle of incarnations whereas a single incarnation would suffice in the former tablet.

The fact that a "weary circle" is mentioned would lead one to believe that the inscriber was referring to cyclic transmigration of souls and that therefore metempsychosis is an Orphic doctrine since these tablets are described as being Orphic. The reason they are so described is because they look like the so-called Orphic material in Plato. Of course, the reason that Plato is linked to Orphic doctrine is that it is generally believed that some of his ideas came from the Orphics. Here we have a rampant circular argument that neither shows that the tablets were Orphic nor that Plato bases his dialogs on Orphic beliefs.

In the two tablets shown above we have a possibility of two different doctrines: one having multiple incarnations and the other not. Are both Orphic?[176] I will argue that there is at least one variant of the Orphic/Pythagorean tradition that holds to no doctrine of metempsychosis at all. This will be based on the evidence of silence from the Petelia tablet[177] and more scientifically on the positive statement on the bone tablet found at Olbia in 1978 that states simply: βίος θάνατος βίος and a word indicating Orpheus ὀρφιχοίοr ὀφιχῶν.[178] This has been taken to show that the orphic belief was in a cyclic rebirth where "temporary death is replaced with a new birth."[179] My contention is that no cycle of life—temporary death—then reincarnation is implied here. Rather this indicates that these Orphics believed in an original life in the divine realm, followed by a death into

---

[176] Walter Burkert, for example, says that there are traditions of both the Orphic and Pythagorean doctrines of metempsychosis. Burkert, *Greek Religion* trans. John Ruffan (Cambridge: Harvard University Press, 1987), 298-301.

[177] Also, similarly in the more recently discovered Pelinna lamellae dated to the late fourth century. See Fritz Graf, "Dionysian and Orphic Eschatology: New Texts and Old Questions," in Thomas H. Carpenter and Christopher A. Faraone, *Masks of Dionysus* (Ithaca: Cornell University Press, 1993), 240.

[178] These bone tablets are dated to the later fifth century. Zhmud' says that one of the three plates of "Orphic grafitti from Olbia (Vth century B.C.)" has the phrase "βίος θάνατος βίος ἀλήθεια Διος ύσω ὀρφιχοί" which proves that there was an organized Orphic community in the 5th century. He also claims that they believed in metempsychosis because one of the plates had ψυχήand σῶμα on the recto (Leonid Zhmud', "Orphism and grafitti from Olbia," *Hermes* 120 [1992]: 159-168). His first claim may be true, however I disagree with the latter claim and contend that the phrases are better interpreted as: life—death—true life, to Dionysus from Orphics. They did indeed believe that the soul (ψυχή) was fallen into a body (σῶμα), but that it could return to true life once again.

[179] Zhmud', "Orphism and grafitti from Olbia," 168.

the earthly flesh, followed by rebirth into true life as a divine being once more.[180] Furthermore, the fragments of Heraclitus do not require multiple incarnations, although those of Empedocles and Pindar do. Interestingly, Plato's first eschatological myth in the *Gorgias* contains no reincarnation doctrine. That was to come later, in the *Phaedo*, after his visit to Sicily and his indoctrination into Pythagoreanism.

For these reasons, I am persuaded that the Pythagoreans believed in metempsychosis but the earlier Orphics did not.

However, one could safely assume that, where Pindar, Heraclitus, Empedocles and the gold leaves agree, they probably are deriving ideas from the same or similar, by now syncretistic, sources.

Summary

In this chapter, we have seen that the very little information concerning the afterlife found in Homer did not make much of an impression on his mainland successors. The mysteries at Eleusis promised some benefit to the initiated, but Hesiod, Solon, Theognis and even the later Democritus represent those intellectuals who manifest no belief in a beneficent afterlife. Of course, it seems that all Greeks held to the fact of an afterlife—but in the form of the predominant Homeric concept of undifferentiated shades in Hades.

In the western Greek world new ideas, such as reincarnation, were coming to the fore. Pythagoras incorporated, embellished upon and promoted the ideas of the Orphics. Since they believed in the conduct of this life influencing the next one, ethical considerations became more prominent in post-mortem rewards and punishments. Heraclitus, Pindar and Empedocles express these newer ideas in their poetry and thereby set the stage for Plato, who will incorporate them into his own eschatological teachings.

Now, let us look at this chapter's texts that have an explicit reference to an afterlife, using the summary chart on the following page.

---

180 Also, the Pelinna lamellae have only one incarnation in the translation found in Graf, "Dionysian and Orphic Eschatology," 239–42. Zuntz denies that the Orphics held to metempsychosis based on there being no statement of such until Proclus. Zuntz, *Persephone*, 337n5.

SUMMARY CHART

of

Rewards and Punishment for Conduct and Behavior in Hesiod, Pindar's Olympian 2 and Dirges, and Fragments in Heraclitus and Empedocles.[181]

Author/Work/ Passage	Conduct/Behavior	Reward/Punishment
Hesiod		
Works		
158	more just, better	Isles of Blest[182]
Pindar		
Olympian		
2.16	justice, injustice	immortality
2.53	virtues, sins, oaths, courage, unjust, just	judged in realm of Zeus, go to Isle of the Blest
Dirges		
129	pious	in paradise
130	impious	in black gloom
133	ancient grief, wisdom	reborn as best men
137	see these rites	a new life
214	pious and just	sweet hope
Heraclitus		
fragments		
24/5	death in battle, honor	better destiny
27	not stated	things not dreamed

---

[181] Also, see Appendix K, Table 7.

[182] Not for the current race of people, but just for the previous race of Heroes. Homer and Pindar also spoke of an afterlife only for heroes, albeit of our race.

28	falsehoods	Justice will catch
63	not stated	rise up guardians
66	not stated	judged in fire

Empedocles

<u>Purifications</u>

112	good deeds, honor	mortal no longer
115	error, murder broke oath	exiled from the gods
117	pre-natal wrong	reincarnated
118	pre-natal wrong	to unfamiliar place
119	pre-natal wrong	lose honor-happiness
121	pre-natal wrong	wander in darkness
124	pre-natal wrong	mortality is scene of sorrow
126	pre-natal wrong	reincarnated
146	pre-natal good	return as best men

A fuller citation of all pertinent statements concerning the afterlife for all of the writers discussed in Chapters 2, 3 and 4 is found in Appendix H: "Passages from Greek Authors Concerning the Afterlife."

CHAPTER 4

The Development of the Afterlife Concepts in Pre-Platonic Greece: The Dramatists

Aeschylus, Sophocles, Euripides and Aristophanes

Aeschylus

> And if any other mortal who has wronged a god or a stranger, with impious action, or his dear parents, you shall see how each has the reward Justice ordains. For Hades is mighty in holding mortals to account below the earth, and with mind that records them in its tablets he surveys all things (*Eumenides* 267-275).[183]

It has been claimed that this is the first reference to a judgment in the afterlife, except for perjury, in the Greek world.[184] This may be true but almost impossible to prove since the same claim has been made for his contemporary, Pindar.[185] The question of priority is less important than the fact that two Greeks on opposite sides of the Greek world came to a similar conclusion on some form of a post-mortem judgment at approximately the same time. As was asked in the previous section concerning Pindar, we can ask again here: why did this happen?

Aeschylus was born in 525 BCE at Eleusis and wrote his first tragedy ca. 499 BCE. Nine years later, in 490, he fought the Persians at Marathon. Significantly,

---

[183] All *Eumenides* translations are by Hugh Lloyd-Jones, *The Eumenides by Aeschylus* (Englewood: Prentice-Hall, 1970), 27.

[184] The same claim has been made for Pindar who has both rewards and punishments in an afterlife. See K.J. Dover, *Greek Popular Morality* (Berkeley: University of California Press, 1974), 263.

[185] *Ol.* 2.58ff. But Aeschylus never offers a reward for good conduct. So Pindar is positive and Aeschylus is negative on this.

he ventured to Sicily in 476 and again in 470 at the same time that Pindar, Simonides and Bacchylides were flourishing.[186] His plays in which the afterlife punishments are most prominent are *The Persians* (ca. 472 BCE), *The Suppliants* (463),[187] and *The Eumenides* (458).

Aeschylus may have been influenced by the same religious thinking that influenced Pindar to write *Olympian* 2 in 476 BCE. However, it is also possible that he was simply influenced by the Homeric *Nekyia* or even the Mysteries closer to home.

The Greek mainland had had their Eleusinian mysteries for many centuries, but those mysteries had promised only a 'better' lot after death for the initiated than for the non-initiated.[188] However, the Eleusinian Mysteries did not claim to offer "a future state of compensation for the good and evil deeds of this world," and anyone could be initiated regardless of their virtues.[189] Now, with Aeschylus, we are seeing a moral reason for suffering punishments after death, which is something new.[190]

---

[186] Dates and biography in: Alan H. Sommerstein, *Aeschylus: Eumenides* (Cambridge: Cambridge University Press, 1989), 17; Anthony J. Podlecki, *The Persians by Aeschylus* (Englewood Cliffs: Prentice-Hall, 1970), xii.

[187] This play was long thought to be early but a papyrus published in 1952, the *Oxyrhynchus Papyri* 2256 fr. 3, shows that it was written later in Aeschylus' life. Note that his later plays develop the idea of an afterlife judgment. See discussion in A.F. Garvie, *Aeschylus' Supplices: Play and Trilogy* (Cambridge: University Press, 1969), vi-28.

[188] Isocrates allowed only that the Mysteries' initiation "inspires in those who partake of it sweeter hope regarding both the end of life and all eternity" (*Isocrates Panegyricus* 28; see George Norlin, *Isocrates* (New York: G.P. Putnam's Sons, 1928), 135.

[189] Erwin Rohde, *Psyche*, 239. There is an ancient and modern scholarly debate on whether 'ethics' was involved since murderers were excluded from the Mysteries. The question is why where they excluded—for ritualistic pollution or for injustice to one's fellow persons? If for ritual only, as complained of by Diogenes, then we see that an ethical conduct did not yet count for the afterlife at Eleusis.

[190] However, in the western Greek world over 60 years earlier, Pythagoras had already claimed that a person was reincarnated over several lifetimes and that conduct did matter in determining the quality of one's next incarnation. Unfortunately, there are no details on the mechanics of his rebirth theory so we do not know what happened, if anything, in the interval between incarnations. Pythagorean reincarnation is not the same thing as an afterlife judgment, although later, Plato will combine the two concepts very effectively.

Afterlife affirming. Aeschylus has only a few references to punishments in the after-life, and those are irrefutably taking place in the underworld. In *The Eumenides*, Orestes is fleeing from the Eyrines and it is claimed that, "That man [Orestes] shall be never be free; though he flee beneath the earth, he shall never gain his liberty. He shall come stained with the guilt of murder" (*Eum.* 175). This passage, of course, uses the language of pollution,[191] but later at *Eum.* 267ff (cited at the beginning of this chapter), we have the prohibition of offences against the gods, strangers or parents. Then, at *Eum.* 337ff, Aeschylus has an even stronger statement of what was said at 175, "That after mortals to whom has come wanton murder of their own, I shall follow, until they descend below the earth; and after death no wide liberty is theirs" (*Eum.* 338-40). At 387, the Eumenides claim that they "are mindful of wrongs," and that they will punish the sighted (living) and the sightless (dead) alike in the sunless slime. Finally, at 440 and 718, Aeschylus alludes to the story of the parricide Ixion, who was purified by the pity of Zeus and taken up into heaven.[192]

In the *Suppliant Maidens*, Aeschylus first clearly links conduct and behavior in this life with a judgment in the afterlife where he has Danaus say: "And how can man be pure who would wrest from an unwilling sire an unwilling bride? Nay, for such an act, not even in the realm of Hades, after death, shall he escape arraignment for outrage [unnatural act]. There also, so men tell, among the dead another Zeus holds a last judgment upon misdeeds" (δικάζει▯Ζεὺς ἄλλος ἐν καμοῦσιν ὑστάτας δίκας; *Suppl.* 225-31).[193] In *Suppl.* 413-6 vengeance after death is promised to one who would violate the sanctuary of a suppliant.

Even in Aeschylus' earlier work, *The Persians*, written in 472 BCE, he has an explicit "ghost" scene where Darius' queen Atossa conjures him up from the dead:[194] "But friends, sing over these libations to the dead songs of good omen,

---

[191] A stain or pollution can be like blood of one's victim clinging to one's hands (*Eum.* 41f) and can be transmitted to others by some form of contact (see Robert Parker, *Miasma* [Oxford: Clarendon Press, 1983], 104ff). One can be morally just and still be ritually polluted as we will see with Oedipus in the "Sophocles" section.

[192] This is a reference to a reward in the afterlife, but not for morality. Ixion, "he who was the first to kill [and make] supplication", later sinned greatly in heaven and was then eternally punished, being bound to a wheel in the underworld.

[193] Translated by Herbert Weir Smyth, *Aeschylus*, vol. 1 (New York: G.P. Putnam's Sons, 1926), 23. Cf. *Suppl.* 158 for reference to the underworld Zeus.

[194] This and other ghost conjuring scenes leads Lloyd-Jones to note that, "the belief that a dead hero could influence events on earth must have been firmly held by Aeschylus' original audience" (Lloyd-Jones, *The Eumenides*, 60).

and conjure up the Spirit (daimon) of Darius" (*Per.* 620).[195] Darius' son Xerxes had been guilty of hubris in his blind attempt to conquer the Greeks and now the queen and Darius are concerned for Xerxes' and their country's welfare. Xerxes had "wounded God with overboastful rashness" (832), and had violated the axiom that "mortal man should not think more than mortal thoughts" (820). Now, "Zeus is standing by, the punisher of thoughts too overboastful, a harsh and careful scrutineer" (827).

In this work we see that the spirits of the dead are quite alive, similarly to *Odyssey* book 24, and Darius, being a king, even holds a great position in Hades.

There are very few words connoting "good" conduct and behavior in the above passages; however, Aeschylus had much to say about the kinds of "bad" behavior that could merit a post-mortem punishment.

Denying an afterlife. We have noted that Pindar's *Olympian 2* and some of his dirges expressed an anomalous opinion compared to the majority of his other works. Pindar's positive afterlife considerations had conflicted significantly with his negative assertions and this is also true of Aeschylus. In many passages he seems to indicate that the dead are anything but consciously alive, and Aeschylus' dead are treated more in the same manner as they were in the non-*Nekyia* passages of Homer.

Discussing the troubles of the past, the Herald in the *Agamemnon* tells the Leader that: "Our labour's past; past for the dead so that they will never care even to wake to life again" (*Ag.* 568-9).[196]

---

[195] Darius is conjured out of concern for Xerxes' overbearing overboastful ignorance. For terms that describe Xerxes' vices, see Persians 676 for mistake and 725 for loss of wits and 744-50 for blind, impetuous, foolish and 808-31 for hubris, blasphemy. Cf. Darius as god's counselor at line 653. There is no judgment of the dead here, but vices that might provoke such a judgment are enumerated. Translated by Podlecki, *The Persians by Aeschylus*, 78.

[196] Translated by Herbert Weir Smyth, *Aeschylus*, vol. 2 (London: William Heinemann, 1926), 51. Note that in Murray's translation, the 'troubles' themselves appear to be in the grave; not the dead person (Gilbert Murray, *The Agamemnon of Aeschylus* [New York: Oxford University Press, 1920], 25). Actually, the troubles (πόνος) are past but the dead (τεθνηκόσιν) are the ones who do not care to rise again.

The statements in the *Choephori* waffle on the afterlife. There Electra and Orestes are asking their dead father to help avenge his murder; "murderous stroke let murderous stroke atone." Orestes doubts that he can summon his ghost, but the Chorus says "the dead man's mind is not subdued by the fire's ravening jaw" (306ff). Then, seemingly contradictorily, at 517-8 Orestes says, "But to the unconscious dead it was a poor solace that she sent [Clytemnestra's libations]."[197]

Doubting an afterlife, the Homer-like statements in *Seven* 683ff have Eteocles hoping only for a good name after death: "If ill luck must come, it must come without disgrace; such fame alone profits the dead; but ill luck plus disgrace—that brings no renown."[198] This is exactly the same kind of sentiment we saw expressed by Sarpedon in the *Iliad*.

In fragment 266, Aeschylus claims that the dead "feel not or joy or grief." It is up to Justice [the gods righteous resentment] to avenge wrongs since the dead are unable.[199] This statement directly contradicts what the Chorus at *Choephori* 324ff said to Orestes.

We do not know the context of the preceding fragment 266, so it is difficult to explain the apparent contradiction. Of course, we should not be too surprised by what is said in poetry and drama since these kinds of passages are not necessarily intended either as dogmatic theology nor philosophy. In addition, the author himself may or may not hold to the speeches he puts into the mouths of his characters.

Sophocles

> Thrice—blessed are those mortals who have witnessed these initiation rites and departed to Hades. For it is permitted to them alone to live there, while the rest fare badly in all things (frag 837).[200]

---

[197] Translated by Hugh Lloyd-Jones, *The Libation Bearers* (Englewood Cliffs: Prentice-Hall, 1970), 28, 39.

[198] Translated by Christopher M. Dawson, *The Seven Against Thebes* (Englewood Cliffs: Prentice-Hall, 1970), 89-90.

[199] Translated by Smyth, *Aeschylus*, 472.

[200] Translated by Dana Ferrin Sutton, *The Lost Sophocles* (Lanham: University Press of America, 1984), 164.

Sophocles was born ca. 496 BCE at Colonus near Athens just six years before Aeschylus fought at Marathon. The *Philoctetes*, in which a probable reference to the afterlife appears, was written three years before his death in ca. 409 BCE.

The fragment quoted above raised the question in antiquity of whether an evil initiate indulging in a ritual would fare well after death while a virtuous non-initiate would not.[201] Of course, fragment 837 is simply a restatement of the famous lines in the Homeric Hymn to Demeter that had been around for around 200 years and were the basis of the Eleusinian mysteries. The Homeric Hymn says:

> Blessed is the mortal on earth who has seen these rites, but the uninitiate who has no share in them never has the same lot once dead in the dreary darkness (480ff).[202]

Before this famous passage, we have some indication that those who "commit injustice [ἀδκησάντων] and fail to appease Persephone (367f)" will suffer eternal punishment. This could be a very early citation of a judgment in the afterlife antedating Pindar, Aeschylus or Sophocles by over one hundred years if the accepted date of composition for the Hymn of 650-550 BCE is accurate.[203]

Adkins notes that the Aeschylian belief in punishment in the next life "seems not to be shared by the other tragedians."[204] Does this mean that Sophocles lacked what was to be the growing moral sense of Socrates and Plato? Or do his lines, taken out of any context, represent such a simple Homeric Hymn restatement—

---

201 Plutarch records Diogenes the Cynic as denying any ethical considerations playing a part in the Mysteries: "do you mean that Pataecion, the robber, will have a better portion after death than Epaminondas, just because he is initiate?" (Plutarch *Moralia*, 21f; trans., Frank Cole Babbitt, *Plutarch's Moralia* [Cambridge: Harvard University Press, 1949], 113).

202 Translated by Foley, ed., *The Homeric Hymn to Demeter* ((Princeton: Princeton University Press, 1994), 26. Pindar also said as much, "Prosperous is he who having seen these things passes below the earth. He knows the end of life and its god given beginning" (frag. 137). Cf. *Ol.* 2.56 for knowing rites vs. ethical considerations.

203 For the date of composition see Foley, *The Homeric Hymn to Demeter*, 29-30. This did inspire the Eleusinian Mysteries but would not likely have inspired Pythagorean belief in reincarnation, but may well have influenced early Orphic poetry.

204 Adkins, *Merit and Responsibility*, 144. It would also seem to me that the judgment passage in the Hymn did not impress any other of our mainland Greek writers either.

possibly by a character in a play. We will have to look elsewhere for the answer to this question.

Afterlife-affirming. There are other instances in Sophocles where he does positively claim a conscious afterlife. Perhaps the most significant, albeit controversial, one besides the fragment already quoted, is at *Philoctetes* 1440ff where he says that "Reverence for the gods does not die along with mortals; whether they live or die, it never perishes."[205] This reading seems to have 'reverence' never perishing. But, Richard C. Jebb has the same passage read: "for piety dies not with men; in their life and in their death, it is immortal." Jebb says "the effect of εὐσέβεια does not cease with man's life on earth, but is imperishable. That is, it brings happiness to the εὐσεβής in the life beyond the grave." Linforth claims that Jebb was wrong and that the passage means only that the name and fame of the pious survives among men after death.[206] The Greek actually says:

Οὐ γάρ ηὐσέβεια συνθνῄσκει βροτοῖς·
Κἂν ζῶσι κἂν θάνωσιν, οὐκ ἀπόλλυτια.

If Jebb is correct and Linforth wrong, then this passage is a most significant instance of Sophoclean belief in immortality and of a blessed reward for those who conduct themselves piously.

However, some other positive afterlife possibilities are at *Antigone* 74ff "for there will be a longer span of time for me to please those below than there will be to please those here"; and at *Ant.* 459, Antigone counts dying before her time as gain. The most confident statement of Antigone's belief in an afterlife reward comes at 891ff where she knows that she will go to Persephone to be among the dead and "that I shall come dear to my father, dear to you, my mother, and dear to you, my own brother."

In the *Electra* we find that the dead below can offer help to those above, "first you will earn credit for piety from our dead father below, and also from our brother" (965f). At *Elec.* 453, she says, "Kneel and pray him to come in kindness from

---

[205] All Sophocles translations, unless noted, are from Hugh Lloyd-Jones, *Sophocles*, 2 vols. (Cambridge: Harvard University Press, 1994).

[206] R. C. Jebb, *Sophocles: The Plays and Fragments* (Cambridge: University Press, 1907), 222-3; Ivan M. Linforth, "Philoctetes, the Play and the Man," in *Studies in Sophocles* (Berkeley: University of California Press, 1963), 149-50.

below the earth to help us against our enemies…my sister, perform this service in aid of…the dearest of all mortals, the father of us both who lies in Hades."[207] At 1066, the Chorus says "cry out a sad message to the Atreidae below…tell them that their house suffers." None of the above citations from *Electra* claims a link between behavior and afterlife reward/punishment, but lines 244, 417 (cited in note below) and 453 suggest that the dead do live on and are capable of exacting their own punishment against the impious living.

Oedipus the King has a clear statement of the afterlife and the result of misdeeds where Oedipus says, "With what eyes could I have faced my father in the house of the dead, or my poor mother" (1370).[208] Then he says that not even death could atone for his crimes.

Oedipus at Colonus 1645ff, reports the apotheosis of Oedipus. This apotheosis is not for reasons of his morality or, even as Homer's with Elysium, a reward for marrying well.[209] Rather it is because Oedipus was punished for events far beyond his control and justice demanded some restitution:

> According to the law I am clean! It was in ignorance that I came to this! (548);
> I pray that the stranger may arrive at the plain of the dead that holds all below
> and at the house of Styx without pain and with no grievous fate! For after
> many futile troubles have beset him, once more a just god would be exalting
> him (1560ff).[210]

---

[207] Cf. 244ff. and 417ff to 453ff. "For if the dead man is to lie there as earth nothingness, unhappy one, and they are not to pay the penalty, murdered in their turn, that would be the end of reverence and the piety of all mortals" (244ff). And, "They say that she was once more in company with your father and mine, who had come to the world of light" (417ff).

[208] Translated by Bernard M. Knox, *Oedipus the King* (New York: Washington Square Press, 1972), 98.

[209] It may be recalled in Homer that Menelaus received his reward for being the son-in-law of Zeus. A reward for marrying a god or the child of a god is a common theme that we will see again with Cadmus in Euripides' Bacchae.

[210] Twenty years after writing Oedipus the King, Sophocles seems to have reconsidered the injustice of the pollution concept that had condemned a just man and has Oedipus, then the chorus, say in Colonus: νόμῳ δὲ καθαρός, ἄϊδρις εἰς τόδ᾽ ἦλθον (548);…πολλῶν γὰρ ἂν καὶ μάταν πημάτων ἱκνουμένων πάλιν σφε δαίμων δίκαιος αὔξοι (1565; trans. Hugh Lloyd-Jones, *Sophocles* (Cambridge: Harvard University Press, 1994). Hence Oedipus at Colonus rectified Oedipus the King.

<u>Denying an afterlife</u>. On the other hand, as in Aeschylus, Sophocles also has passages that deny the afterlife, some of which are in the very same plays as his more positive afterlife assessment.

At *Elec.* 137-9, Electra is told that, "you will never raise up your father from the lake of Hades, to which all must come, by weeping or by prayers," and at 955, Electra admits that her brother is dead and therefore no longer able to help her. At *Trachis* 1173, Heracles says that he thought he'd be released from labor through prospering, but he is released only because he's dead and the dead do not labor. At *Oedipus at Colonus* 955, Creon says that "anger knows no old age, till death; and no pain afflicts the dead." Finally, Odysseus sees that all who live are nothing more than phantoms or fleeting shadows (*Ajax* 125).

Even so, there are several afterlife scenes in Sophocles, but only *Elec.* 983 and *Phil.* 1440 appear to involve a judgment of the dead based on one's earthly conduct.

Euripides

> May Hermes of the Underworld and Hades receive you kindly! And if in that place the good have any advantage, may you have a share in it and sit as attendant beside Hades' bride (*Alcestis* 742ff)![211]

This is ambivalent to say the least. There seems to be no question that there is some form of an afterlife in Hades, but whether morality here plays any role in one's lot, in my opinion, is an open question.

Euripides was born ca. 485 in Phyla in Attica. All of his plays were written between 441 BCE and 406 BCE, when he died within one year before Sophocles. Like Aeschylus before him, he also spent time in Sicily. There are several plays that discuss a concept of an afterlife: *Alcestis* (438 BCE), *Hippolytus* (428), *The Suppliants* (420), *Helen* (412), and *The Bacchae* (406).

<u>Afterlife-affirming</u>. In the *Alcestis*, Admetus tells Alcestis that if he had the "lips of Orpheus and his melody to charm the maiden daughter of Demeter," he would

---

[211] Translated by David Kovacs, *Euripides* (Cambridge: Harvard University Press, 1984), 237.

win her back from death, but as it is he asks only that she "wait for me, then, in that place, till I die, and make ready the room where you will live with me" (357ff).[212]

Euripides' characters make a good case for an "aetherial" afterlife in several places. At *Suppliants* 532ff, the corpses are to be hidden in the earth but "let soul release to air, body to earth. We do not own our bodies, but are mere tenants there for life," and again at 1138 the dead is "gone into air. Their bodies have melted into ash and fire, to the Underworld they have flown."[213]

Helen 1014-17 has a passage that combines the idea of the soul (here as εἴδωλον) passing and merging into the immortal ether, with its accountability for deeds performed in life.

> For all men, in the world below and in the world above must pay for acts committed here. The mind of those who have died, blown into the immortal air, immortally has knowledge, though all life is gone.[214]

However, there is no individual survival here but rather a type of return to universal soul, which retains consciousness of moral obligations.[215] The story of *Odyssey* 4.563 is repeated at lines 1676f where Menaleus goes to the Isles of the Blest, which contrasts with the foregoing statement but is in line with the preferential treatment of the famous in the lines from the *Andromache* cited below.

At *Bacchae* 1338, Cadmus will eventually be translated to the Isles of the Blest as Dionysus tells him, "Ares will rescue you and Harmonia and establish your life in

---

212 Translated by Richmond Lattimore, *The Complete Greek Tragedies* eds., David Grene and Richmond Lattimore, vol. 3 (Chicago: University of Chicago Press, 1992), 20.

213 Translated by Rosanna Warren and Stephen Scully, *Euripides: Suppliant Women* (New York: Oxford University Press, 1995), 39, 60.

214 Translated by Richmond Lattimore, *The Complete Greek Tragedies*, David Grene and Richmond Lattimore, eds., vol. 3 (Chicago: University of Chicago Press, 1992), 455.

215 Lattimore translates the lines, "For all men, in the world below and in the world above must pay for acts committed here...though all life is gone" (Lattimore, *Complete Greek Tragedies*, 454). Also see A.M. Dale, *Euripides: Helen* (Oxford: Clarendon Press, 1967), 132; James Morwood, *Euripides* (Oxford: Clarendon Press, 1997), 148.

the land of the blessed."[216] But at 1361, Cadmus claims that he will not cease from sufferings when going to the underworld because he will not even have death to end the grief over what he will have had to suffer from the curse of Dionysus.[217]

In the *Rhesus* we have another allusion to the ascent of the soul, but now linked to Persephone, where the Muse tells Hector, "No, he will not go to the black plain under your world. The Bride beneath the earth, child of Demeter, mother who creates the grain, will let his soul ascend...[in order] to honor the family of Orpheus," but Rhesus will never again see daylight for he will be hidden in a cave as "a wakeful, deathless spirit, man, and god" (962-73).[218] One Euripidean fragment specifically alludes to an afterlife based on conduct: "A man who reverences his parents in life is, while both alive and dead, dear to the gods" (frag 852).

Denying an afterlife. Just as Aeschylus and Sophocles do before him, Euripides also makes several claims against a beneficent afterlife:

> Afterward: is there an afterward? I hope not. If there's then no end to our troubles, where do we go on from there—since death itself, they say, supplies the cure for everything that ails (*Heracleidae* 588-596)?[219]

---

[216] Translated by Richard Seaford, *Euripides: Bacchae* (Warminster: Aris & Phillips, 1996), 139. This is another Homer-like bodily translation in death because of marriage to a god's daughter.

[217] See E.R. Dodds, *Euripides: Bacchae* (Oxford: Clarendon Press, 1960), 236ff; Seaford, Euripides: Bacchae, 139, 141, 254f.

[218] Translated by Richard Emil Braun, *Euripides: Rhesos* (New York: Oxford University Press, 1978), 69-70. Mikalson calls these lines "a muddle of vocabulary, concepts, and categories...not even internally consistent" (Jon D. Mikalson, *Honor Thy Gods* [Chapel Hill: University of North Carolina Press, 1983], 43). Rhesus was a cousin of Orpheus. The contradictory ascent yet eternal cave dwelling offers an eternal life of sorts based, not on morality, but on a relationship to the gods. Euripides has the soul ascending but the body goes under the ground, not to die as it does in *Suppl.* 532ff, but rather to have eternal life still in possession of his body. This, as we shall see, compares to Egyptian concepts very closely. Also, see the story of Salmoxis who claimed immortality under the earth in Herodotus IV 93-6.

[219] Translated by Lattimore *Complete Greek Tragedies*, 137.

At *Orestes* 1084ff Orestes claims that "we dead are deprived of all welfare," but Pylades responds, saying that "may the fruitful soil not accept my blood nor the bright air my soul if ever I betray you."[220]

At *Troades* 632ff Andromache tells Hecuba that "Death, I am sure, is like never being born…since the dead with no perception of evil feel no grief."[221]

The Nurse in the *Hippolytus* asks if there is such a thing as an afterlife, but says "no man can tell us the stuff of it, expounding what is, and what is not: we know nothing of it. Idly we drift, on idle stories carried (195)."[222] At *Hipp.* 952, Hippolytus is accused of acting like an Orphic—

> Now you may plume yourself, now by a vegetable diet play the showman with your food, and with Orpheus for your lord hold your covens and honour all your vaporous screeds.[223]

—an accusation that is not meant to be a compliment.[224] The *Andromache* at 775f claims that for those without fame and resources to match, it is better not to have been born, but for those aristocratic good men, they have no end to their glory via fame and a good name. In Homer we saw that a good man was one who practiced the manly virtues, but here we see an ethical content, although there is no indication of an afterlife reward. One's virtue is to do nothing disgraceful that would "knock awry all law" and to adhere "to this manner of life…may no unjust sway flourish in family affairs."[225]

---

[220] Here Orestes is denying any beneficent afterlife, whereas Pylades is affirming an 'ethereal' afterlife. Translated by M.L. West, *Euripides: Orestes* (Warminster: Aris & Phillips, 1987), 135.

[221] Translated by Lattimore, *Complete Greek Tragedies*, 637.

[222] Translated by Lattimore, *Complete Greek Tragedies*, 171.

[223] Translated by W.S. Barrett, *Euripides: Hippolytos* (Oxford: Clarendon Press, 1992), 342.

[224] Cf. Euripides' negative view of Orphics with the similar ones of Plato in the *Republic*. Although the Orphics were early religious innovators, by the 5th century many of them were no longer respected. Nevertheless, their influence persisted.

[225] Translated by Lattimore, *Complete Greek Tragedies*, 591.

Suppliants 86 plainly says that death is oblivion and at 1000-8 death will end the weary life of pain. *Media* 1224, as we saw in *Pythian* 8.95 and *Ajax* 125, has our life thought to be a shadow and it claims that no mortal ever achieves blessedness.

Once again we find evidence of a considerable range of afterlife beliefs in a single author, and sometimes in a single work (e.g., the above cited *Electra* passages of Sophocles).

The 5th century BCE was a time of mixed religious views. The intellectuals were denying an afterlife altogether, while the mysteries were allowing a better lot after death for the initiated. And, coming out of the west were the newer ideas that the soul passed through many lives with each depending on the moral conduct of the last.

This variety, which must have seemed bewildering and/or disturbing to many, provided the background for the irreverent comedy of Aristophanes.

Aristophanes

> For on us alone do the sun
> and the daylight shine,
> all of us who are initiated
> and who led a righteous [εὐσεβῆ]
> way of life towards strangers
> and towards ordinary folk (*Frogs* 454-459).[226]

Later than the Tragedians, Aristophanes was born around the middle of the 5th century and died around 385 BCE just about the same time that Plato was setting up his academy. He is considered the greatest comic writer in Greek and is credited with over forty plays. His play the Clouds in which he satirizes Socrates as a Sophist may have contributed to the false charges that caused Socrates' death in 399.[227]

---

[226] All translations are from Alan H. Sommerstein, *Frogs* (Warminster: Aris & Phillips, 1996), 75.

[227] Plato's Socrates mentions this play in *Apology* 19c.

Kenneth Dover says, "the notion that good people will be rewarded in the after-life and bad people punished was well-established and widespread in Aristophanes's time. So was the notion that initiation at Eleusis ensures preferential treatment in the underworld."[228] This awareness was not always perceived as a good thing as attested by Democritus: "Some men, ignorant of the dissolution of mortal nature, but conscious of the miseries of their life, crawl, during their lifetime, in troubles and fears, inventing falsehoods about the time after death" (frag 297).[229]

The passage from the *Frogs* cited above is stating that the mystic initiate will be rewarded in the afterlife, but only if he strives for righteous behavior with his fellow man. Just as significantly, sinners are punished:

> And then a vast sea of mud and ever-flowing dung, in which there lies anyone who has ever, say, broken the laws of hospitality, or slyly grabbed back a rent-boy's money while having it with him, or struck his mother, or given his father a sock in the jaw, or sworn a perjured oath, or had someone copy out a speech by Morsimus. (*Frogs* 145-151).[230]

It should be remembered that this is a comedy and as such it is full of spoofs. The spoof of the rent-boy and Morsimus are obvious but what is not so obvious is the probability that the entire thing is a spoof. We have no guarantee that Aristophanes actually believed any of this and indeed, that is a problem in all such 'fiction'. However, what we can believe is that the spoof was against a real set of beliefs held by some people and we can take the playwright's words as evidence of these beliefs.

Other places in Aristophanes where the afterlife is alluded to are:

---

[228] Kenneth Dover, *Aristophanes: Frogs* (Oxford: Clarendon Press, 1993), 57, 251.

[229] Translated by Jonathon Barnes, *The Presocratic Philosophers*, vol 2 (London: Routledge & Kegan Paul, 1979), 155. Democritus was a contemporary of Aristophanes. The Nurse in the Hippolytus also called the afterlife nothing more than tales, but Democritus is more adamantly negative about it. Democritus also played a great part in the nomos -vs- physis conflict that figured in Plato's works. Democritus, in frag B9, had claimed that attributes of things (such as color, taste, etc.) are so only by convention (nomos), whereas atoms exist in reality or nature (physis). This raised the question of whether the virtues and laws also exist by nature or simply by convention. See citations in C.C.W. Taylor, *The Atomists: Leucippus and Democritus* (Toronto: University of Toronto Press, 1999), 9, 143.

[230] Translated by Sommerstein, *Frogs*, 51.

Frogs 274 has father-beaters and perjurers punished in the afterlife. Then at 354ff there is a punishment, but not in the afterlife, for a long list of vices that would keep one from participating in the mysteries and consequentially attaining the desired afterlife.[231]

At *Birds* 696, Aristophanes has the birds tell of the creation, which includes some Orphic cosmology.[232]

Trygaeus tells Hermes that if he has to die now to "please lend me a sucking-pig; I must get initiated before I die" (*Peace* 374).[233] He was looking for the promised afterlife happiness. Then at line 830-2 we see that dithyrambic composers flit about catching exordia and it is said of them and others "that when we die we become stars in the sky."[234]

---

[231] Since non-participants are said to have an unhappy afterlife, can we therefore assume that they are to experience a form of postmortem punishment also? The alternative is the existence of the Homeric shades; neither punished nor rewarded. The text of 354 follows: Let all speak fair, and let these stand out of way of our dances whoever is unfamiliar with words such as these—or has thoughts that are **not clean**—or has not seen or danced in the secret rites of the true-bred Muses nor been initiated in the Bacchic verbal mysteries of bull-devouring Cratinus—or delights in words of **buffoonery** from men who choose the wrong time to behave thus—or does not endeavor to resolve the internal **strife** that threatens us and is **not peaceable** towards other citizens, but **stirs it up and fans its flame** out of a desire for private advantage—or is an office-holder who takes **bribes** to harm the city when it's struggling in heavy seas—or **betrays** a fort or a fleet—or is a damnable five-percent-collector like Thorycion who **exports contraband** [**smuggles**] from Aegina, sending oarportleathers, flax and pitch across to Epidaurus—or induces anyone to **supply money for our adversaries' navy**—or is a soloist in cyclic choral performances who **shits on the offerings to Hecate** [**sacrilege**]—or is a politician who goes and nibbles away at the fees of poets after having been satirized in the course of the ancestral rites of Dionysus. To these I proclaim, and again I proclaim the ban, and again a third time do I proclaim the ban, that they stand out of the way of the initiates' dances, but do you awaken the voice of song and begin the all-night revels which befit this our festival (Sommerstein, *Frogs*, 67).

[232] The Orphic egg worked well for a bird's cosmology. See M.L. West, *The Orphic Poems* (Oxford: Clarendon Press, 1983), 198-203.

[233] Translated by Alan H. Sommerstein, *Peace* (Warminster: Aris & Phillips, 1985), 39.

[234] Translated by Sommerstein, *Peace*, 81.

Summary

With the Dramatists we are back firmly on Greek mainland soil. Both Aeschylus and Pindar were born on opposite sides of the Greek world around 520 BCE, just within a generation of the death of Pythagoras. They have both been credited with being the first to posit an afterlife consequence for one's conduct in this life.[235] But, where Pindar was more positive, Aeschylus could only offer punishment for negative behavior.

Upon deeper analysis, we see that although all of the dramatists had much to say about an afterlife, there are actually very few strong statements linking conduct and behavior to the quality of that afterlife. Let us examine a few such statements.

Aeschylus' *Eumenides* 255ff has an unequivocal link between conduct and a judgment after death.

Sophocles alludes to the afterlife in several places but in only one does he explicitly link conduct with reward. *Philoctetes* 1140 seems to say that a person's piety is immortal, and therefore the person. However, this passage has been contested.

Euripides brings in some hitherto unexpounded ideas of an afterlife where he posits an ethereal soul that is released to the air while the body goes to the earth. In fragment 252 there is a link between conduct and a promise of a beneficial afterlife where the ancient virtue of reverence to parents makes one dear to the gods both in this life and in death.

Finally, with Aristophanes *Frogs* we see a spoof of the mysteries that indicate a belief, at least by a minority, of an afterlife where one's conduct (whether ritualistic or ethical) determines one's afterlife condition.

In order to summarize the Dramatists' passages that deal with conduct and behavior that determines reward or punishment in the afterlife, see the chart on the following page. A more detailed account is found in Appendix H: "Passages from Greek Authors Concerning the Afterlife."

---

[235] However, my alternative claims in Chapter two that the Homeric texts already allude to post-mortem punishment, in my opinion, may have made these claims more tenuous.

SUMMARY CHART

of

Passages in the Dramatists that Associate Earthly
Conduct and Behavior with an Afterlife
Reward or Punishment[236]

Author/**Work**/ Passage	Conduct/Behavior	Reward/Punishment
Aeschylus		
Choephori		
306	murder	conjuration to aid punishment
324	murder, guilt	contra fr. 266—dead do help
Eumenides		
95	murder	shame and verbal abuse
175	murder	lose liberty below earth
267	impious to:	
	god	
	stranger	
	parents	held to account below earth
337	murder	after death no liberty below
387	wrongs	fulfillment in sunless slime
441	hubris	bound to wheel in underground
Persians		
654,	god's	
691	counselor	exercised authority in Hades
676	mistake	[676-827 are vices of Xerxes
725	lose wits	
744	blindness	

---

[236] Also, see Appendix K, Table 7.

744	impetuous	and
744	foolish	
808	hubris	
808	impiety	Darius is conjured
820ff	pride	
	rashness	
	overboastful	
	ignorance	because of them]

Suppliants

225	unnatural act, wrong	chars final vengeance
413	violate sanct.	vengeance after death
701	piety to: gods parents	reward

Sophocles

Antigone

74	pious, honor	longer time to please below
449	unwritten law, justice	death is a gain
897	honor, wise	see one's dead family

Electra

236	shame, rever.	not neglect the dead
442	murder	dead not welcome tribute
453	pious, wise	dead can help punish
965	piety, noble	praise from dead below
983	manly courage	glory in life and death

Philoctetes

| 1440 | piety | immortality |

Oedipus Tyrannus

1370	crimes	not face dead family

Oedipus Colonus

1645	not stated	apotheosis of Oedipus

fragments

837	initiation	live or fare badly

Euripides

Alcestis

741	courage, noble generous, good	sit beside Persephone

Bacchae

1338	unwise, unjust, insult	exiled by the god
1361	blasphemy	immortality allows suffering

Helen

1014	honor father, piety, just.	pay for acts in immortal air
1676	god relation	Isles of Blest

Hippolytus

197	fidelity	questioned postmortem reward

Orestes

395	murder	madness
1629	god relation	immortality

Rhesus

| 962 | god relation | wakeful deathless man & god |

Suppliants

| 526 | defeated honorably | soul to air, body to earth |

fragments

| 852 | rev. parents | dear to gods alive and dead |

Aristophanes

Frogs

145	wronged stranger parents perjury	lie in dung
274	father-beater perjury	stay in filth & darkness
353	clean buffoonery not peaceable (disagreeable) civil strife bribes betrays smuggles sacrilege	banned from mysteries
454	initiation righteousness (piety)	stay in divine sunshine

Peace

374	initiation	have happy afterlife
830	be composer	catch exordia (preludes)
832	be composer	become stars in sky

CHAPTER 5

Conclusions on the Greek Authors: the Pre-platonic's Influence on Plato's Myths

Introduction

Our investigation into earlier writers has shown that the literature of the western Greek world was expounding on concepts such as the immortal soul, the soul's rebirth through cyclic lives and an afterlife consequence for one's conduct while alive. At this same time the mainland Greek writers were still holding on to the predominant Homeric idea, that of no beneficial afterlife.

The Sophistic movement was creating a morally relativistic society where the laws were being questioned as having no support other than the conventions of the majority.[237] Into this societal breakdown came Socrates with his ideas of respect for the virtues and the laws. Plato followed through with support beyond mere convention, explaining in his dialogues and myths, that the virtues were based in a much deeper reality.

However, Plato did not create these great dialogues and myths in a vacuum, for all of the writers we have reviewed helped set the stage for what he was later able to accomplish—some with ideas in eschatology and some in ethics.

Eschatology

Olympiodorus in his *On the Phaedo* has said that Plato paraphrases Orpheus everywhere.[238] Perhaps that is a bit strong, but Plato certainly used the material

---

[237] Plato holds this opinion in his dialogues against Callicles and Thrasymachus in the *Gorgias* 481ff and the Republic book I.

[238] Plato does mention Orpheus many times: *Crat.* 400c; *Gorg.* 493a; *Rep.* 364b; *Symp.* 179c; *Euthyd.* 277d; *Meno* 81a and *Laws* 715e.

that, in the *Gorgias* 493a, he attributes to certain wise men from "perhaps some inhabitant in Sicily or Italy."[239] As we've seen, these can only be the Pythagoreans and/or Orphics who were the forerunners of Heraclitus, Pindar and Empedocles.

In the *Meno* 81b, Plato is supposed to have summarized the Orphic eschatology[240] where, "They say a man's soul is immortal, sometimes it ends its existence which is called death and sometimes it comes into being again." Did he really get that from the Orphics? They had only contended, somewhat differently from Pythagoras,[241] that a human being contained a divine spark that was punished by being entombed in the flesh.[242] The Orphic goal was to return to whence one came in a 'life in the divine world—death in the body—back to life' scenario. This fits with what both Heraclitus and Empedocles (except for his multiple lives) had to say on the subject. It also fits with the bone tablets of Olbia where we see the inscription: *bios—thanatos—bios*. Therefore, the lines in *Meno* 81b also fit the Orphics but Plato will put a cyclic rebirth spin on it just as did Pindar.[243]

---

[239] Also in Gorg 493a: "Sages say that we are now dead and the body (σῶμα) is our tomb (σῆμα)."

[240] Socrates tells of what he has heard from wise men and women (priests and priestesses) and from Pindar whose fragment 133 he quotes. I believe that the fist part (*Gorg.* 493a) cited above is Orphic but that Pindar's quote (at *Meno* 81b) allowed Plato to say that the soul "has been born many times." Cf. Heraclitus frag 63, Pindar frag 133, Empedocles frag 146 and Plato *Meno* 81bc.

[241] Pythagoras is supposed to have claimed that the soul wanders through countless lives, as humans and plants and animals too. Actually, we know very little of Pythagoras from contemporary sources. Frankel enumerates "the sum total of our trustworthy early evidence" by quoting four passages from three writers. Xenophanes (frag 7) and Empedocles (frag 129) make reference to his belief in reincarnation and the younger Heraclitus (frags 40, 129) condemns him for deceit and lack of understanding. See Hermann Frankel, *Early Greek Poetry and Philosophy* (New York: Harcourt Brace Jovanovich, 1973), 272-5.

[242] Socrates equates this doctrine with "the Orphic poets" at Cratylus 400c. Dodds calls the 'body equals tomb' contention by some scholars a "hoary error" and explains that Plato did not do any such thing. Dodds, *Greeks and the Irrational*, 169 n. 87.

[243] As with everything else where the facts are sparse, there is a scholarly debate over whether the Orphics taught the doctrine of metempsychosis. Rohde and Dodds hold that they did. Rohde says, "Least of all did they [Orphics] need to derive the doctrine of the migration of souls and its application from this source [Pythagoreans]," therefore it was their own. Later he says that, "The Orphics retained, in spite of everything, the doctrine of transmigration" (Rohde, *Psyche*, 336-342, 346; Dodds,

Pythagoras is supposed to have claimed that a person passed through several life-times, and Empedocles echoes this claim with his statement that he has passed through many types of existence.

Nevertheless, the mechanics of their reincarnation theory is unclear. The Orphic material that we have is late and Pythagoras did not write anything down so we do not know for sure what they said happens after one's death and before another rebirth. Most of the popular concepts we have of the Pythagoreans and Orphics have been filtered through the gauze of Platonic myth so it is difficult to tell what they really believed as opposed to what Plato embellished. Even so, it seems that we can take the testimony of Pindar and Empedocles as attesting to the metempsychosis theory of Pythagoras[244] and the Heraclitean and 'bone tablets' as attesting to the life-death-life concept of the Orphics.[245] It remains to look at both of these cases to determine if an afterlife judgment makes any sense.

Does the Pythagorean believe that one reincarnates immediately at death? In that case, there is no need for any place like a Hades in which to be judged. Or, do they spend an interval between incarnations in which case there certainly is a requirement for such a holding place.

Does reincarnation allow or even require a judgment for one's living conduct? I would have to say yes to both allowing and requiring some form of judgment, since in all cases, one's ultimate destination depends on what one has done in past lives.

Plato is very clear about his belief, excepting the earlier *Gorgias* which posits no reincarnation, in that he holds to an interval between incarnations and specifies

---

Greeks and the Irrational, 149, 170 n. 94). And, Dodds allows that the Orphics did believe that the body was the prison of the soul where it is punished for past sins and that this doctrine is supported by the belief "in a preexistent detachable soul." I maintain that the Orphics did not necessarily hold to the doctrine of metempsychosis since the preexistent soul need only support the life-death-life scenario.

[244] Xenophanes' (560-470) frag 7 is an early attestation of the reincarnation belief of Pythagoras where he orders the maltreatment of a dog to stop because the dog is the soul of a friend.

[245] Heraclitus disagreed with Pythagoras at frags 40, 81, 120, 129. His statements that, "mortals are immortals and immortals are mortals" implies a life from death and a death from life, but not necessarily a cyclic reincarnation. Heraclitus' statement is closer to the inscription on the bone tablet of Olbia than to the doctrine of metempsychosis taught by Pythagoras.

that one will be judged each time one dies. Nevertheless, his judgment scenes evolve over time, ranging from the final judgment found in the *Gorgias* where actual judges examine the scars left by bad conduct, to his later myths where the judgment becomes more automatic and finally, in the *Phaedrus*, where there are no judges at all. Pythagorean reincarnation is not the same thing as an afterlife judgment, although Plato will combine these two concepts very effectively.

Pindar is the first major poet to speak of a judge below the earth who passes sentence on wrongdoers. He also allows that those who abstain from wrongdoing through three lifetimes are destined for the Isle of the Blessed. There is no need for a judge below the earth for either Pythagoras or the Orphics, and Pindar's story might be seen as a syncretism of the afterlife punishments found in Homer added to the rebirth ideas of Pythagoras.

Now, does the Orphic believe that he or she experiences a reincarnation after death? We do not really have enough facts to know the answer. However, since the punishment for the Orphic is the fall into flesh for a perceived original sin, there is no reason to posit a rebirth doctrine in their eschatology. As to a judgment, we may ask why did one receive the punishment of being incarnated if some form of a judgment had not already taken place? If the bone tablet scenario accurately describes Orphic beliefs, then this judgment must take place in the first life as a divine or semi-divine being. There must be an implicit judgment for some primordial sin that condemns one to an incarnation.

This incarnation concept does not match that of the *Gorgias* myth but the 'life-death-life' scenario is exactly what is happening in the *Phaedrus*. The evolution of the idea is that, instead of a single life-death-life, Plato has incorporated the Pindaric (and therefore Pythagorean and Empedoclean) concept of multiple reincarnations.

We might ask, if the Orphic's punishment was to be born into the flesh, why does Plato speak of other punishments like "the barbaric slough of the Orphic myth" (*Rep.* 533d, cf. 363d). This "everflowing dung" type of punishment also showed up in the earlier *Frogs*. But was it Orphic? Possibly, but it was most certainly Eleusinian and therefore associated with the presumed 'founder' of the mysteries, Orpheus.

By the time of Plato's *Republic*, some Orphics, who by now must have been practicing a disreputable form of Orphism, were being condemned for their "babble of books." Nevertheless, the "barbaric slough" and the "everflowing dung" seem to have no place in eschatology of the gold leaves and the bone tablets.

Ethics

If Plato got his metaphysics mostly from western Greek writers, he surely got his terms for conduct and behavior from a long line of writers from the mainland all the way from Homer to Euripides. Therefore, at this point, it seems relevant to look at some of the terms and their definitions that Plato used in determining virtue or vice in relation to the judgment myths. This is not an easy endeavor, for even though Aristotle says that Plato's Socrates searched for universal definitions,[246] it is clear that Socrates never was able to fully finalize these definitions.[247] However, Plato claims many times throughout his works that there are such virtues that he attempts to define.[248] Some of these virtues are of paramount order; those we have come to call the cardinal virtues of courage, justice, temperance, wisdom and sometimes also holiness.[249] Due to the importance[250] of these

---

[246] Aristotle claims that Socrates was the first to seek a general definition and credits him with two innovations: the general definition and inductive reasoning. Aristotle *Metaphysics* 1078b.

[247] We can, at least, say of the Socratic dialogs that he concluded that: the individual virtues cannot be defined or possessed separately (*Gorg.* 507a-c); that all virtues are a unity; that virtue is knowledge of good and bad (*Meno* 88d, 89a, *Gorg.* 460a-c); that it cannot be taught but only discovered or recollected (*Meno* 96c); that knowing it brings happiness; and that one with this knowledge would never do evil. However, final definitions remained elusive and even these conclusions would change in the later works of Plato.

[248] Richard Robinson notes that Socrates invented the notion of definition and that it was always to be definitions of things or res (i.e., real definition), and never about nomina or words or concepts. He also notes that in most of Plato's works "the definition is never achieved" (Richard Robinson, *Definition* [Oxford: Clarendon Press, 1962], 4, 7-8, 149, 170).

[249] At *Laws* 631c all of the cardinal virtues are mentioned. "And wisdom, in turn, has first place among the goods that are divine, and rational temperances of soul comes second; from these two, when united with courage, there issues justice, as the third." At *Laws* 963, 964 and 965, it is said that the laws must aim at one object—virtue, which consists of four things: courage, temperance, justice and wisdom. The four cardinal virtues may just be a literary conceit since holiness or piety clearly qualifies as do such qualities as high-mindedness, liberality, and others [e.g., see *Rep.* 402c].

[250] These cardinal virtues are important in many of Plato's works, however all five are mentioned only in the Phaedo myth. In the Phaedo all of the 'virtues', including the cardinal, are subsumed under the heading of 'well-ordered and wise'. This associates the cardinal virtues with such terms as: comos, logos, *Dike* and the Egyptian *Ma'at*.

virtues they will be examined, if not really defined, first. Then we will look at the unwritten laws of the gods.

The Cardinal Virtues[251]

Assuming that the *Phaedo* is indeed earlier than the *Republic*, we can say that the four cardinal virtues are mentioned here (69b), before the *Republic*,[252] as being:

Justice	δικαιοσύνη
Moderation	σωφροσύνη
Wisdom	φρόνησις
Courage	ἀνδρεία

These four terms are repeated again in the *Phaedo* myth, with pious added, at 114b-115a.[253] They reappear in Agathon's speech in the *Symposium* at 196d, but now wisdom is σοφία rather than φρόνησις.

---

[251] To the standard four cardinal virtues are added a fifth—holiness at *Protagoras* 329c and 349b.

[252] Paul Shorey says that the *Republic* "formulates for the first time the doctrine of the four cardinal virtues" (Paul Shorey, *The Republic*, vol. 1 [1937; reprint, Cambridge: Harvard University Press, 1978], 427).

[253] Plato *Phaedo* 114b-115a, with the cardinal virtues.

οἱ δὲ δὴ ἂν δόξωσι διαφερόντως πρὸς τὸ ὁσίως βιῶναι, οὗτοί εἰσιν οἱ τῶνδε μὲν τῶν τόπων τῶν ἐν τῇ γῇ ἐλευθερούμενοί τε καὶ ἀπαλλαττόμενοι [114c] ὥσπερ δεσμωτηρίων, ἄνω δὲ εἰς τὴν καθαρὰν οἴκησιν ἀφικνούμενοι καὶ ἐπὶ γῆς οἰκιζόμενοι. τούτων δὲ αὐτῶν οἱ φιλοσοφίᾳ ἱκανῶς καθηράμενοι ἄνευ τε σωμάτων ζῶσι τὸ παράπαν εἰς τὸν ἔπειτα χρόνον, καὶ εἰς οἰκήσεις ἔτι τούτων καλλίους ἀφικνοῦνται, ἃς οὔτε ῥᾴδιον δηλῶσαι οὔτε ὁ χρόνος ἱκανὸς ἐν τῷ παρόντι. ἀλλὰ τούτων δὴ ἕνεκα χρὴ ὧν διεληλύθαμεν, ὦ Σιμμία, πᾶν ποιεῖν ὥστε ἀρετῆς καὶ φρονήσεως ἐν τῷ βίῳ μετασχεῖν· καλὸν γὰρ τὸ ἆθλον καὶ ἡ ἐλπὶς μεγάλη....

ἀλλὰ τούτων δὴ ἕνεκα θαρρεῖν χρὴ περὶ τῇ ἑαυτοῦ ψυχῇ [114e] ἄνδρα ὅστις ἐν τῷ βίῳ τὰς μὲν ἄλλας ἡδονὰς τὰς περὶ τὸ σῶμα καὶ τοὺς κόσμους εἴασε χαίρειν, ὡς ἀλλοτρίους τε ὄντας, καὶ πλέον θάτερον ἡγησάμενος ἀπεργάζεσθαι, τὰς δὲ περὶ τὸ μανθάνειν ἐσπούδασέ τε καὶ κοσμήσας τὴν ψυχὴν οὐκ ἀλλοτρίῳ ἀλλὰ τῷ αὑτῆς κόσμῳ, σωφροσύνῃ τε καὶ [115a] δικαιοσύνῃ καὶ ἀνδρείᾳ καὶ ἐλευθερίᾳ καὶ ἀληθείᾳ, οὕτω περιμένει τὴν εἰς Ἅιδου πορείαν.

These four are again described in the *Republic* where Plato is comparing the ideal city to the human soul at 504a in this form:

Justice	δικαιοσύνη
Moderation	σωφροσύνη
Wisdom	σοφία
Courage	ἀνδρεία

'Wisdom' has changed from the Greek term meaning practical wisdom or prudence to the term for cleverness or skill. But, this is perhaps an insignificant change since it occurs often in Plato and Greek works generally. What is really surprising is that <u>none</u> of the four terms occurs in the *Republic's* eschatological myth.

Another consideration is that, if the scholarly consensus on dating the Platonic corpus is correct, we find that the *Protagoras* may actually lay claim to being the first of Plato's dialogs to name the four cardinal virtues where he also had specified a fifth, so that at 349b we now have:

Justice	δικαιοσύνη
Moderation	σωφροσύνη
Wisdom	σοφία
Courage	ἀνδρεία
Piety[254]	ὁσιότης

All of these five virtues, or their <u>underlined</u> similar root words, occur in Plato's eschatological myths and may be charted thus:[255]

---

[254] Prot. 330c equates ὁσιότης (holiness or piety) with ὅσιος (pious) It is the latter term that appears in the myths.

[255] The cardinal virtues appear in the four dialogs with which we are concerned. An x = in the eschatological myth, but a citation = in the body of the work itself but outside the myth. This chart shows that all of the virtues are at least mentioned in all of the dialogs in which the myths appear except the Phaedrus. * note that wisdom is just outside the myth which ends at 249d.

	justice	moderation	wisdom	courage	piety
Gorgias	justly	519a	492a	475d	x
Phaedo	x	x	x	x	x
Republic	just	591b	621c	609c	x
Phaedrus	x	x	250d*	239c	NOT

Note that the fifth cardinal virtue appears <u>nowhere</u> in the *Phaedrus*. It is almost as surprising that several of the other cardinal virtues do not appear in the eschatological myths. At least, it would be surprising if we had not looked in vain for the cardinal virtues to be important to the earlier writers. None of the earlier writers have them all, although Aeschylus does come close in *Seven* 610 where he has: σώφρον, δίκαιος, ἀγαθὸς ανδ εὐσεβής. Unfortunately, they are not in a passage dealing with the afterlife.[256]

This seems to indicate at least two things: the cardinal virtues were in the public domain as concepts when Plato named them and they were not always of the paramount importance to Plato as they would become in his later works and in later ages.

Let us now review some definitions of these cardinal virtues:

Courage—Ἀνδρεία. This virtue retains its meaning throughout the period from Aeschylus to Plato and beyond. Homer and Pindar had expressed the concept by *agathos* and *aristos*. Even Aristotle says that fearlessness in battle or other dangers to one's safety are of primary importance, although he does allow that there are other instances. Plato, in the *Laches* 190e-192e, also says that standing firm in battle is primary but also that endurance and other attributes qualify, where it says, "courage is a sort of endurance of the soul." *Rep.* 429cd even allows "that courage is a kind of preservation," meaning the withstanding of more spiritual temptations. *Prot* 359c says: "cowards go where there is safety, and the brave go where there is danger."

In the *Definitions* 412ab, we find the following mostly traditional definitions: "unmoved by fear, knowledge of the facts of warfare, boldness in obedience to

---

[256] Pindar ascribes five virtues (some form of the terms for moderation, piety, justice, courage and wisdom) to the Aeacids in *Isthmian* 8. See Helen North, *From Myth to Icon* (Ithaca: Cornell University Press, 1979), 93.

wisdom, being intrepid in the face of death, calm in the soul about what correct thinking takes to be frightening or encouraging things."

Justice—Δικαιοσύνη. This term does not appear in Homer, Pindar or the Dramatists, however, the term *Dike* does so in all of them. It occurs in two of Plato's myths.

The *Republic* is generally recognized as dealing with the theme of justice. It asks the question: "whether it is also true that the just have a better life than the unjust and are happier." The answer Plato arrives at is, yes they do. This flies in the face of the traditional meaning of "helping friends and harming enemies" that Plato attributes to Simonides (*Rep.* 331e-2a), and it is most difficult to prove that it benefits the agent and not just other people. The Sophistic conflict between living according to the dictates of nature (φύσις) rather than convention (νόμος) was the major catalyst for the evolution of this word's meaning.

Justice in Plato's city is the perfect coordination of the three classes of citizen just as justice in the individual is complete harmony of the three parts of the soul (*Rep.* 444de). "Justice is the health of the state (*Prot.* 346)". Lack of harmony in the soul is considered a disease (445ab), and, the best way of life is to practice justice (*Gorg.* 527e).

Many believed that "justice is the whole of virtue," such as for example, Theognis 147ff, Plato *Prot.* 325a, 337-50 and Aristotle *Nic. Ethics* 1129b-1130a.

Finally, in the *Definitions* 411de, we have: "unanimity of the soul, good discipline of the parts of the soul with respect to each other, the state that distributes to each person according to what is deserved, social equality."

Moderation—Σωφροσύνη. Homer has the term σαοφροσύνη twice, at *Od.* 23.13, 20, but Pindar not at all, then it was used extensively by the Dramatists.

This is the only other cardinal virtue mentioned in two myths, *Phaedo* and *Phaedrus*, where it is subsumed under the heading 'well-ordered and wise' and 'good' respectively. In the *Republic* the common meanings of the word are given as subordination to appropriate authority and control of the appetite [see 389de]. Plato says that: "Soberness is a kind of beautiful order and a continence of certain pleasures and appetites, as they say, using the phrase 'a man is master of himself' (*Rep.* 430e)." *Sophrosyne* is the main subject of the *Charmides* and may be thought of as being the opposite of arrogance, insolence and self-assertiveness. It is translated as temperance, moderation, soberness and self-control. At the *Charmides* 155ce, Plato implies that it is self-control in the face of lust. At 159be, he suggests that the virtue is doing everything in an orderly and calm way. At 160e, it is shame or modesty (αἰδοώς, which is another virtue). At 161d, it is said that temperance is minding one's own business and not meddling in other's affairs (both, πραττέιν and πολυπραγμοσύνη, are additional virtues). Finally, at 165a: "Know yourself" and 'Be Temperate' are said to be the same because those who know who they are will not be intemperate enough to aspire to be gods. See also *Laws* 710ab "a restraint in the search for pleasure", *Prot.* 322ce "a sense of shame", *Tim.* 72a "only a man of sound mind may know himself". The term is defined at *Rep.* 432a as the mean between extremes "is rightly called moderation."

In *Definitions* 411e: "moderation of the soul concerning the desires and pleasures that normally occur in it, Harmony…Concord…Discipline…in the soul, rational agreement within the soul about what is admirable and contemptible."

Wisdom—Φρόνησις. The term is not used in Homer through Aeschylus, however *Sophia* is used by all, and sometimes Φρόνησις is interchangeable with Σοφία, a practical shrewdness in life and in craft. This is the lower wisdom of which it is said, "they should not neglect the higher wisdom for the sake of that wisdom which is concerned with the necessities of human life" (*Letter* 6.322e). At *Char.* 174 it is implied that wisdom is only utilization of knowledge. Again, a single virtue is equated with the whole as: "Wisdom is the essence of virtue" (*Epin.* 977d). In *Phaedo* 68ab, 69bc, "wisdom itself is a kind of purification." *Phaedo* 79d has it as "that state in which soul, resting from its wanderings while animating a body, remains always the same with what is changeless, it is communion therefore with recollection."

In *Definitions* 411d: "the ability which by itself is productive of happiness, the knowledge that produces happiness, the knowledge of what is good and bad, the disposition by which we judge what is to be done and what is not to be done."

Piety or Holiness—Ὁσιότης. In the form of ὅσιος it is used from Homer onward.

This is the only cardinal virtue to be mentioned in three myths (all except *Phaedrus* where Socrates seems more interested in the love that grows wings rather than piety being the vehicle that allows a return to the celestial realm). The term is subsumed under 'just and pious', 'well-ordered and wise', and 'righteous'.

This virtue can be seen in a wide range of meaning; it can be a simple ritualistic approach to honoring the gods or it can be associated with justice. Some believed that one could stay on good terms with the gods by proper attendance to sacrifice and other actions did not matter. For example: "Holiness or piety is the art of attending to the gods" (*Euth.* 13). On the other hand, some claimed that the gods were in charge of justice and would punish injustice. Plato condemned the ritualistic approach[257] and supported the latter.[258]

A difficult question was: "is the holy loved because it is holy, or is it holy because it is loved" (*Euth.* 10)?

In *Definitions* 415a: "service to a god which is agreeable to the god".

Virtue as a unity. At *Protagoras* 349b we have: "Wisdom, temperance, courage, justice, and piety—are these five names for the same thing…?" So, virtue is a unity!

The Unwritten Laws of the Gods

In Homer we find a few basic laws of conduct that will echo down the centuries through the generations of the poets, philosophers and dramatists we have reviewed. The ancient Homeric condemnations of false oaths and prohibitions against conduct and behavior that wrongs gods, parents and strangers still seem to hold sway for Plato's afterlife judgment.

These conducts, as opposed to the cardinal virtues, are ancient and appear in almost every writer.[259] They include the first to cause a punishment after death

---

[257] Plato condemns the ritualistic approach in *Rep.* 364b-e: Begging priests and prophets frequent the doors of the rich and persuade them that they possess a god-given power founded on sacrifices and incantations…. And they present a noisy throng of books by the Musaeus and Orpheus…with which they perform their rituals…. These initiations, as they call them, free people from punishment hereafter, while a terrible fate awaits those who have not performed the rituals.

[258] Starting at *Euth.* 4bc, Socrates shows that the old piety is replaced by a new type of piety and justice.

[259] We know that Socrates discussed some of the unwritten laws since they appear in Xenophon as: fear the gods, honor parents, avoid incest and repay benefactors (*Mem.* 4.4.19-20).

(false oaths in the *Iliad* at 3.276, 19.256) and are the cause of retribution by the gods throughout all Greek literature.

The conduct that wrongs parents, strangers and gods does not exact an afterlife retribution in Homer nor in Hesiod but is nevertheless punished by the gods (see *Od.* 5.447, 9.270, 14.404, *Works* 185-212).

Heraclitus and Empedocles condemn false oaths at frag 28 and frag 115 respectively. Pindar condemns false oaths at *Ol.* 2.67. With both Pindar and Empedocles this vice is associated with an afterlife consequence.

By the time of the Dramatists, we see that the wronging of parents, strangers, guests, suppliants and the gods result in dire consequences for the afterlife.

Aeschylus has Hades judging the wrongdoers under the earth in *Eumenides* 255ff. Sophocles speaks of the "unwritten and unfailing statutes given to us by the gods" and seems to associate adhering to them with an afterlife consequence in *Antigone* 449ff. Euripides proposes that one is dear to the gods after death if he honors his parents in frag 852. Finally, Aristophanes combines them all in the *Frogs* where he puts these violators in "a great slough (βόρβορον)[260] of ever-flowing dung (σκῶρ)(135ff, 274ff, 354ff)."

In using these unwritten laws in his myths, Plato was incorporating an ancient body of virtues and vices into his afterlife rewards and punishments, whereas, the development of the concept of the cardinal virtues appears relatively late and it is only with Plato that the actual terms are used.[261]

---

[260] This is the so-called 'Orphic' slough found in Plato *Rep.* 533d.

[261] However, recall that four virtues are mentioned in Aeschylus as: σώφρων, δίκαιος, ἀγαθός and εὐσεβής (Seven 610). Here temperance and justice are obvious, and we can note that the Homeric good (ἀγαθός) man was one who was brave and one who revered the gods(εὐσεβής) was wise.

CHAPTER 6

Conduct and Behavior as Determinants for the Afterlife in Ancient Egypt: The Classical Judgment

Introduction

> The judges who judge the oppressed, thou knowest that they are not lenient on that day of judging the miserable...A man remaineth over after death and his deeds are placed beside him in heaps...But he that cometh unto them without wrong-doing, he shall continue yonder like a god, stepping boldly forward like the Lords of Eternity.
>
> *Merikare*[262]

Religious Texts

Egyptology may be said to have entered the modern age of scholarship with the ability to understand the ancient Egyptian writings, which began with the work of Champollion in 1824.[263]

Although much could be learned from non-textual archeological sources and from classical authors such as Herodotus and Plutarch, nothing of written primary source knowledge could be gained before the translation of the principal religious texts in the mid-nineteenth century.

---

[262] *The Instruction for King Merikare* of the 9/10th Dynasty. Translated by Adolf Erman, *The Ancient Egyptians* (1923; reprint, New York: Harper & Row, 1966), 77-8.

[263] Champollion was the first to decipher hieroglyphics using the famous Rosetta Stone which had been promulgated by the priests at Memphis in 196 BCE and found by Napoleon's troops in 1799.

The first Egyptian religious text to be studied was the *Book of Going Forth by Day* (also called the *Book of the Dead*) which began with Karl Richard Lepsius's 1842 publication of a Ptolemaic-period papyrus.[264] Thus, the historically latest texts were translated earliest and would therefore be the first to impress their ideas of the Egyptian afterlife on modern thinking. These texts made an unfavorable moral and religious impression on the early Egyptologists[265] and thereby caused early scholarship to misjudge the extent of the ethical content of the Egyptian religion. This misconception continues somewhat to this day.

For example, although he was generally favorable to the earlier Egyptians, James Breasted writing in 1912 claimed that morality advanced in the succeeding periods of their history. Then, eventually with the "magic" of the later *Book of the Dead*, he claims that this developing spiritual expression was checked by the corruption and greed of the priests.[266]

While the *Book of the Dead* does encompass a variety of means for obtaining a successful afterlife, including ritual and even threats to the gods, this thinking must not blind the observer to the moral elements contained therein.

Next the *Pyramid Texts* were translated, and first published by Gaston Maspero between 1882-1893.[267] These texts would be shown to be among the earliest that dealt with the ancient Egyptian afterlife.

---

[264] The Ptolemaic period was from 332 to 31 BCE. Leonard Lesko, "Egyptian Religion: History of Study," in *Encyclopedia of Religion*, vol. 5, ed. Mircea Eliade (New York: Macmillan Publishing Company, 1987), 66.

[265] Erman said in his 1905 book, "Magic is a wild offshoot of religion; it attempts to coerce the forces that govern the fate of mankind…beside the noble plant of religion flourishes the rampant weed of magic" (Adolf Erman, *Die Ägyptische Religion* [Berlin: G. Reimer, 1905], 148). Maspero, in 1908, accused the early Egyptians of savagery and cannibalism. G. Maspero, *New Light on Ancient Egypt* (London: T. Fisher Unwin, 1908), 126-7.

[266] Breasted decries the evolution of religion that results in a mechanical observance and which attempts to secure moral vindication by magical means. In his mind, this seems to be a general fault of religions when the priests take over. He calls the Book of the Dead a priestly product and a force for evil. This understanding of religious evolution is simplistic, though common to earlier scholarship of ancient cultures (cf. Julius Wellhausen). James Henry Breasted, *The Dawn of Conscience* (New York: Charles Scribner's Sons, 1934), 264f.

[267] Lesko, "Egyptian Religion," 66.

Finally, in 1904-1906, Pierre Lacau published the *Coffin Texts*.[268]

Although discovered and translated in the sequence stated above, these texts were originally produced in the reverse order. The *Pyramid Texts*[269] were written in the 5th and 6th Dynasties (after c. 2400 BCE) where they were carved on the interior walls of the pyramids as a set of spells to assist the king into a felicitous afterlife. The *Coffin Texts* were composed later (after c. 2200 BCE) for the benefit of the nobility where they were painted on the interiors of their coffins and served a similar function as did the *Pyramid Texts* for the king. Appearing around the mid-fifteenth century BCE and remaining in use until the Roman period were spells written on papyri that were now available to everyone who could afford them. This large corpus of spells developed into the *Book of the Dead* which would do for the common people what the earlier *Pyramid* and *Coffin Texts* did for the king and the elite.

Spanning this entire period were a fourth and fifth type of literature: the instructions or wisdom texts, and the autobiographies of non-royalty inscribed in their tombs or on funerary stelae. These latter texts will prove to be most significant to our inquiries.

The above, then, are the primary texts that describe the concepts of the afterlife held by the ancient Egyptians from the Old Kingdom (2705-2180)[270] through the Middle Kingdom (1987-1640) to the New Kingdom (1540-1075) and beyond.

---

[268] Lesko, "Egyptian Religion," 66.

[269] These texts "had been transmitted for centuries before they were cut in stone…they conspicuously contain both earlier and later ideas" (Rudolf Anthes, "Egyptian Theology in the Third Millennium B.C.," *Journal of Near Eastern Studies* XVIII no. 3 [Jul. 1953]: 170).

[270] All major dates will be taken from two books of Hornung's, but dates not given by Hornung will be cited as they occur in the text. See a more detailed chronology at the end of this Introduction. Erik Hornung, *Idea into Image: Essays on Ancient Egyptian Thought*, trans. Elizabeth Bredeck (Princeton: Timkin Publishers, 1992), 187-188, first published as *Geist der Pharaonenzeit* (Zurich and Munich: Artemis, 1989); *The Ancient Egyptian Books of the Afterlife*, trans. David Lorton (Ithaca: Cornell University Press, 1999), xxi-xxii. See also among the many alternative datings (e.g., by Klaus Baer) in Sue D'Auria, Peter Lacovara and Catharine H. Roehrig, *Mummies and Magic: The Funerary Arts of Ancient Egypt* (Boston: Museum of Fine Arts, 1988), 9.

Historical Framework

The major divisions (i.e., the three Kingdoms) of Egyptian history are mentioned above. However, in order to more fully understand the concepts of our inquiry, we must briefly investigate how these divisions came into being.

Before ca. 3000 BCE, pre-dynastic Egypt existed as a group of independent provinces that were loosely associated with either upper Egypt in the south and lower Egypt in the northern Nile delta. The first politically significant event was the unification of upper and lower Egypt by Menes, the king of Upper Egypt.[271] Menes established a new capital at the boundary between the two lands at Memphis and established himself as the king of the two lands.

This conquest initiated the archaic dynastic era with Dynasties I and II preceding the Old Kingdom.[272]

The Old Kingdom, consisting of Dynasties III through VI, was the time of the great pyramid building and strong kings who were thought of as the divine keepers of the universal order expressed by the Egyptian term *ma'at*. The late 5th Dynasty saw the inception of the *Pyramid Texts*. The Old Kingdom disintegrated during the 6th Dynasty and the power of the king was diluted among the provincial nobles for what is now called the First Intermediate Period (c. 2180-1987 BCE) between the Old Kingdom and the advent of the Middle Kingdom.

With the Middle Kingdom the power of the king was returned during Dynasties XI through XII after which another intermediate period of provincial usurpation of power occurred. After this Second Intermediate Period, the power of the central kingship was once more restored during Dynasties XVIII through XX. When the New Kingdom drew to a close, Egypt fell under a series of dynasties often dominated by foreign nations.

---

[271] This is the traditional explanation according to the Egyptian historian of the 3rd century BCE, Manetho. Our divisions of Egyptian chronology into Kingdoms and Dynasties is attributable to him. The palette of Narmer (c. 3000 BCE) shows the conquest of the north over the south. Narmer may have been the same character as Menes.

[272] Depending on the scholar, Dynasty III is a transitional period placed either in the archaic period or the Old Kingdom.

Our inquiry starts with the archeological evidence of pre-dynastic times and terminates with the evidence of the *Book of the Dead*, which was essentially finalized by the New Kingdom.[273]

For a more detailed outline of Egyptian history, see Appendix J: "Egyptian Chronological Summary Chart".

Types of Judgment

One of the problems of an inquiry into the details of any subject is that of definition. In our case the question is: exactly what constitutes a judgment of the dead? Therefore, it would be fruitful to investigate what is believed to define the judgment for modern scholarship.

As we will see below, many of the scholars of the late nineteenth and early twentieth centuries interpreted some of the oldest texts as referring to a judgment and took it to imply that the moral judgment, as it appears in the later *Book of the Dead*, was of long standing. Some scholars (e.g., Griffiths and Spiegel)[274] credit Junker[275] with providing evidence that the beginnings of the concept of some

---

[273] See the end of this Introduction section for a chronological chart of dates and issues of interest to this inquiry.

[274] Spiegel says: "Vgl. SPIEGEL, Totengericht, und JUNKER, Pyramidenzeit. Gegenüber der von mir vertretenen Auffassung, daß die "Idee vom Totengericht" erst aus den Wirren am Ende des Alten Reiches erwächst, hat JUNKER mit Recht darauf hingewiesen, daß ihr Bestehen bereits in der 6. Dynastie nachweisbar ist. Erst der Zerfall dieser Ordnung, der—wie ich in meinem Buch "Totengericht" noch nicht gesehen habe—bereits am Ende der 5. Dynastie, also lange vor dem äußeren Zusammenbruch des Alten Reiches, eintritt, führt die "Idee vom Totengericht" herauf" (Joachim Spiegel, *Das Werden Der Altagyptischen Hochkultur* [Heidelberg: F.H. Kerle Vertag, 1953], 411, 662 n. 54). Here, Spiegel agrees that Junker established the origin of the idea of the judgment of the dead for the end of the Old Kingdom. But, he does not believe that at that time it implied a general examination of conduct here on earth. See also, J. Gwyn Griffiths, *The Conflict of Horus and Seth* (Liverpool: Liverpool University Press, 1960), 79.

[275] Junker is credited as being the first scholar who claimed to show that both a judicial court and the beginnings of a general judgment appear in the Pyramid Texts. He discusses some judgment scenes in the Pyramid Texts: "Ein weiteres Bekenntnis des vor den Richtern stehenden Königs ist in 2082f. der Pyramidentexte wiedergegeben. Vielleicht stellte es ebenfalls ursprünglich einen selbständigen in der ersten Person abgefaßten Spruch dar; im Kapitel 688 wurde dieser aber hinter einen Text vom

form of the post-mortem judgment on one's conduct in this life appears as early as the *Pyramid Texts*. This would influence many others in later years, rightly or wrongly, to see in those early texts the precursors to the judgment as it appears in the *Book of the Dead*.

On the other hand, well into the 20th century some scholars started to differentiate between a moral judgment as found in the *Book of the Dead* and what they saw as earlier references to judicial court hearings, which are a different matter.[276] This differentiation is a key step, because there is a significant distinction between an automatic judgment based on ethical living for all people and an *ad hoc* court case that only occurs if a specific complaint is lodged against the deceased. The judgment of all the dead based on their ethical living is here referred to as the general judgment, whereas the court case against an accused is simply a judicial proceeding.

We will look at these opposing views beginning with The Questions section below.

Elements of the Person: *ba, ka, akh*

Although later we will look more deeply at the Egyptian ideas of what is usually translated as the 'soul', it would be helpful at this point to explain some of the basic concepts concerning the elements that were said to make up the human personality.[277]

The person at various times during his or her life and death was thought to consist of many elements besides just the body. Three of the most important were the *ba, ka,* and the *akh*.

Aufstellen der Leiter gesetzt…Ein dritter Text = Pyr. 2029 f…Er zeigt uns, wie der Herrscher einem Verhör unterzogen werden soll, und wie er sich durch Zauber der gerichtlichen Verhandlung zu entziehen sucht…Die Tatsache, daß selbst der Konig auf seinem Weg zum Himmel mit einem Gericht zu rechnen hatte" (Hermann Junker, *Pyraminenzeit* [Zurich: Koln, 1949], 83).

[276] Cf. Breasted, *The Dawn of Conscience*, 125, 249.

[277] The soul is a Platonic idea, so the Egyptian concept of 2000 years earlier should not be expected to correspond very closely to it. For a summary comparison to the Platonic soul, see Appendix M: "Attributes and Features of the Egyptian Soul, Table 9."

These three entities appear very early in the Egyptian *Pyramid Texts* and were almost certainly part of Egyptian thinking before being committed to writing on the pyramids' walls.[278]

The *ba* is divine. It can refer to a manifestation of the power of the god that can appear on earth.[279] It also was originally exclusive to the king, the aspect that could rise up from the tomb and ride in the solar bark with the sun-god.[280] Thus the *ba* was thought of as the mobile quality of the deceased and was often represented as a human-headed bird.[281] Later, it became an element of all persons when the spells of the *Pyramid Texts* were 'democratized' for non-royalty in the *Coffin Texts* and the *Book of the Dead.*

The *ka* is not necessarily divine, since both people and gods have one or more *ka*'s. For a person, the *ka* is that entity that exists eternally in the tomb. It is sometimes called the double of the person[282] since it can still exist even if the body is destroyed, usually in a statue of the deceased. The *ka* can receive the food and other offerings given at the tomb by the living.[283]

The *akh* was the spirit of the dead person, much like the *ka*, but it is differentiated by its ability to commune with and help the living, whereas the *ka* is helped by the living. Letters to the dead seeking help were addressed to the *akh*, but food was given to the *ka*.[284]

---

[278] The *ka* and the *akh* both appear as early as the Early Dynastic Period (c. 3000-2705) in the 1st Dynasty. However, the first appearance of the *ba*, according to most scholars, is in the Pyramid Texts themselves. See Werner Forman and Stephen Quirke, *Hieroglyphics and the Afterlife* (Norman: University of Oklahoma Press, 1996), 10, 31, 72.

[279] Louis V. Zabkar, *A Study of the Ba Concept in Ancient Egyptian Text* (Chicago: University of Chicago Press, 1968), 160.

[280] "I assume my pure seat which is in the bow of the Bark of Re" (Spell 710 of the Pyramid Texts).

[281] Alan B. Lloyd, "Psychology and Society in the Ancient Egyptian Cult of the Dead," in *Religion and Philosophy in Ancient Egypt*, ed. William Kelly Simpson (New Haven: Yale University Press, 1989), 119.

[282] Lloyd, "Psychology and Society in the Ancient Egyptian Cult of the Dead," 118.

[283] H. Frankfort, *Ancient Egyptian Religion* (New York: Harper and Brothers, 1948), 93.

[284] Edward F. Wente, "Funerary Beliefs of the Ancient Egyptians," *Expedition* (Winter 1982): 20.

More will be said of these complex and often misunderstood concepts in what follows.

The Questions

There are four major questions to be addressed in our inquiry concerning the Egyptian afterlife beliefs:

1. What entity is being judged?
2. When did a blessed afterlife become available to all persons?
3. What exactly constitutes the Egyptian judgment of the dead?
4. At what point in the development of the concept of a blessed afterlife did conduct and behavior begin to matter?

These questions will be addressed in order below. Our first inquiry concerns just what is the entity or element of the human personality that partakes of an afterlife.

The Entity Being Judged

At the dawn of written religious texts, that is, in the *Pyramid Texts*, we see many religious concepts that are almost as complete as they will later be in the *Book of the Dead.* Already there appear to be multifarious elements of the human personality (*ka, ba, akh* as discussed above) and already the two gods, Re and Osiris, come into play, sometimes as competitors.[285] The afterlife is full-blown, albeit in this set of spells composed by the priests of the Heliopolitan theology,[286] for the

---

[285] Re and Osiris are the two main gods attested throughout Egyptian history. There seems to be some periods when one is superior to the other and then again when they are equal or even merged. An interesting question is: Which of the two gods was the first on the scene. Many scholars have debated this question and I shall briefly inquire into it further, later in this chapter.

[286] Heliopolis was the Greek name for the Egyptian Iwnw or On as it appears in the Bible. It was the center of worship of the sun-god Re and by the 4th Dynasty and had so much influence that the kings became known as the sons of Re. By the 5th Dynasty the priests had developed the Pyramid Texts for the benefit of the king's afterlife. The name of On appears in *Pyramid Text* 1655: "O you Great Ennead which is in On..." Thus, on this and other internal evidence, the Pyramid Texts contain the Heliopolitan theology of On, and it is certain that their priests are the creators and/or compilers of the Texts.

king only. Furthermore, we see that conduct and behavior may already have begun to count as a determinant in that afterlife. In order to better understand the Egyptian concept of what it is that continues after death as it has developed in the earliest texts, we need to briefly review the older periods prior to the *Pyramid Texts*.

Pre-History

Some scholars[287] have attempted to discover the origins of Egyptian culture. Their search has led them back to Paleolithic times (before c. 10,000 BCE) when a belief in the afterlife is already indicated.

We see evidence of burials from the Paleolithic period[288] right up to the pre-Dynastic period[289] (before c. 3000 BCE) when the body has been carefully placed[290] in its tomb and surrounded by articles that would be useful in an afterlife. There is evidence that the body was sometimes disassembled[291] with the expectation being that it would be reassembled in the future life. We see echoes of this practice in the *Pyramid Texts*, where the King's body will be reconstituted.[292]

---

[287] Some early scholars include: Alexander Moret, *The Nile and Egyptian Civilization* (London: Kegan Paul, Trench, Trubner, 1927), 38ff; W.M. Flinders Petrie, *Religion and Conscience in Ancient Egypt* (1898; reprint, London: Benjamin Bloom, 1972), 11ff. A recent study is John Baines, "Origins of Egyptian Kingship," in *Ancient Egyptian Kingship*, eds. David O'Conner and David P. Silverman (Leiden: E.J. Brill, 1995), 95-156.

[288] S.F. Brandon, "The Origin of Death in some Ancient Near Eastern Religions," *Religious Studies* I, no. 2 (1966): 217-218.

[289] A display of the burial of a man, surrounded by useful grave goods, in the Naqada II period (c. 3650-3300 BCE) is in the Carnegie Museum. James A. Romano, *Death, Burial, and Afterlife in Ancient Egypt* (Pittsburg: The Carnegie Museum of Natural History, 1990), 2; Also, Leonard Lesko, "Death and Afterlife in Ancient Egyptian Thought," in *Civilization of the Ancient Near East*, ed. Jack M. Sasson, vol. III (New York: Charles Scribner's Sons, 1995) 1763-1774; H. Frankfort, Ancient Egyptian Religion, 90.

[290] Usually in a fetal position and facing west.

[291] This idea is supported by: A.J. Spencer, *Death in Ancient Egypt* (New York: Penguin Group, 1982), 39-44; and Anthes, "Egyptian Theology in the Third Millennium," 206; but is questioned by J. Gwyn Griffiths, *The Origins of Osiris and His Cult* (Leiden: E.J. Brill, 1980), 25, 51f.

[292] There are many of these reconstitution texts in the *Pyramid Texts* besides the ones cited above, (e.g., spells 572, 736, 828, 840, 1675, 1685, 1732, 1916, 1981).

You have your water, you have your flood, you have your efflux which issued from Osiris; gather together your bones, make ready your members, throw off your dust, loosen your bonds.[293]

Pyramid Text 2007-9

Hail to you, Tait [the Divine weaver]…Guard the King's head, lest it come loose; gather together the King's bones, lest they become loose.[294]

Pyramid Text 738f

Oho! Oho! Rise up, O Teti!
Take your head,
Collect your bones,
Shake the earth from your flesh![295]
Take your bread that rots not,
Your beer that sours not,
Stand at the gates that bar the common people!
…
The gatekeeper…
Sets you before the spirits, the imperishable stars.[296]

Pyramid Text 654

These texts obviously imply the expectation of a bodily restoration even though a much more spiritual concept of the future life is also now propounded in

---

[293] All Pyramid Texts are translated, unless otherwise noted, by R.O. Faulkner, *The Ancient Egyptian Pyramid Texts* (Oxford: Clarendon Press, 1969), 289.

[294] Faulkner, *The Ancient Egyptian Pyramid Texts*, 137.

[295] The texts for this must have come from a time when the dead were still buried in the desert sands and this attests to a far greater age than the 5th Dynasty of many of the spells in the Pyramid Texts. Many of these earlier references to 'shaking off the earth or dust' appear, (e.g., spells 645, 736, 748, 1068, 1363, 1732, 1878, 1917, 2008).

[296] Translated by Miriam Lichtheim, *Ancient Egyptian Literature* 3 vols. (Berkeley: University of California Press, 1973, 1976, 1980), 1.41f. Not only does this text give evidence for a disassembled corpse, but also more importantly, it suggests that commoners were barred from the king's afterlife, which was still conceived in terms of joining the stars as opposed to the later solar afterlife. A very good indication that the stellar afterlife was desired appears in the 4th Dynasty Great Pyramid of Cheops where two small passage-ways connect the burial chamber to the outside walls. These passage-ways are aimed directly at the heavenly bodies of Sirius and Orion which are mentioned in Pyramid Text 723 where the king reaches the sky as Orion and his soul is as effective as Sothis (Sirius).

other *Pyramid Texts* where the king's spirit [*akh*] or soul [*ba*] join the gods in the heavens:

> O Re-Atum, this King comes to you, an imperishable spirit [*akh*]…May you traverse the sky…

and,

> I come to you, O Nut…I have left Horus behind me, my wings have grown into those of a falcon…my soul [*ba*] has brought me…[297]
>
> Pyramid Text 152 and 250

This seeming contradiction between an existence both in the tomb and in the heavens is one of many that we see the Egyptians holding, and it makes us wonder how they could simultaneously hold multiple mutually opposed concepts in spite of the logical consequences. A possible explanation of this facet of Egyptian religion might be given by an almost exact analogy from a modern religion.

The belief in the resurrection of the body is simultaneously held with the belief in the immortality of the soul in present day Christianity. These two different beliefs entered Christianity from two diverse places and times. Our investigation of Plato's immortal soul in the first two chapters of this paper adequately explains the origin of the soul idea. The resurrection idea, on the other hand, has Jewish roots, and may have had an even more ancient origin in the Zoroastrianism of the sixth century BCE.

As Christianity spread into the cultural milieu of the Greek world in the second century CE it encountered Plato's idea of the immortal soul and incorporated it into its developing dogma. Subsequent theologians were able to take these two diametrically opposed concepts and weave them into an integrated whole that has survived to this day.

This is analogous to what happened in ancient Egypt. The pre-Dynastic physical renewal has been skillfully integrated into the Dynastic-era spiritual concepts such as the king's rising to the sun-god Re.[298] This culminated in the priestly the-

---

[297] Faulkner, *The Ancient Egyptian Pyramid Texts*, 44, 58.

[298] "I assume my pure seat which is in the bow of the Bark of Re." As referenced above in Spell 710 of the Pyramid Texts.

ology of Heliopolis and that integrated material made its way into the *Pyramid Texts* of the late 5th Dynasty.[299]

Somewhere along the way, the human personality became endowed with a multiplicity of spiritual aspects (i.e., the *ba*, *ka*, and *akh*). Whatever the cause of all of these apparently disparate spiritual ideas, the same kind of theological juggling act that we have seen being required for integrating the bodily resuscitation and the spiritual rising to the heavens must have been at work here also.

One conclusion that may be drawn, therefore, is that for centuries prior to Egypt's first religious texts the restoration of the body was one element of the afterlife and was then combined with the idea of the deceased's spiritual incorporation or union with the stars and the sun.

The Spiritual Afterlife

However the Egyptians' multifaceted physical and spiritual afterlife may actually have developed, whether by a single group or, more likely, by a syncretism from diverse groups,[300] these seemingly conflicting ideas appeared to form a functional system for the ancient Egyptians.[301]

As to why the non-physical concepts of the *ba*, *ka* and *akh* arose at all is lost in the mists of time. Nevertheless, we can conjecture based on the premise of two facts that clashed—an afterlife was desired and the body did disintegrate after death.

The preservation of the body in the hot dry sand of the Egyptian desert may have lent credence to the belief in the individual's physical continuity,[302] but as sandy

---

[299] See footnote 277 on Heliopolis given above.

[300] Note that at least one scholar argues for a "coherent vision of the afterlife" in the Pyramid Texts. James P. Allen, "The Cosmology of the Pyramid Texts," In *Religion and Philosophy in Ancient Egypt*, ed. William Kelly Simpson (New Haven: Yale University Press, 1989), 19.

[301] Of course, the coherence could have either been syncretized from diverse entries into the Texts, or it may have been created in toto by the Heliopolitan priests. From our remote frame of reference we see conflicting ideas that need to be reconciled.

[302] Edward F. Wente, "Funerary Beliefs of the Ancient Egyptians," 18-9. Also, James H. Breasted, *Development of Religion and Thought in Ancient Egypt* (London: Charles Scribner's Sons, 1912), 49.

graves evolved into more elaborate tombs, the natural bodily preservation no longer sufficed. In spite of efforts to preserve the body, it still decayed, requiring the employment of alternative methods of preservation, hence, the advent of mummification.

Now the fear arose that the mummy itself might be lost, so a duplicate body was prepared in the form of a statue.[303] As the mummified body was ritually revitalized by what became known as 'the opening of the mouth' ceremony, the duplicate body in the form of a statue might be likewise revitalized. A statue of the person could be ritually transformed[304] and given the same kind of life in the tomb previously enjoyed by the body should the mummy be destroyed. The person's statue was filled with the double or *ka* of the deceased person which could move from the statue to the food offerings left by the family and priests.

Also, at this same time, a statue of a god was thought to hold the manifestation of that god called the *ba*.[305] Since the king was also thought to be a god, he and his statue both would have a *ba* and this entity would be what soared to the heavens to be with the sun god.

Both of these elements now were thought, in the *Pyramid Texts*, to be non-physical[306] elements that duplicated the king. Later theological developments would have them become integrated elements of personhood in general.

---

[303] Griffiths, *The Origins of Osiris and His Cult*, 72; Frankfort, *Ancient Egyptian Religion*, 93.

[304] Transformation of the person into a variety of other things developed greatly in later times.

[305] Herman Te Velde, "Theology, Priests, and Worship in Ancient Egypt," in *Civilization of the Ancient Near East*, ed. William Kelly Simpson, vol. III (New York: Charles Scribner's Sons, 1995), 1732, 1747.

[306] There is some indication that these elements or forms were thought to be corporeal rather than spiritual, and "in each of these forms the deceased acts and lives as a full individual…[each form was] considered to be full physical entities and not 'spiritual components of a human composite'" (Zabkar, *A Study of the Ba Concept in Ancient Egyptian Text*, 97).

The Blessed Afterlife for Everyone

Was an afterlife available only to the king?[307] It does seem that, in the Old Kingdom, he was the only one to have a *ba* since the *ba* is not attested in private tomb inscriptions before the New Kingdom.[308] This restriction of b*a* to the king alone makes sense inasmuch as the "*ba*" originally referred to divine power or manifestation, and both the gods and the king were divine, while other humans were not.

Since, in the *Pyramid Texts*, the *ba* was the spiritual aspect that soared beyond the tomb and was able to dwell with the sun-god Re in the celestial realm, the king was indeed the only one to have a celestial afterlife with Re.

In early Old Kingdom royal mastaba tombs we already find boats[309] for the king to ride into the sky that the later *Pyramid Texts* will call 'the boat of a million years'. Since some entity was thought to be soaring to the heavens in the 1st Dynasty, the *ba* may therefore have been a well established idea by this early time (3000-2890), well before the Pyramid Texts of the 5th Dynasty.[310]

In spite of the fact that the king was the only one with a *ba*, there is little reason to suspect that others had no afterlife at all since the solar afterlife was only one type of post-mortem existence possible. The idea of survival in the tomb (possibly

---

[307] The fact that the *Book of the Dead* is found in many tombs of persons of varied social statuses attests to a "democratization" of the afterlife which, according to some scholars, was supposedly available in earlier times to the king alone. How did this democratization occur and is it really the case that in earlier days everyone was excluded from the afterlife except the king?

[308] "Unless our tradition is deceptive, the soul (ba), as distinct from the vital force (ka), was during the Old Kingdom the property of the King alone" (Siegfried Morenz, *Egyptian Religion*, trans. Ann E. Keep [London: Methuen; Ithaca: Cornell University Press, 1973], 206. First published as *Agyptische Religion Religionen der Menschheit* 8 [Stuttgart: Kohlhammer, 1960]. Also see Forman and Quirke, *Hieroglyphs*, 31; J. Gwyn Griffiths, *Atlantis and Egypt* (Cardiff: University of Wales Press, 1991), 170 n32.

[309] As early as the 1st Dynasty. See Alan Gardiner, *Egypt of the Pharaohs: An Introduction* (Oxford: Clarendon Press, 1961), 77.

[310] The term 'ba' also appears in names of the 1st Dynasty. Zabkar says, "the last king of the 1st Dynasty is listed as...Baunetjer (divine of Bas)" (Zabkar, *A Study of the Ba Concept in Ancient Egyptian Text*, 58).

associated with Osiris[311]) was still available to other people as shown by this text that addresses the newly deceased king.

> Open up your place in the sky among the stars of the sky, for you are the Lone Star, the companion of Hu; look down on Osiris when he governs the spirits, for you [the king] stand far off from him, you are not among them [the other people's spirits] and you shall not be among them.[312]
>
> Pyramid Text 251[313]

The king goes to the celestial realm where he will look down on Osiris who rules the other spirits [the *akh*'s] in the Netherworld. Thus, it would seem that even the non-royal people had an afterlife, at least as an *akh* in the realm of Osiris.[314]

---

[311] Lichtheim, *Ancient Egyptian Literature*, 1.33. Osiris is an ambivalent character. He first appears in the Pyramid Texts, here as king of the underworld and only later does he rise to the heavens to be on a par with Re.

[312] Faulkner, *The Ancient Egyptian Pyramid Texts*, 58.

[313] Note that all Egyptian citations are summarized in Appendix N: "Passages from Egyptian Texts Concerning the Afterlife."

[314] Here, since we have now reviewed *Pyramid Texts* 738, 152, 654 and 251, we shall address the primacy of Re or Osiris. The king goes up to the celestial realm of Re who is the god of heaven and looks down on Osiris who is the god of the underworld. In Pyramid Text 738, we saw that the king was to gather up his bones and shake the dust from his body, a clear reference to more ancient ideas where the dead were under the earth. This would seem to indicate that the underworld was the more ancient place for people to populate after death, and a chthonic god would be the most reasonable to expect to be there. Also, in the Pyramid Text 152, the king has acquired a new type of spiritual element—the ba, which ascends to the heavens. There the common people are barred from entering (Pyramid Text 655) and the king looks down on Osiris where he holds power over the other dead (Pyramid Text 251). The common dead have had an afterlife long before the priests of Heliopolis devised the celestial scheme for the deification of the king. They survived as akhs and kas in the underworld of Osiris where Re had not yet been placed by the priests. My conclusion, based on the foregoing texts, is that Osiris was the older of the two gods but was initially overshadowed by the priestly Re in the 5th Dynasty, then Osiris came to the fore again by the 6th Dynasty, then at various later times, their position oscillated, sometimes attaining equality.

Petrie, who argued for a solarization of Osirian texts, would probably agree with me. But Breasted who argued for Osirianization of solar texts would not. Petrie, *Religion and Conscience in Ancient Egypt*, 74-75; Breasted, *The Dawn of Conscience*, 148.

In *Pyramid Text* 474 it is said that "The spirit (*akh*) is bound for the sky, the corpse is bound for the earth."[315] Compare this early text with one a thousand years later where an 18th Dynasty subject of Queen Hatshepsut, Hepusonb, has these words in his tomb: "my Ba in heaven, my corpse in the graveyard."[316] Here the word *ba* has replaced the word *akh* as the entity that goes to heaven. Although the *akh*[317] later was to become a theological marvel of integration, it was at first considered only a ghost and may have existed in or for all persons.[318] If it did, then it may not be too much of a conjecture to assume that the *akh* of a non-royal person might also have had a celestial afterlife as early as the time of the *Pyramid Texts* since all people definitely had an *akh* by that time.

The *ba*[319] seems to have been attributed to the king by the 5th Dynasty Heliopolitan priests, but the same was probably not true of the *ka*. Early evidence suggests that non-royals had it also since the *ka* first appears in the First Dynasty during the reign of King Djer. It is found on a stela for the tomb of a non-royal woman, where it says simply: "*ka n* [picture of a woman]."[320] There is also a stela of a courtier named Wedjka of King Djet, also of the 1st Dynasty, with the carved phrase *wd-ka*.[321]

---

[315] Faulkner, *The Ancient Egyptian Pyramid Texts*, 94.

[316] Translated by Miriam Lichtheim, *Maat in Egyptian Autobiographies and Related Studies* (Gottingen: Vandenhoeck & Roprecht, 1992), 51. This phrase is repeated a thousand years later for the Athenian dead at Potidaea.

[317] The term *akh* first appears in inscriptions of the First Dynasty. H. Frankfort, *Ancient Egyptian Religion*, 100.

[318] As alluded to it the Introduction, the akh would later become the state achieved when the *ba* and the *ka* are rejoined. Lloyd, "Psychology and Society in the Ancient Egyptian Cult of the Dead," 119-120. James P. Allen, "Funerary Texts and Their Meaning," in *Mummies and Magic*, eds. Sue D'Auria, Peter Lacovara and Catharine H. Roehig (Boston: Museum of Fine Arts, 1988), 45.

[319] The *ba* is not like the Platonic soul. The *ba* originally was not a part of the king until after his death. It was only with the Coffin Texts (see especially 99-104) that the *ba* evolved into an element of the person, somehow inside him, to be released at death, like the soul of much later times. See Ronald J. Williams, "Reflections on the Lebensmude," *Journal of Egyptian Archaeology* 48(1962): 52.

[320] "The *ka* of [picture of a non-royal woman]". Stela from Abydos, Umm el-Ga'ab from Dynasty 1 in D'Auria, *Mummies and Magic*, 74.

[321] The name Wedjka means to "order/command the *ka*". H.M. Stewart, *Egyptian Stelae, Reliefs and Paintings*, Part Two (Warminster: Aris & Phillips, 1979), 4.

In addition to the evidence provided by inscriptions we also have that provided by the suggestive names and titles of the Early Dynastic officials who were buried in close proximity to their king. "They [the non-royal names or titles] tell us that for the King rites were performed relating to his Ka and his Akh—that is, to the deified Substance and to the divine Spirit which the King rejoined in the next world."[322] Therefore, the *ka* and the *akh* of common people clearly were thought to participate in an afterlife well before the *Pyramid Texts* were written.[323]

So, we see that whether the afterlife was available to the king alone depends on the nature of the afterlife in question. Asking just the right question could eliminate the confusion that has had many scholars denying an afterlife for anyone but the king during the time of the *Pyramid Texts*. The same would be true on the related question of an afterlife judgment based on conduct.

The Classical Egyptian Judgment of the Dead

As has already been said in chapter 2 of the religious ideas of Homer, we can again say here of the similar ideas of the Egyptians: 1) there is an afterlife; 2) there is some entity that is experiencing an afterlife; and 3) the afterlife depends on one's conduct and behavior in this life (i.e., a judgment of the dead). However, as with Homer, the devil is in the details and these three issues need to be examined much more closely. They also need to be traced through time from Egyptian prehistory until the point at which the beliefs have coalesced into the form taken in the *Book of the Dead*.

Following the procedural format of the first five chapters of this project, we will first investigate our terminal time period then we will start at the beginning and chronologically trace the evolution of the Egyptian ideas of conduct and behavior

---

322 Moret, *The Nile and Egyptian Civilization*, 143, 171. See also Zabkar, *A Study of the Ba Concept in Ancient Egyptian Text*, 59-60.

323 As to whether it was of a celestial type remains possible, but unsubstantiated, on the available evidence. David Silverman's comment that "the concept of the afterlife was originally limited to royalty" is in error unless he was restricting the form of the afterlife to a celestial one, which here he was not. Later Silverman says, "Once Coffin Texts had been compiled...their funerary spells became available to the high nobility" (David P. Silverman, "Divinity and Deities in Ancient Egypt," in *Religion in Ancient Egypt*, ed. Byron E. Shafer [Ithaca: Cornell University Press, 1991] 46, 72-3]. The implication being that they were not so in the Pyramid Texts.

as related to their significance for an afterlife judgment. Whereas, in our Greek chapters, the beginning was Greek pre-history and the terminus was the works of Plato, in this Egyptian chapter, the beginning and end points will be Egyptian pre-history and the *Book of the Dead.*

As stated in the Introduction, the *Book of the Dead* is a large corpus but only a few of the spells deal directly with the judgment itself. In order to make the available texts manageable, we will use spells 30 and 125 as a representative subset of the whole.[324]

The *Book of the Dead* is examined here in order to show the New Kingdom Egyptian conception of the judgment against which the earlier texts may be compared. The <u>underlining</u> in the texts quoted is to indicate and highlight positive or negative types of behavior.

The Book of the Dead

> O my heart which I had from my mother! O my heart which I had from my mother! O my heart of my different ages! Do not stand up as a witness against me, do not be opposed to me in the tribunal, do not be hostile to me in the presence of the Keeper of the Balance, for you are my ka which was in my body,[325] the protector who made my members hale. Go forth to the happy place whereto we speed;[326] do not make my name stink to the Entourage who make men. Do not tell lies about me in the presence of the god; it is indeed well that you should hear!
>
> Thus says Thoth, judge of truth, to the Great Ennead which is in the presence of Osiris: Hear this word of very truth. I have judged the heart of the deceased, and his soul stands as a witness for him. His <u>deeds are righteous</u> in the great balance, and <u>no sin</u> has been found in him. He did <u>not diminish the</u>

---

[324] Spells (or sometimes referred to as chapters) 30 and 125 are the major judgment of the dead spells in the *Book of the Dead.*

[325] Interestingly, by this time, the ka was believed to be in the body much as Plato's psyche also was in the body.

[326] The first part of this verse has been found carved on the underside of a heart scarab included in the tomb of the high steward Nebankh of the 13th Dynasty (c. 1730 BCE). It is the earliest known dated reference to the classical Egyptian judgment of the dead. Forman and Quirke, *Hieroglyphics and the Afterlife*, 104.

offerings in the temples, he did not destroy what had been made, he did not go about with deceitful speech while he was on earth.

Thus says the Great Ennead to Thoth who is in Hermopolis: This utterance of yours is true. The vindicated Osiris N is straightforward, he has no sin, there is no accusation against him before us, Ammit shall not be permitted to have power over him. Let there be given to him the offerings which are issued in the presence of Osiris, and may a grant of land be established in the Field of Offerings as for the Followers of Horus.

Thus says Horus son of Isis: I have come to you, O Wennefer, and I bring N to you. His heart is true, having gone forth from the balance, and he has not sinned against any god or any goddess. Thoth has judged him in writing which has been told the Ennead, and Maat the great has witnessed. Let there be given to him bread and beer which have been issued in the presence of Osiris, and he will be for ever like Followers of Horus.

Thus says N: Here I am in your presence, O Lord of the West. There is no wrong-doing in my body, I have not wittingly told lies, there has been no second fault. Grant that I may be like the favoured ones who are in your suite, O Osiris, one greatly favored by the good god, one loved of the Lord of the Two Lands, N, vindicated before Osiris.

Book of the Dead—Spell 30B[327]

Spell 30B from the *Book of the Dead* as quoted above comes from after 1500 BCE[328] and stands toward the evolutionary end of a long history of religious beliefs. In this spell from the New Kingdom we see several interesting things concerning the judgment of the dead.

The dead person begs that his heart not witness against him. He further claims that his heart is his *ka* which was in his body and was the protector who made him hale while living. This either equates the heart and the *ka* or enfleshes the *ka* within the body or both.

---

[327] All translations of the Book of the Dead are from Faulkner unless otherwise noted. Raymond O. Faulkner, *The Ancient Egyptian Book of the Dead* (Austin: The University of Texas Press, 1993), 27f.

[328] Faulkner, *The Ancient Egyptian Book of the Dead*, 11, 14-15. However, as stated in footnote 332 referencing Forman and Quirke, a form of spell 30 appears on the underside of a heart scarab from the 13th Dynasty (c. 1730 BCE), over 200 years earlier than thought by Faulkner at the time of his publication in 1969.

Thoth is the judge of truth who weighs the heart in the balance and declares that it is sinless. Next, the Great Ennead[329] says that the vindicated 'Osiris N' is to be given a place in the Field of Offerings instead of being given over to the destroyer Ammit.[330]

Finally, Horus introduces the dead person to his father, Osiris, and claims that he or she should be forever like the Followers of Horus. The dead person then speaks to Osiris and asks that he or she may be vindicated and favored in the house of Osiris.

In this single excerpt from the *Book of the Dead*, which gives an excellent overview of what is involved in the judgment of the dead, we find the fully evolved ideas comprising the judgment of the dead that were to remain important themes throughout subsequent Egyptian history. This spell, along with spell 125, gives us the classical version of the Egyptian judgment. In the *Book of the Dead* there also appeared pictorial scenes or vignettes that illustrated the judgment in great detail, showing the all important scale that weighed the heart against the feather of *ma'at* (truth, order).

Interestingly, although there is a pronouncement of innocence by a judge, the person's heart is simply weighed in a balance to compare it with the feather of truth (*ma'at*); if the heart is heavier, the person is annihilated, but if lighter, the person moves on to see Osiris. Here we have one of those automatic judgments[331] where the person has already convicted himself by the physical

---

[329] The Great Ennead was a group of nine gods. In the Heliopolis cosmology they consisted of: Atum (Re); Shu (air) and Tefnut (moisture); their offspring Geb (earth) and Nut (sky); and their offspring Seth, Osiris, Nephthys and Isis. Osiris was the ruler of the world but jealous Seth killed him. Isis restored him and Osiris came to rule the realm of the dead. This story of the death of Osiris, and his restoration by Isis, forms the basis of the mythology that undergirds the Book of the Dead.

[330] The "pictorial representations [of the Book of the Dead] began in the 18th Dynasty," and the destroyer was added in the Ramesside period. Erik Hornung, "Ancient Egyptian Religious Iconography," in *Civilizations of the Ancient Near East*. vol. III, ed. Jack M. Sasson (New York: Charles Scribner's Sons, 1995), 1721.

[331] It seems to be strictly automatic because, "the so-called 'Negative Confession' in spell 125 appears to have had no real effect on the final judgment. The verdict was given independently as a result of the weighing of the dead man's heart against Truth" (Anne Burton, ed., *Études Préliminaires Aux Religions Orientales Dans L'Empire Romain: Diodorus Siculus, Book 1, A Commentary* [Leiden: E.J. Brill, 1972], 270).

indicators of the kind of life he led. This is analogous to what happens in Plato's *Gorgias*, where physical scars indicate one's conduct in life although there are also judges present.

The key concept, about which this chapter inquires, is that of the link between good conduct and behavior and a favorable judgment after death. Many of the spells in the *Book of the Dead* appear to use magic in the sense of invoking formulas believed to be ritually effective, without consideration of moral worth, to absolve the dead persons of their actual past sins. However, the link between morality or ethical behavior and conduct and a real judgment is unmistakably present in these spells as shown in the following sketch of vices and virtues from the <u>Book of the Dead</u>.[332]

Conduct and Behavior in The Book of the Dead

The negative conduct.

The two judgement spells are examined here.

<u>In spell 30</u>:
The negative statements are extracted here for this spell.

> <u>No sin</u> has been found in him.
> He did <u>not diminish the offerings in the temples,</u>
> <u>he did not destroy what had been made</u>
> <u>He did not go about with deceitful speech</u>
> while he was on earth
> He <u>has no sin</u>
> <u>There is no accusation against</u> him before us
> He has <u>not sinned against any god or any goddess</u>
> There is <u>no wrongdoing in my body</u>
> I have <u>not wittingly told lies</u>
> There has been <u>no second fault</u>

---

[332] This declaration of innocence (originally and inappropriately called the negative confession) has been said to be a magical incantation to insure entrance into the blessed afterlife. Even if that is so, it is still an excellent summary at this time in Egyptian history of the conduct and behavior that the Egyptians ideally wished to avoid.

In addition to the chapter/spell 30, noted above, there is another chapter that is key to understanding the Egyptian afterlife, the lengthy chapter or spell 125 partially quoted here:

In spell 125:

> Hail to you, great god, Lord of justice! I have come to you, my lord…I know the names of the forty-two gods…who live on those who cherish <u>evil</u> and who gulp down their blood on that day of reckoning of characters in the presence of [Osiris]…I have come to you, I have brought you <u>truth</u>, I have expelled <u>falsehood</u> for you…I have not [the <u>first list of evils</u> followed by—]
> I am pure, pure, pure, pure!
> [then a <u>second list of evils</u>—described as the "negative confession" or the "declaration of innocence"].

There are two of these lists, both of which may be called declarations of innocence in Chapter 125. They are generally said to be repetitious but that is not the case at all. The second declaration appears to have a much more abstract concept of conduct and behavior than the first does. In order to show that this is true we will state each case and analyze them. Each translation comes from Faulkner[333] with the *term* of interest in *italics* and with other scholars', mainly Wilson and Renouf, various translations of (that term) set off in parentheses in order to provide for greater clarity of meaning. My comments are in square brackets.

Declaration 1:

1) I have not done *falsehood* against men. (committed evil, done wrong)
2) I have not *impoverished* my associates. (mistreated cattle, slayeth kindred)
3) I have done no *wrong* in the Place of Truth. (committed sin, telleth lies)
4) I have *not learnt* that which is not. [pried into the affairs of the gods]
5) I have done no *evil.* (seen evil, been doer of mischief)
6) I have not daily *made labour in excess* of what was due to be done for me. [expected more than my due]

---

[333] Faulkner, *The Ancient Egyptian Book of the Dead*, 29-31. Other translations used for the terms of interest include: John A. Wilson, in *Ancient Near Eastern Texts*, ed. James B. Pritchard (Princeton: Princeton University Press, 1955), 34-6; Also Peter Le Page Renouf, *The Life Work of Sir Peter Le Page Renouf: Volume IV, The Book of the Dead* (Paris: Ernest Leroux, 1907), 222-230.

7) My *name has not reached* the offices of those who control slaves. [expected praise or to be exalted]

8) I have not *deprived the orphan* of his property

9) I have not *done what the gods detest.* (abominate, abhor)

10) I have not *calumniated* a servant to his master. (defamed a slave, hurt servant)

11) I have not *caused pain.*

12) I have not *made hungry.* (made sick, caused famine)

13) I have not *made to weep.*

14) I have not *killed.* (not a murderer)

15) I have not *commanded to kill.* (given order to kill, give orders for murder)

16) I have not *made suffering* for anyone. (caused suffering)

17) I have not *lessened the food-offerings* in the temples. (cut down on, reduced)

18) I have not *destroyed the loaves* of the gods. (damaged bread, lessen cakes)

19) I have not *taken away the food* of the spirits. (taken loaves, robbed the dead)

20) I have not *copulated.* (had sexual relations with a boy, been an adulterer)

21) I have not *misbehaved.* (defiled myself, am undefiled)

22) I have not *lessened the food-supplies.* (diminished the grain measure)

23) I have not *diminished the aroura.* [added to or stolen land]

24) I have not *encroached upon fields.* (falsified a half-aroura of land, cutteth short the field measure)

25) I have not *laid anything upon the weights* of the hand-balance. (added to the weight, put pressure on the beam)

26) I have not *taken anything from the plummet* of the standing scales. (weakened the plummet, tampered with the tongue)

27) I have not *taken the milk* from the mouths of children. (snatched milk from infants)

28) I have not *deprived the herds* of their pasture. (driven cattle away, driven cattle from pastures)

29) I have not *trapped the birds* from the preserves of the gods. (snared, net)

30) I have not *caught the fish* of their marshlands.

31) I have not *diverted water* at its season. (held up, stop not)

32) I have not *built a dam on flowing water.* (divided an arm of water)

33) I have not *quenched the fire* when it is burning. (extinguished lamp)

34) I have not *neglected the dates for offering* choice meats. (defrauded gods)

35) I have not *withheld cattle* from the god's-offerings. (driven away from god's property, drive away from sacred estate)

36) I have not *opposed a god* in his procession. (stopped a god when he commeth forth)

Declaration 2: The second declaration of innocence is likewise from the translation of Faulkner with possible alternate terms set off in parentheses. All declarations start off with an address to a god, mistakenly thought to be the god of each of the 42 nomes of Egypt, and the statement that "I have not—":

1) done falsehood. (committed evil, been doer of wrong)
2) robbed. (stolen, done violence)
3) been rapacious. (covetous, evil minded)
4) stolen. (robbed, been rapacious)
5) killed men.
6) destroyed food-supplies. (diminished grain measure, been fraudulent in measure)
7) done crookedness. (fraud)
8) stolen the god's-offerings. (stolen property of the gods, been robber of sacred property)
9) told lies.
10) taken food. (taken away, robber of)
11) been sullen. (contentious, sluggish)
12) transgressed.
13) killed a sacred bull. (slain the cattle of god, slaughtered sacred animals)
14) committed perjury. (practiced usury, dealt fraudulently)
15) stolen bread. (stolen bread-ration, been land-grabber)
16) eavesdropped. (gossiped)
17) babbled. (have mouth gone on unchecked, have prating tongue)
18) disputed except as concerned my own property. (argued over property, only trouble self with own affairs)
19) committed homosexuality. (committed adultery, committed adultery with another's wife)[334]

---

[334] Various translators have assigned alternate meanings for the hieroglyphic (n nk sexual determinative) which, in numbers 19, 20 and 27, can vary from 'not lain with men' to 'not debauched the wife'. Cf. Declaration 1, line 20. See note in J. Gwyn Griffiths, "The Faith of the Pharonic Period," in *Classical Mediterranean Spirituality*, ed. A. H. Armstrong (New York: Crossroad, 1986), 34, 36 n. 51.

20) misbehaved. (defiled myself, been unchaste)

21) made terror.

22) transgressed. (trespassed)

23) been hot-tempered. (over heated, hot of speech)

24) been deaf to words of truth. (unresponsive in matter of justice, lent deaf ear to words of Righteousness)

25) made disturbance. (been quarrelsome, been boisterous in behavior)

26) hoodwinked. (winked at justice, caused weeping)

27) misconducted myself nor copulated with a boy. (had sexual relations with a boy, been given to unnatural lust)

28) been neglectful. (swallowed my heart, indulged in anger)

29) been quarrelsome. (abusive, given to cursing)

30) been unduly active. (over energetic, of aggressive hand)

31) been impatient. (of hasty heart, of inconstant mind)

32) transgressed my nature [or] washed out the picture of a god. [neglected god's satisfaction, vengeance on god]

33) been voluble in speech. (voice too much about matters, noisy in speech)

34) done no wrong, seen no evil. (committed and done evil, liar or doer of mischief)

35) made conjuration against the king. (been abusive against a king, curseth the king)

36) waded in water. (put check on water in its flow)

37) been loud voiced.

38)

39) reviled God. (been abusive against a god, cursed a god)

40) …(made puffing up, been swollen with pride)

41) made distinctions for myself. (made discriminations, made unjust preferences)

42) wealthy except with my own property. (my portion not too large, no strong desire except for my own property)

43) blasphemed God in my city. (blasphemed against my local god, offendeth the god of my domain)

Analysis of the declarations.

In analyzing these lists I will separate the terms under two headings in the summary comparison below. One set of terms may be thought of as imperatives that concern one's <u>relationships with others</u> (i.e., people and gods) and possible infractions of their rights, while the other set of terms may be thought of as representing one's <u>inner qualities of character</u>.[335] This representation shows that there is a fair amount of overlap in the 'relationships with others' category but also that the first declaration was very weak on 'inner qualities of character'.

A Comparison of the Two Declarations.

<u>Terms from the declarations</u>	<u>Line numbers</u>	
<u>Qualities of Character</u>	<u>Declar.#2</u>	<u>Declar. #1</u>
rapacious, covetous, evil minded -	3	
falsehood, crookedness, lies, fraud, evil, perjury, wrong, calumniated	1, 7, 9, 14	1, 5, 10
sullen, contentious, sluggish -	11	
babbler, gossip, mouth unchecked, eavesdropper, prating -	16,17	
hot-tempered, hot of speech, overheated -	23	
deaf to words of truth, deaf to words of righteousness, unresponsive to injustice -	24	3
quarrelsome, abusive, cursing, disturbing, boisterous -	25, 29	-
unduly active, over energetic, aggressive-	30	
neglectful, angry -	28	
impatient, hasty heart, inconstant mind -	31	
voluble in speech, noisy, loud voiced -	33, 37	
puffed up, swollen with pride -	39	7
made distinctions for myself -	40	
wealthy except with my own property, no desire except for my own, portion too large -	41	

---

[335] This same analysis is done in chapter 8 for Plato's terms where he also expresses both "relationships with others" and "inner qualities of character" in his myths.

Relationships with Others	Declar.#2	Declar. #1
robbed, mistreated, stolen, violence, impoverished -	2	2, 8
stolen, robbed, lessened, altered balance, diminished, encroached -	4	6,22,23,24,25,26
killed men, ordered to kill -	5	14, 15
destroyed food-supplies, damaged grain -	6	
stolen the god's-offerings or property -	8	18, 35
taken food, milk, made hungry, famine -	10	12, 27
transgressed, trespassed, caused pain, caused suffering -	12, 22	11, 16
killed a sacred bull, slain sacred animals, trapped birds, caught fish -	13	29, 30
stolen bread, land-grabber -	15	17
disputed as concerned my own property, my own affairs -	18	-
committed homosexuality, committed adultery with another's wife -	19	20
misbehaved, defiled self, been unchaste -	20	21
made terror -	21	-
hoodwinked, caused weeping -	26	13
misconducted myself nor copulated with a boy, unnatural lust -	27	-
transgressed my nature [or] washed out the picture of a god, neglected god's satisfaction, vengeance on god -	32	36
done no wrong, seen no evil, sin, liar, mischief -	34	-
made conjuration against the king, cursed the king, abusive to king -	35	-
waded in water, diverted water, built dam-	36	31, 32
reviled God, cursed a god, abusive to god, defrauded a god -	38	34
blasphemed God in my city, done what god abhors or abominates -	42	9

robbed the dead -	-	19
deprived the herds, driven away cattle -	-	28
quenched fire, extinguished lamp -	-	33

The positive conduct.

In addition to the negative statements analyzed above, there are also some statements found in our two primary judgment Chapters 125 and 30 that deal with conduct and behavior in a positive manner.

In spell 30:

The positive statements are extracted here for this spell.

> His deeds are righteous
> Osiris N is straightforward
> His heart is true, having gone forth from the balance

In spell 125:

The following phrases and terms express the deceased's virtues in a positive manner:

> I brought truth
> > repelled falsehood
> > come to you without:
> > > falsehood
> > > crime
> > > evil
> > live on truth
> > have done that which the gods are pleased
> > propitiated god
> > gave :
> > > bread to hungry
> > > water to thirsty
> > > clothes to naked
> > > boat to boatless
> > > offering to god
> > > offering to spirits
> > am pure of:
> > > mouth
> > > hand

                succor the gods
                bear witness to truth
                set the balance in its proper place
                have done right for the Lord of Right
                am pure
    my brow is clean
                hinder parts cleansed
                middle is the Pool of Truth

This positive conduct and behavior is, indeed, interspersed with some 'magical'/ritual expectations and that has provoked some scholars [e.g., Erman and Breasted] into denigrating the moral climate of the Egyptians at the time of the *Book of the Dead*. However, one can hardly look at the terms for conduct and behavior expected of the average Egyptian and deny that they should meet any characterization of what we would today call ethical standards. In fact, the Egyptian ideals are comparable to the ethics of Plato, as we shall see in the final chapter.

Having looked at the classical judgment as epitomized by the 18th Dynasty *Book of the Dead*, we now turn our attention to the earlier periods of Egyptian writings and scholarship.

CHAPTER 7

Conduct and Behavior as Determinants for the Afterlife in Ancient Egypt: The Early Periods

I desire to be vindicated by what I have done.

You will cause me to sit because of my righteousness and I will stand up because of my blessedness.

Pyramid Texts 316 and 1219

When Did Conduct and Behavior Begin to Count in the Afterlife?

Did the ancient Egyptian always envision this connection between good (or at least lack of bad) conduct and behavior and a blessed afterlife or was this a late development appearing only with the *Book of the Dead*? If it existed earlier, how did it develop and at what points in Egyptian history do we see evidence of it?

The Scholarship Against an Early Period Judgment.

There is no question that conduct and behavior was linked to the judgment of the dead well before the appearance of the *Book of the Dead* in the New Kingdom, no later that the Second Intermediate Period at the latest.[336] The only question is, how far back can we take it—to the Middle Kingdom, to the First Intermediate Period, or can we see it even in the Old Kingdom?

---

[336] None of the scholars in the subsequent review have questioned this. All agree that the judgment was a fact of Egyptian religion no later than the Second Intermediate Period.

Some scholars have questioned whether the 'general' judgment of the dead appeared before the Second Intermediate Period.[337]

If all we had of the ancient Egyptian religious texts were the various recensions of the New Kingdom *Book of the Dead*, we might be justified in believing that, for all periods of Egyptian history, all persons of whatever status were expecting an afterlife in which they would be judged by the god Osiris based on their conduct and behavioral practices while alive. We do, however, have the even older texts and these have caused many to doubt the justification of this belief.

There are many modern scholars who hold to the idea that the judgment of the dead was, indeed, a post—Old Kingdom development in the religious thinking of the ancient Egyptians, and it would be beneficial to examine these scholars' claims of a later period date for the judgment before this chapter attempts to argue otherwise. Here we will look at some of these scholars who have claimed that the judgment does <u>not</u> appear in the earlier periods of Egyptian history and then we will look at some contrary evidence.

For a summary of scholars opinions on the dating of the Egyptian judgment of the dead, see Appendix L: "Synopsis of Scholars' Conclusions Concerning the Dating of the Judgment of the Dead, Table 8."

Some important scholars holding a post-Old Kingdom date for the origin of the judgment of the dead are: Joachim Spiegel, John Wilson, Rudolf Anthes, Jean Yoyotte, Jan Assmann, Stephen Quirke and Eric Hornung.

Joachim Spiegel says that the idea of the judgment of the dead begins to form at the time of the disintegration of the Old Kingdom (i.e., the First Intermediate Period, c. 2200). "Vom Geist dieser Zeit mußte hier zunächst gesprochen werden, weil er die Grundlage der folgenden Entwicklung bildet…die nach der Zersetzung des ursprünglichen Zustandes am Ende des Alten Reichs in der

---

[337] Most notably is Stephen Quirke whose scholarship is reviewed below. He is a scholar who differentiates between a judicial and general judgment and says a judicial judgment first appears in the Coffin Texts, but the general appears only in the 2nd Intermediate Period. Not all scholars specify this differentiation so, sans specification, I will allow a general judgment by implication.

ägyptischen Religion Einfluß zu gewinnen beginnen. Auch die Idee vom Totengericht, die in dieser Zeit sich zu formen beginnt…"[338]

John Wilson claims that the judgment of the dead concept is not supported before the time of the *Instruction of Merikare* in the 9th dynasty of the First Intermediate Period (c. 2100 BCE).[339] The *Instruction* is from the old king to the next and it stresses the life of morality and a judgment in the afterlife. Wilson says that in the Old Kingdom, the texts do not indicate a need for a code of ethics to insure the afterlife.[340] Although Wilson accepts the fact that the afterlife would become morality-based in the First Intermediate Period and New Kingdom,[341] he says that the higher moral values did not come to the fore until after the materialistic values of the Old Kingdom were shattered.

Rudolph Anthes also claims that the trial of the judgment is not to be found in the *Pyramid Texts*. In fact, like Wilson, he says it is not even in the later *Coffin Texts* but rather comes from the non-funerary *Instruction for King Merikare* which dates to c. 2200 BCE. Anthes argues that, "the classical conception of the trial in the beyond originated in the intellectual temper of the 'Instruction' and not in the *Coffin Texts*." The trial did not appear specifically in mortuary texts until the *Book of the Dead* around 1500 BCE.[342]

Jean Yoyotte says that although there are traces of ethics associated with the judgment of the dead in the 5th and 6th dynasties, he sees the full-fledged judgment only in the 9th Dynasty (c. 2100) and later. "Du code de morale negatif et positif inclus dans le chapitre 125 [the major judgment chapter in the *Book of the Dead*], on possede des traces des le V et VI dynasties…La doctrine du jugement des morts, en ses multiples aspects, est clairement atteste/e pour la premiere fois a l'e/poque des rois heracleopolitains des IX et X dynasties (Textes des Sarcophages

---

338 Joachim Spiegel, *Die Idee vom Totengericht in der agyptischen Religion* (Leipziger Agyptologische Studien, 2. Gluckstadt: J.J. Augustin, 1935), 14.

339 See the opening quotation of chapter 6 for a key passage from the Instruction. John A. Wilson, *The Burden of Egypt: An Interpretation of Ancient Egyptian Culture* (Chicago: University of Chicago Press, 1951), 119.

340 Wilson, *The Burden of Egypt: An Interpretation of Ancient Egyptian Culture*, 104.

341 Wilson, *The Burden of Egypt: An Interpretation of Ancient Egyptian Culture*, 114.

342 Rudolf Anthes, "Mythology in Ancient Egypt," in *Mythologies of the Ancient World*, ed. Samuel Noah Kramer (Garden City, New York: Anchor Books, 1961), 56.

et Instruction a Merikare)."[343] He also claims that it is not until the time of the Middle Kingdom (after c. 2000 BCE) that the survival of the deceased as an Osiris was dependent on the individual's morality.[344]

Jan Assmann holds that the judgment of the dead is already recognizable toward the end of the 3rd millennium, but he believes it only became dominant and obligatory in the New Kingdom. He further states "its [the judgment of the dead's] canonical form, as found in Chapter 125 of the Book of the Dead, has….no known predecessors in the older funerary literature."[345]

Stephen Quirke argues that the judgment "as a passport control point for permission to enter [the afterlife]"[346] appears only in the transition from the Middle Kingdom to the New Kingdom (the Second Intermediate Period, after c. 1640 BCE). Quirke agrees with Anthes that the Middle Kingdom *Coffin Texts* held to a "view of an afterlife without a judgment of the dead."[347] However, he places the concept later than Anthes since he feels that it is unlikely that the judgment of the dead concept was formulated earlier than around 1800 BCE and, even then, not in the *Coffin Texts* where there is only "a standard court in which the divine authorities could give hearings for cases of complaint," [i.e., what is best called a judicial proceeding].[348]

Eric Hornung says, "The Judgment of the Dead is itself an ancient Egyptian concept, although it does not occur as a visual image until Dynasty 18" in the New Kingdom (after c. 1540).[349] "The idea of the universal judgment of the dead took shape after the end of the Old Kingdom, and pictorial representations—

343 Jean Yoyotte, "Le Jugement des Morts dans L'Egypte ancienne," in *Le Jugement des Morts*, Sources Orientales, 4 (Paris: Seuil, 1961), 63-64.

344 Jean Yoyotte, "The Egyptian world-picture," *The Unesco Courier.* no. 9 (Sept 1988): 25.

345 Jan Assmann, "Death and Initiation in the Funerary Religion of Ancient Egypt," in *Religion and Philosophy in Ancient Egypt*, ed. William Kelly Simpson (New Haven: Yale University Press, 1989), 147.

346 Stephen Quirke, *Ancient Egyptian Religion* (London: British Museum Press, 1992), 66.

347 Quirke, *Ancient Egyptian Religion*, 162.

348 Quirke, *Ancient Egyptian Religion*, 162.

349 Hornung, *Idea into Image: Essays on Ancient Egyptian Thought*, 101.

with the scales in the center and the ibis-headed Thoth as scribe who registered the result—began in the Eighteenth Dynasty." It was not until the Ramesside period (in the late New Kingdom when several pharaohs named Ramses ruled around the twelfth century BCE) that the idea of the devourer of the dead, Ammit, was added.[350]

Hornung does allow that "from the time of the *Pyramid Texts*...we also find appeals of the deceased to various gods to protect him from all the dangers and obstacles of the next world."[351] This would seem to imply that attaining the afterlife involved some sort of trials. Nonetheless, he says that the judgment scene in all its detail is not mapped until the New Kingdom.

The Judgment in the Earlier Periods

In light of the foregoing section, in order to determine if these scholars are in some way mistaken, we will have to investigate possible instances of the judgment before the New Kingdom *Book of the Dead*. If we are to look for evidence for a judgment of the dead being dependent on one's conduct and behavior in this life, a good starting point would be in the 5th Dynasty *Pyramid Texts* of King Unas. Therefore we will start with the Old Kingdom and then move forward chronologically to investigate increasingly more certain instances.

There is no question of the existence of an afterlife in the minds of the Egyptians who wrote the earliest surviving religious compositions now known as the *Pyramid Texts*. The question is, more specifically, are there also indications that the post-mortem judgment is based on one's life conduct and behavior in these texts?

In this writer's survey of the literature, the majority of the scholars reviewed saw some form of a judgment, either judicial or general, in the *Pyramid Texts* and/or other mortuary texts of the Old Kingdom. However, our inquiry is this: Is a full-fledged judgment based on one's life conduct attested rather than just instances of post-mortem judicial court proceedings in the case of a specific lawsuit against

---

350 Hornung, "Ancient Egyptian Religious Iconography," 1721.

351 Erik Hornung, *Conceptions of God in Ancient Egypt: The One and the Many*, trans. John Baines (Ithaca: Cornell University Press, 1982), 206. First published as *Der Eine und die Vielen: Agyptische Gottesvorstellungen* (Darmstadt: Wissenschaftliche Buchgesellschaft, 1971).

the deceased? Put even more basically, does one's life conduct and behavior matter for attaining an afterlife?

The Old Kingdom Texts and Scholarship

The Pyramid Texts.

The following are texts found in the pyramids of Unas (5th Dynasty) and Teti and Pepi (6th Dynasty).

Pyramid Text 167:

> Atum, this thy son is here,
> Osiris, whom thou hast preserved alive—he lives!
> He lives—this Unas lives!
> He is not dead, this Unas is not dead:
> he is not gone down, this Unas has not gone down:
> he has not been judged, this Unas has not been judged.
> He judges—this Unas judges![352]

This refrain, a part of Utterance 219, is repeated over several times as addressed to a different god each time. The key phrase is: "he has not been judged."

In this particular spell, the priests of Heliopolis protest against the king having to stand for judgment. This suggests, at least, there would have to have been a judgment for someone other than the king in order for such a thought to have arisen. Indeed, the king himself is said to do the judging rather than being the passive subject of judgment as non-royalty presumably was or had been at some earlier time.

Pyramid Text 309:

> The King is bound for the sky, on the wind, on the wind! He will not be excluded, and there will be no session on him in the Tribunal of the God, for the King is unique, the eldest of the gods.[353]

---

[352] Translated by Alexandre Piankoff, The Pyramid of Unas (Princeton: Princeton University Press, 1968), 64. Faulkner, however, translates Piankoff's word 'judged' as 'mourned' for this text.

[353] Faulkner, The Ancient Egyptian Pyramid Texts, 68.

Raymond Faulkner[354] uses this text to argue that the King is exempt from the judgment after death. He stresses the phrase "there will be no session on him" to mean that the dead king is not to be judged before the divine tribunal, contrary to the fate of others. Again, the implication is that there must have been such a concept as the judgment of the dead in the Old Kingdom which was normal for others, but not for the king. On the other hand, see the next spell:

Pyramid Text 316:

> O Geb, Bull of Nut,
> A Horus is Unas, the heir of his father.
> Unas is he who went and came back,
> The fourth of four gods
> Who have brought the water, who have made a purification,
> Who jubilates over the strength of their fathers.
> * He wishes to be justified [*maa kheru*][355]
> In what [through that] he has done.
> Unas, a small orphan (tefen),
> Went to the law with his sister (Tefnet).
> The Two Truths judged, *
> While Shu was a witness.
> The Two Truths have decreed
> That the thrones of Geb should come to him
> And that he should raise himself to what he wanted.[356]

* Or alternately as quoted in Moret:

> He wishes to be just in voice by his deeds.
> Tefen and Tefnet have judged Unas;
> ...
> Inasmuch as the Two Justices have given the verdict;

---

354 R. O. Faulkner, review of The Origins of Osiris and His Cult, by J. Gwyn Griffiths, Journal of Egyptian Archeology 57 (1971): 208-209.

355 There is much debate as to what *maa kheru* actually means. An interesting interpretation is discussed in Rudolf Anthes, "The Original Meaning of *maa kheru*" Journal of Near Eastern Studies 13 (Jan-Oct 1954): 21-51. He interprets spell 316 as meaning "to affirm the rightness (*maa*) of an individual by acclaim (*kheru*). The more common translation is 'true of voice' or 'justified'.

356 Translated by Piankoff, The Pyramid of Unas, 36.

He has taken possession of the thrones of Geb,
and he has raised himself there where he wished.
Gathering together his flesh which was in the tomb,
he joins himself to those who are in Nun,
he brings the sayings of Helioplolis to fulfillment.
So Unas goes out this day, in the just form of a living Akh."

Alexander Moret,[357] in 1927, quoted chapter 316 of the *Pyramid Texts* to show that King Unas was judged in the afterlife. Moret argued that by the 5th Dynasty the *Pyramid Texts* clearly show a judgment of the king's action before he was allowed access to heaven.[358] I would agree with Moret here, but other scholars have disagreed and argued that this is simply a judicial court case modeled on the trial of the orphaned Horus against his uncle Seth, where Horus is vindicated as the rightful successor to his father Osiris.[359]

Forty years later in 1967, S.G.F. Brandon writes that he believes that the judgment of the dead concept appears in the Old Kingdom *Pyramid Texts*, at least in the form of a post-mortem court in which complaints might be made against the deceased (i.e., a judicial proceeding). He notes that "the evidence of the *Pyramid Texts* envisaged some post-mortem court, similar to those of magistrates…at which complaints might be made against the deceased."[360] Therefore, he is a scholar who would claim that Spell 316, just quoted above, is a good example of such a judicial judgment.

Brandon allows that there are conflicting notions in the *Pyramid Texts* regarding the judgment of the king. Some texts indicate that in no way is the king judged as stated in spell 309 above. However, he admits that spell 316 does indicate that a

---

[357] Moret, *The Nile and Egyptian Civilization*, 186-7.

[358] The dichotomy of general vs. judicial judgment had not been promulgated at this early time. Junker was to advance the idea for the *Pyramid Texts* in 1949 and Grieshammer was to do the same for the *Coffin Texts* in 1970. Junker, *Pyramnenzeit*, 83; Reinhard Grieshammer, *Das Jenseitsgericht in den Sargtexten* (Wiesbaden: Otto Harrassowitz, 1970), 1-2.

[359] Even if *Pyramid Text* 316 were a judicial case, it would still has great ramifications for our inquiry as to whether conduct counts for the afterlife, since our question is: is one's conduct a determinant of one's afterlife condition? Nevertheless, we will argue for a general judgment in the ancient texts.

[360] S.G.F. Brandon, *The Judgment of the Dead: The Idea of Life After Death in the Major Religions* (New York: Charles Scribner's Sons, 1967), 18.

judgment was anticipated in the lines: "He desires that he be *maa kheru* [usually translated as 'true of voice' or 'vindicated' or 'justified'] through that which he has done."[361] This was the title conferred on Osiris at his own vindication by a divine tribunal and Brandon thinks that it is therefore not to be confused with a general judgment of all the dead but is rather an example of justification in a specific court setting.

J. Gwyn Griffiths would later support Brandon's contention by saying that the judicial judgment does make its first appearance in the <u>Pyramid Texts</u>. Griffiths mentions that the following text—

<u>Pyramid Text</u> 892:

> This Pepi <u>blasphemes not the king</u>,
> He <u>defames not [the goddess] Bastet</u>,
> He does <u>not make merry in the sanctuary</u>.[362]

—is very like the 'negative confession' in the *Book of the Dead*.[363] Griffiths, nonetheless, claims that there is no clear evidence that the King in the Old Kingdom was amenable to the discipline of moral assessment by the gods for success or failure in this life. Thus he seems not yet to see a full-fledged general judgment of the king in the *Pyramid Texts*. He says that the general moral judgment of the dead does, however, seem to be present in the lore of *Ptahhotep* in the 5th (or probably 6th) Dynasty and definitely by the *Instruction for King Merikare* in the 9th or 10th Dynasty.[364]

---

[361] S.G.F. Brandon, *Man and His Destiny in the Great Religions* (Toronto: University of Toronto Press, 1962), 50.

[362] Translated by James H. Breasted, *Development of Religion and Thought in Ancient Egypt*, 173. Faulkner has alternatively: "I have not opposed the King, I have not succoured Bastet, I will not act the dancer (?) as the great one of the carrying-chair." This still looks like the phrasing of the negative confession of the general judgment in the *Book of the Dead*.

[363] Griffiths, *The Conflict of Horus and Seth*, 79. This passage appears to have been carelessly lifted from older text that originally referred to a non-king and was used here simply by plugging in Pepi's name.

[364] Griffiths, *The Divine Verdict: A Study of Divine Judgement in the Ancient Religions*, 165, 218; also *The Divine Tribunal* (University College of Swansea, 1975), 9.

Still, the idea of judgment for the king in terms of individual judicial complaints that involve court cases does appear as early as the *Pyramid Texts* in the following where any complaint against the king is in fact denied:

Pyramid Text 386:

> There is no accuser (about) a living one against Unas,
> there is no accuser (about) a dead one against Unas.
> There is no accuser (about) a goose against Unas,
> there is no accuser (about) a bull against Unas.[365]

It is clear that spell 386 simply involves an accuser in a judicial court case, but the following is less clear:

Pyramid Text 462ff:

> There is no word against Unas on earth among men.
> There is no crime of Unas in the sky among the gods.
> Unas has done away with the word against him,
> he has annulled it, in order to rise towards heaven.[366]

Here, the priests are attempting to annul a judgment against the king, as Piankoff notes, by a negative confession. So, as Griffiths had also noted with spell 892, this is a kind of Negative Confession as later found in the *Book of the Dead*, which undisputedly has a general judgment.

The following are some other *Pyramid Text* which seem to indicate that a judgment does take place in the afterlife.

Pyramid Text 1174c:

> I have removed myself from the Tribunal of the Magistrates of the Abyss at the head of the Great Ennead.[367]

---

[365] Translated by Piankoff, *The Pyramid of Unas*, 43.

[366] Translated by Piankoff, *The Pyramid of Unas*, 21.

[367] Faulkner, *The Ancient Egyptian Pyramid Texts*, 189.

This is just like spell 309, where the king denies having to be judged, but is judged just the same (e.g., spell 316).

Pyramid Text 1188:

> O thou who ferriest over the just who is without a ship.
> Ferryman of the Field of Rushes,
> King Merire (Pepi) is just before the sky
> and before the earth.
> King Pepi is just before that island of the earth
> to which he has swum and arrived there.[368]

Pyramid Text 1219 and 1238:

> Thou (O Morning Star) makest this Pepi to sit down because of his righteous-ness and to rise up because of his reverence.
> and,
> There is no evil in which King Pepi has done.
> Weighty is this word in thy sight, O Re.[369]

Pyramid Text 1160-1:

> I will set a record of myself among men and the love of me among the gods. It is said: 'Say that which is, do not say that which is not, for the god detests falsity of words.[370]

The king is protected because of his record of doing right by the truth.

The foregoing quotations show that the king was indeed judged on his conduct in the Old Kingdom and that the general judgment was in place at least by the time of Pepi in the 6th Dynasty.[371]

James Breasted provides us with an early 20th century view of Egyptian scholar-ship. He was among the first, in 1912, to claim a need for moral worthiness in the

---

[368] Breasted, *Development of Religion and Thought in Ancient Egypt*, 172

[369] Breasted, *Development of Religion and Thought in Ancient Egypt*, 172

[370] Faulkner, *The Ancient Egyptian Pyramid Texts*, 188

[371] See also my summary and conclusions at the end of this chapter.

deceased in order to face the judgment of the dead in the Old Kingdom. He felt that even the king is not exempt from the need for moral worthiness, which is contrary to the views of those scholars who think moral concerns were not thought to be relevant to the deceased King's afterlife. Of course, his early argument did not have the benefit of the later more precise delineation between a judicial vs. a general judgment.

Nevertheless, one of his arguments is based on the *Pyramid Texts* for 6th dynasty King Pepi, where Breasted noted that he is called "justified" in Utterances 265-6 which are concerned with the king crossing the sky on reed floats. Since the earlier 'reed-float' text variants for Unas and Teti, Utterances 263 and 264, do not contain this statement of justification, it appears that by at least the 6th dynasty, moral justification had become deemed necessary even for the King.[372]

Breasted says that the "pyramids of Gizeh…are…the silent but eloquent expression of a supreme endeavor to achieve a blessed immortality by sheer physical force."[373] The earliest and largest pyramids into the 5th dynasty had no texts written inside them. Prince Hardjedef (4th or early 5th dynasty) also relied on a materialistic afterlife as seen in the fragmentary text attributed to him.[374] This dependence solely on materialism changed with the later 5th dynasty and Breasted says that morality started to play a part in attaining the afterlife. After the decline of the materialism of the 4th and early 5th dynasty, the pyramids

---

[372] Breasted, *Development of Religion and Thought in Ancient Egypt*, 172, 177-178. For another example of ambiguity, note that: on the one hand, we see in the Pyramid Texts an appeal to morality, as in Utterance 270: "No one alive accuses Unas, No dead accuses Unas, No goose accuses Unas, No ox accuses Unas," therefore Unas is morally pure. On the other hand, there is ritual as in Utterance 273-4: "Unas is the bull of heaven Who rages in his heart, Who lives on the being of every god, Who eats their entrails When they come, their bodies full of magic From the Isle of Flame," which implies gaining magical gnosis by eating the god. Finally, there is royal submission to the god as in Utterance 309: "Unas is god's steward…Unas squats before him…Unas does what Unas is told" (trans., Lichtheim, *Ancient Egyptian Literature*, 35, 36, 39). In short, the Pyramid Texts show some variety in worldview.

[373] Breasted, *The Dawn of Conscience*, 150f.

[374] Hardjedef says: "Found your household…take a hearty wife…build a house…Make good your dwelling in the graveyard, make worthy your destination in the West…The tomb is for life and the priest of the tomb is more important than your own son" (trans., Lichtheim, *Ancient Egyptian Literature*, 58). There is no concern for righteous living in the extant text.

became smaller and texts were added to their walls as a sign of resorting "to less tangible agencies." With the recognition of a requirement for moral worthiness in 5th dynasty texts, he claims that there was a greater expression of spirituality.[375]

Siegfried Morenz argues that the conception of the judgment of the dead was in place by the 5th Dynasty. He claims that the "automatic general judgment upon every mortal" can be traced to the fifth maxim of *Ptahhotep* in the late 5th [or likely 6th] Dynasty because the later *Instruction for King Merikare*, which assumes such judgment, quotes it. He says that still in the 4th Dynasty, Prince Hardjedef thought the future of the deceased depended on fine funerary furnishings, but by the 5th, it depended on ethical adherence to *ma'at* (defined as, "truth/order/justice").[376]

Jan Zandee claims that already in the Old Kingdom something similar to Chapter 125 of the Book of the Dead was known. He says however that, in the Old Kingdom, the judgment expressions are always judicial, where Re oversees a court where complaints may be lodged against the dead person.[377] In the *Pyramid Texts*, "the idea occurs that the righteous judges together with Re."[378] It is useful to compare this scenario with what happens in the *Book of the Dead* where Osiris is the judge and where judgment takes place whether a specific complaint has been lodged against the deceased or not and all the dead are silently judged by the weight of their heart. This comparison marks the distinction between a judicial and a general judgment.

Reinhard Grieshammer argues for a differentiation between a judicial court and a general judgment. The former is attested in the (sic) 4th Dynasty, the latter seems to have grown out of the maxims of *Ptahhotep* in the (sic) 5th Dynasty. He says:

> The presentation of a judgment after death is already attested in the 4th Dynasty....[together] with a judgment before the great god. This certainly does not yet witness the belief that underlies a general judgment of the dead.
> ...
> Harder to answer, but also frequently asked, is the question about the time of origin of a general ethical judgment of the dead. For a long time there was

---

375 Breasted, *The Dawn of Conscience*, 264f.

376 Morenz, *Egyptian Religion*, 127-129.

377 Jan Zandee, *Death as an Enemy According to Ancient Egyptian Conceptions* (Leiden: E.J. Brill, 1960), 32, 275.

378 Zandee, *Death as an Enemy According to Ancient Egyptian Conceptions*, 40.

unanimity about the fact that the idea, in the sense of a coupling of life conduct and fate after death, can be found in the Instruction for King Merikare. Newer investigations have now revealed that it was already in the time of the teachings of Ptahhotep, more exactly in the 5th Dynasty.

...

Through it the idea of an ethical judgment of the dead was very probably made at the time of the outgoing 5th Dynasty.[379]

He adds that in the Instruction of Hardjedef from the 4th dynasty these thoughts as yet played no role. There, the grave and its equipment alone suffices for survival in the hereafter. This agrees with the earlier contentions of Breasted and Morenz.

John Baines claims the judgment of the dead concept started in the Old Kingdom, but the text that enacts the deceased's successful passage through the judgment was not attested until the 18th Dynasty. He further offers that "the date of origin of this idea is disputed and can hardly be resolved on available evidence."[380] Baines prefers the interpretation that the concept started in the Old Kingdom, but claims that all Old Kingdom allusions pertain to "litigation in the hereafter, as opposed to ethical judgment."[381] This again makes a distinction between the general and a simply judicial judgment.

---

[379] Die Vorstellung von einem Gericht nach dem Tode ist bereits in der 4. Dynastie bezeugt…mit einem Gericht vor dem Grossen Gott. Diesen Zeugnissen liegt gewiss noch nicht der Glaube an ein allgemeines Totengericht zugrunde…Schwieriger ist die Frage nach der Entstehungszeit eines allgemeinen ethischen Totengerichtes zu beantworten, und darüber ist auch recht häufig gehandelt worden. Es herrscht seit langem Einmütigkeit darüber, dass in der Lehre für Konig Merikare diese Idee im Sinne einer Kopplung von Lebensführung und Schicksal nach dem Tode fassbar ist. Neuere Untersuchungen haben nun ergebe, dass bereits in der Lehre des Ptahhotep, genauer gesagt in der 5. Dadurch ist die Idee eines ethischen Totengerichtes für die Zeit der ausgehenden 5.Dynastie sehr wahrscheinlich gemacht worden (Grieshammer, *Das Jenseitsgericht in den Sargtexten*, 1-2). His dates are probably off somewhat. Ptahhotep is now thought to be from the 6th Dynasty and there is no extant text from the 4th Dynasty

[380] John Baines, "Society, Morality, and Religious Practice," in *Religion in Ancient Egypt: Gods, Myths and Personal Practice*, ed. Byron E. Shafer (Ithaca, New York: Cornell University Press, 1991), 151.

[381] Baines, "Society, Morality, and Religious Practice," 151 n. 79.

Non-funerary texts of the Old Kingdom.

The following spell for a king, *Pyramid Text* 1278-9, may be compared to those that appear in the contemporary autobiographies of the nobles which will be examined in this section.

> As for anyone who shall lay a finger on this pyramid and this temple which belongs to me and to my double [*ka*], he will have laid his finger on the Mansion of Horus in the firmament, he will have offended the Lady of the Mansion…his affair will be judged by the Ennead and he will be nowhere and his house will be nowhere; he will be one proscribed, one who eats himself.[382]

Here we see that the tomb defiler is threatened and both the offender and his family will lose their chance of an afterlife, after he has appropriately been judged by the great gods.[383]

Non-royal people also had aspirations to a blessed afterlife in the Old Kingdom. We see this in their tomb autobiographies and their instructions in wisdom texts. What follows below are some representative texts that show such aspirations. Of course, we are looking for a post-mortem judgment dependent on conduct and behavior which many scholars, whom we have reviewed above, have claimed is not there.

Henku (5th Dynasty):

> O all ye people…who shall pass by this tomb…
> I gave bread to all the hungry of the
> Cerastes—mountain;
> I clothed him who was naked therein;
> I filled its shores with large cattle,
> and its lowlands with small cattle…
> I never oppressed one in possession of
> his property, so that he complained
> because of it to the god of my city;

---

[382] Faulkner, *The Ancient Egyptian Pyramid Texts*, 202.

[383] There is no indication of where this judgment of the offender will take place, but the offender's afterlife is definitely threatened by the phrase 'he will be nowhere'. This is a significant case, which supports the implied judgment of commoners occurring in the Pyramid Texts. This punishment of future generations for the sins of the father will play a comparable role in the later ancient Greek religious and secular texts.

I <u>spake and told that which was good</u>;
<u>never was there one fearing</u> because of one
stronger than he,
So that he complained because of it to the god.
I <u>speak no lie</u>, for I was one
<u>beloved </u>of his father, praised of his mother,
Excellent in character to his brother,
and amiable to his sister.[384]

This is an obvious case of acting out of a sense of duty to those in an inferior position. There is no other indication that Henku expected a better afterlife for it, except for the fact that it is carved on his tomb, but he does fear any complaint to the god of his city if he should not perform these good deeds. This is, at the very least, a precursor to the expectation of good conduct for a beneficial afterlife.

<u>Inscription of Hetepherakhet</u> (5th Dynasty):

I <u>made this tomb by my very own means</u>,
I <u>never took the property</u> of anyone.
All persons who worked at it for me,
they worked <u>praising god for me</u> greatly for it.
They worked this for me for bread, for beer,
For clothes, for ointment, for much barley and
emmer,
I <u>never did anything by force</u> against anyone.
…
The Senior Elder of the Portal, Hetep-her-akhet,
he says:
I made this tomb on the side of the West,
<u>in a clean place where no person's tomb was</u>,
in order to <u>guard the possessions</u> of one who went
to his *ka*.
Any persons who would enter this tomb <u>uncleanly</u>,
and do something <u>evil</u> against it—
they shall be judged for it by the great god.[385]

---

[384] James Henry Breasted, *Ancient Records of Egypt*, 5 vols. (Chicago: University of Chicago Press, 1906), 1.281.

[385] Translated by Miriam Lichtheim, Ancient Egyptian Autobiographies Chiefly of the Middle Kingdom (Gottingen: Vandenhoeck & Ruprecht, 1988) 10-11.

As early as the 5th Dynasty some people were concerned about a type of behavior that allowed someone to steal another person's tomb and recognized that in order to be treated as they would want that they would have to behave toward others in the same manner. Here conduct is a mixture of a 'negative confession' and a positive affirmation of good deeds. They also appealed to the great god to enforce good conduct by threatening a judgment on a wrongdoer. However, we can not tell from this inscription alone if that judgment was to be during the wrongdoer's life or post-mortem.

The Maxims of Ptahhotep (6th Dynasty):

> If you are a man that leads,
> Who controls the affairs of the many,
> Seek out every <u>beneficent deed</u>,
> That your <u>conduct may be blameless</u>.
> Great is <u>justice</u>, lasting in effect,
> Unchallenged since the time of Osiris.
> One punishes the <u>transgressor of laws</u>,
> Though the <u>greedy</u> overlooks this;
> <u>Baseness</u> may seize riches,
> Yet <u>crime</u> never lands its wares;
> In the end it is justice that lasts...
> ...
> The wise feeds his *ba*[386] with what endures,
> So that it is happy with him on earth.[387]

The Instruction to Kagemni (6th Dynasty):

> The <u>respectful</u> man prospers,
> Praised is the <u>modest</u> one,
> The tent is open to the <u>silent</u>,
> The seat of the <u>quiet</u> is spacious.
> Do not <u>chatter</u>!
> Knives are sharp against the <u>blunderer</u>,
> Without hurry except when he <u>faults</u>.

---

[386] Ptahhotep seems to be addressing the non-royal leaders here. If that is really the case, then this is evidence for a 5th or 6th Dynasty concept of the ba for non-royalty. The right to a solar afterlife was already spreading.

[387] Translated by Lichtheim, *Ancient Egyptian Literature*, 1.64, 1.73.

When you sit with company,
Shun the food you love;
Restraint is a brief moment,
Gluttony is base and is reproved.
A cup of water quenches thirst,
A mouthful of herbs strengthens the heart;
A little something stands for much.
Vile is he whose belly covets when (meal)-time has passed,
He forgets those in whose house his belly roams.
When you sit with a glutton,
Eat when his greed has passed;
When you drink with a drunkard,
Take when his heart is content.
…
He who is gentle, even timid,
The harsh is kinder to him than to his mother,
All people are his servants.

Let your name go forth
While your mouth is silent.
When you are summoned, don't boast of strength
Among those your age, lest you be opposed.
One knows not what may happen,
What god does when he punishes"[388]

The writings of Kagemni and Ptahhotep, both of whom were viziers to a king in the 6th Dynasty, are considered 'wisdom literature' and are partially quoted above. Such statements as theirs may imply that divine justice was thought to be inescapable in any era, although it still is not clear whether it is understood in these passages to be in this life or in the afterlife.[389]

Flinders Petrie[390] argues that conscience developed in the Old Kingdom and ideas in the oldest wisdom literature such as one finds in the above quotations

---

[388] Translated by Lichtheim, *Ancient Egyptian Literature*, 1.59-60.

[389] A good argument can be made for divine justice being in the afterlife by the fact that Ptahhotep speaks of the ba that endures. Is the endurance to be understood as being past death? If so, then we have another 6th Dynasty example of a judgment of non-royalty in the afterlife.

[390] Petrie, *Religion and Conscience in Ancient Egypt*, 86-87, 111.

from *Kagemni* and *Ptahhotep* were the seed of the much later "repudiation of sins", which were necessary for a general moral judgment, in the *Book of the Dead.*[391]

The Autobiography of Harkhuf (6th Dynasty):

> An offering which the king gives and Osiris…
> May he journey in peace on the holy ways to the West…
> May he ascend to the god, lord of heaven…
> …
> I gave bread to the hungry,
> Clothing to the naked,
> I brought the boatless to land.
> O you who live upon this earth,
> Who shall pass by this tomb
> Going north or going south,
> Who shall say: "a thousand loaves and beer jugs
> For the owner of this tomb,"
> I shall watch over them [who make offerings]
> in the necropolis.
> I am an excellent equipped spirit (*akh*),
> A lector-priest who knows his speech.
> As for any man who enters this tomb unclean,
> I will seize him by the neck like a bird,
> He will be judged for it by the great god!
> I was one who spoke fairly, who repeated what was liked,
> I never spoke evilly against any man to his superior,
> For I wished to stand well with the great god.[392]

In this non-royal autobiography we see evidence in the 6th Dynasty (after ca. 2400 BCE) of the judgment where a person's fate in the afterlife is determined by their conduct in this life. Both forms of the judgment appear here: the judicial court proceeding in the lines, "I will seize him…he will be judged" and the general by, "I gave bread, etc." Harkhuf performed all of these good deeds

---

[391] Whether or not a moral conscience, as we moderns understand the concept, developed in this ancient time is a matter of much scholarly contention. However, the development of conscience is not the subject of our inquiry here.

[392] The great god who judges is probably Re since Harkhuf has ascended to the heavens where Re, not Osiris, resides. Translated by Lichtheim, *Ancient Egyptian Literature*, 1.23f.

because he desired that it might be well with him at the great god's judgment. This is consequentialist morality to be sure. Nevertheless, Harkhuf expected that his afterlife depended on his good works.[393]

The Autobiography of Nekhebu (6th Dynasty):

> Never did I beat a man…
> Never did I enslave any people…
> It was I who pacified them.
> I never spent the night angry…
> It was I who gave clothing, bread, and beer to
> all the naked and hungry among them.
> I am one loved of all people,
> I never spoke evil to king or potentate about
> anyone.
> …
> O you who are alive on earth,
> who shall pass by this tomb!
> If you wish to be favored by the king,
> And honored by the great god,
> Enter not this tomb profanely, uncleanly!
> Anyone who enters it profanely despite this—
> I will be judged with him by the great god!
> …
> Not shall you destroy a thing in this tomb,
> I am a spirit [potent] and equipped!
> Anyone who destroys a thing in this tomb—
> I will be judged with them by the great god!
> I am one who speaks the good, repeats the good,
> I never spoke evil against anyone.[394]

In the Harkhuf and Nekhebu autobiographies from the 6th Dynasty as cited above, we can see both types of the judgment appearing.

---

[393] Cf. Plato's consequentialist morality in the Republic's eschatological Myth of Er.

[394] Translated by Miriam Lichtheim, *Ancient Egyptian Autobiographies Chiefly of the Middle Kingdom*, 13-4.

<u>Inscription of Sheshi</u> (6th Dynasty):

> I have come from my town,
> I have descended from my nome,
> I have done <u>justice</u> for its lord,
> I have satisfied him with what he loves.
> I <u>spoke truly, I did right,</u>
> <u>I spoke fairly, I repeated fairly,</u>
> I seized the moment,
> So as to stand well with the people.
> I <u>judged between two so as to content them,</u>
> I <u>rescued the weak from one stronger</u> than he
> as much as was in my power.
> I <u>gave bread to the hungry, clothes <to the</u>
> <u>naked>,</u>
> <u>I brought the boatless to land,</u>
> <u>I buried him who had no son,</u>
> <u>I made a boat for him who lacked one,</u>
> <u>I respected my father, I pleased my mother."</u>
> <u>I raised their children.</u>
> So says he whose name is Sheshi.³⁹⁵

Miriam Lichtheim notes that even in the Old Kingdom there were catalogues of virtues proclaiming the deceased's moral worth. This could certainly lead one to believe that the judgment of the dead was a viable concept at that time. An example from the 6th Dynasty is the above tomb biography of the noble Sheshi, which contained a detailed affirmation of his moral worth. While he doesn't explicitly say that his conduct will earn him an afterlife reward, this is a possible interpretation in view of the fact that similar moral self-defense is later quite plainly needed for an afterlife in the *Book of the Dead*.

Even if we were to fail to make a case for the general judgment of the king in the *Pyramid Texts*, it is certainly in the non-royal autobiographies of the same Old Kingdom period. However, let us not lose track of our basic question—when did life's conduct begin to count for the afterlife?

---

[395] Translated by Miriam Lichtheim, *Ancient Egyptian Literature*, vol. 1, 17.

Texts of the First Intermediate Period and Middle Kingdom

The Coffin Texts.[396]

The following are some representative post-Old Kingdom texts that address our inquiry.

Coffin Text Spell 8, I, 24:

> Hail to you, Tribunal of the God who <u>shall judge me concerning what I have said [and did]</u>[397], I being ignorant at ease and having no care. O you who surround me and stand at my back. May I be vindicated in the presence of Geb, chiefest of the gods. Yonder god <u>shall judge me according to what I know</u>. I have arisen with my plume on my head and my <u>righteousness</u> on my brow, my foes are in sorrow, and I have taken possession of all my property in vindication.[398]

By this time in the development of Egyptian religion there was a post-mortem council of the gods that judged the non-royal deceased based on what he said and did in life. This text looks very similar to that in <u>Pyramid Text</u> 316 where it is said, "He wishes to be justified in what he has done."[399] The non-royal person here could expect to be vindicated of wrongdoing in the same way that Osiris had been vindicated by the council.

Coffin Text Spell 44, I, 181-185:

> The doors of the sky are opened because of your <u>goodness</u>; may you ascend and see Hathor, may your <u>complaint [evil]</u>[400] be removed, may your <u>sin [iniquity] be erased</u> by those who weigh in the balance on the day of <u>reckoning characters</u>.

---

[396] The earliest *Coffin Texts* are usually assigned to the First Intermediate Period. However, a noble named Medunefer of the 6th Dynasty during the reign of Pepy II was buried with texts that had several parallels to and would become part of the Coffin Texts. Forman and Quirke, *Hieroglyphs*, 63-4.

[397] The bracketed words are the translations given in John Gwyn Griffiths, "The Idea of Posthumous Judgment in Israel and Egypt," in, *Fontes Atque Pontes*, ed. Manfred Gorg (Wiesbaden: Otto Harrassowitz, 1983), 198.

[398] All Coffin Texts translated by R.O. Faulkner, *The Ancient Egyptian Coffin Texts*, 3 vols. (Warminster: Aris & Phillips, 1973), 1.4.

[399] So, by analogy, this kind of judgment should apply to the royal also.

[400] Griffiths, "The Idea of Posthumous Judgment in Israel and Egypt," 187.

...

May you sail southward in the Night-bark and northward in the Day-bark; may you recognize your soul [*ba*] in the upper sky, while your flesh, your corpse, is in On.

Here we find the judgment of deceased non-royal persons of the First Intermediate Period associated with the iniquity, evil or goodness of their life. By this time the non-royal person had a *ba* and the opportunity for a celestial afterlife like the king had in the *Pyramid Texts* before him.

This is one of the fist allusions to the balance that will weigh the heart which will become so central to the text and iconography of the *Book of the Dead*.

Non-funerary texts of the post-Old Kingdom period.

Perhaps the most prescient text of this period is the Instruction for King Merikare in that it contains the most explicit allusions to the subject of the Book of the Dead.

The Instruction for King Merikare:

> The Court that judges the <u>wretch</u>,
> You know they are not lenient,
> On the day of judging the <u>miserable</u>,
> In the hour of doing their task.
> It is painful when the accuser has knowledge,
> Do not trust in the length of years,
> They [the judges] view a lifetime in an hour!
> When a man remains over after death,
> His <u>deeds</u>[401] are set beside him as treasure,
> And being yonder lasts forever.
> A <u>fool</u> is who does what they reprove![402]
> He who reaches them without <u>having done wrong</u>
> Will exist there like a god,
> Free-striding like the lords forever!
> ...
> A man should do what profits his *ba*.
> ...

---

[401] One's good deeds are a treasure for a favorable judgment.

[402] What the gods approve, reprove and what is wrong is stated in the Instruction.

So the *ba* goes to the place it knows.

...

Divine are they who follow the king![403]

The old king here details the duties and behavior of a good king to his successor, King Merikare. He advises that the king must show justice and impartiality in order to succeed in the practical world as well as in the spiritual world to come. He insists that good conduct and behavior will be seen by the afterlife judges when they review the life deeds of the deceased person. He calls the judges those who see the whole of one's life span, whether the wretch, the miserable, the fool or the non-wrongdoer, as in a single instant. Although we do not as yet have the detail that later will appear in the Book of the Dead, we need look no further than the 10th Dynasty for by this point the evidence for a general judgment of king and non-royal alike is solid.

Conduct and Behavior in the Old Kingdom Texts

We have now examined representative texts for all periods of interest for our inquiry. Here we will summarize the underlined terms for conduct and behavior as they appear in the texts of the Old Kingdom.

The *Maxims of Ptahhotep* has the greatest number of terms concerning positive and negative conduct. They are stated here and followed by the other Old Kingdom texts:

Ptahhotep:

Positive Conduct	Negative Conduct
wise	arrogant
self-control	aggressive
seek-good thing	transgress
truth	rapacious
rightdoing	baseness
straight forward	wrongdoing
kindly hearing	inspire terror
propitiate friends	plunder
quiet	calumny

---

[403] Translated by Lichtheim, Ancient Egyptian Literature, 1.101-2, 1.106-7.

control self	distortion of truth
wisdom	angry speech
good will	boast
true judgment	speak ill
friendly	errs
graciousness	disobeys
good deed	defies
good	babbles
right	covetous
devoid of falsehood	selfish
honored	repeat slander
justice	hot temper
suppress desires	theft
patient	quarrelsome
good son	haughty
acts rightly	anger
	one-sided
	rob
	steal
	copulate with woman-boy
	hostility
	ill-tempered
	frivolous
	notorious
	error
	fool
	give offense

The others are much shorter and are listed here:

<u>Henku:</u>

gave bread	oppressed
clothed	lie
spoke good	allow fear
gave cattle	
beloved	

Hetepherakhet:

own means	took property
treat people well	force
guard others things	unclean
	evil

Kagemni:

Respectful	chatter
Restraint	blunder
Modest	fault
Silent	gluttony
Quiet	covet
Gentle	greed
Timid	drunkard
	boast

Harkhuf:

gave bread	speak evilly
clothed	
help boatless	
speak fairly	

Nekhebu:

pacifier	beat people
gave bread	enslave
clothed	angry
beloved	speak evil
	profane
	destroy

Sheshi:

| done justice |
| spoke truly |
| did right |

spoke fairly
judged well
rescued weak
gave bread
clothed
helped boatless
buried sonless
respected parents
raised siblings

The Pyramid Texts:

righteousness	oppose (blaspheme)king
reverence	defamation of goddess
just by deeds	act the dancer (make merry) in sanctuary
say that which is	say that which is not
just	falsity of words
	commit wrong
	crime
	evil
	violate the king's tomb

These virtues and vices will be compared to those of the much later Greeks as discussed in the first five chapters.[404]

---

[404] See Appendix O: "Conduct and Behavior that Influences the Afterlife: Egyptian Inverse Index, Table 10," for a complete comparison with Plato's terms. This extensive list contains much more than Plato does in his eschatological myths. Most of these are the kinds of morality that Plato would not call attention to in the myths, presumably, I believe, in order to emphasize conventions (νόμος) more closely related to the natural (φύσις) order of the cosmos. See Table 4 in Appendix E for additional explanation.

Summary and Conclusions

Summary of the Egyptian Chapters

After introducing some important concepts concerning the ancient Egyptians as they appear in the Egyptian source texts, four primary questions are examined and we arrive at the following conclusions:

1. What entity is being judged?

From the earliest periods all people, king and commoner alike, had access to some sort of an afterlife, although before the 5th Dynasty, there is no explicit indication that either was judged for their conduct in this life.

> Spell 251: the king looks down on Osiris where he governs the other spirits.

At the time of the *Pyramid Texts* the king possessed a soul (*ba*), a double (*ka*), and a spirit (*akh*) that rose to the celestial realms, whereas, the commoner had a double (*ka*) and an effective spirit (*akh*) that was probably relegated to the tomb. The idea of a *ka* and an *akh* for all people had already been in place by the 1st Dynasty.

2. When did a blessed afterlife become available to all persons?

All people were believed to experience an afterlife from the earliest times, but here, by a blessed afterlife, is meant the kind of celestial unification with Re in the sun bark that occurs in the *Pyramid Texts* for the king. Our best written evidence shows that, in this period, only the king had a *ba* and was thus the only one to have such an afterlife. Based on the fact of boats being buried with the king from the 1st Dynasty, the king's celestial afterlife and perhaps also the king's *ba* may have been established by that time.

There are some indications that commoners acquired a *ba* very early (by the time the 6th Dynasty Ptahhotep), and when they did, they too may have had such access. Harkhuf, also in the 6th Dynasty, expected to "ascend to the god, lord of heaven" to be judged. All people had a *ba* by the time of the *Coffin Texts* in the First Intermediate Period.

3. What exactly constitutes the Egyptian judgment of the dead?

First, it should be noted that the question of the judgment of the dead is nuanced by such factors as: who has an afterlife and who is being judged (King vs. non-royal commoners) and what type of judgment is involved (judicial vs. general). I believe that these factors have historically confused the question and this has led to much of the divergent scholarly opinion.

The judgment has commonly been thought to be synonymous with the weighing of the heart as found in the *Book of the Dead* at which time there was clearly a judgment based on one's life conduct. This is the classical case but many texts from earlier periods also expressed the idea that one's conduct had some bearing on the kind of afterlife one would enjoy. There is no question that this was the case by the 9/10th Dynasty with the *Instruction for King Merikare.*

The biggest confusion that was not even addressed until the late 1940's was; what do we mean by a judgment. At that time there was a differentiation made between a judicial court case where a charge is brought against a defendant vs. a general automatic judgment on the conduct of a deceased person regardless of a specific complaint being brought. This changed the argument for most scholars, many of whom opted for the date of the inception of the general judgment to be placed well past the Old Kingdom but some others allowing it during the Old Kingdom albeit not in the *Pyramid Texts.*

Our inquiry concerns the link between good conduct and behavior and the attainment of a god, bad or no afterlife. Is that link found prior to the 9/10th Dynasty *Instruction for King Merikare*? More specifically, is it found in the Old Kingdom and especially in the 5/6th Dynasty *Pyramid Texts*?

4. At what point in the development of the concept of a blessed afterlife did conduct and behavior come to matter?

Throughout this inquiry I have taken this to mean—at what point in time did the Egyptians make reference to one's conduct being a determinant on one's quality of afterlife? This is not the same question as—when was the king first judged or when was the commoner first judged or when did conscience first arise? It is this—when did one's living conduct matter to one's afterlife?

My conclusions on this question follow.

Conclusions

My interpretation based on the Pyramid Texts, the wisdom texts and the non-royal autobiographies is that it is quite possible that the ideas of both types of judgment, for both groups of people, existed earlier than the time when they were written down in our extant form. In later periods earlier ideas may be put in the written form we now have for reasons of tradition or convention. Nonetheless, the summary below outlines the evidence as it is attested in extant written form.

Commoners. A general judgment occurs by the time of the 6th Dynasty autobi-ographies of Harkhuf and Nekhebu. *Pyramid Texts* 167, 309, 892 and 1278 indicate that commoners were subject to at least a judicial judgment in the 5th Dynasty and, most likely, long before that since some of the texts are derived from earlier works that are obviously much older that that.

Spells:

> 167—Unas has not been judged. He judges.
> 309—The king...there will be no session on him.
> 892—This N blasphemes not the king.
> 1278—Anyone who shall lay a finger on this pyramid...he will be nowhere.

The King. A judicial judgment occurs in the earliest *Pyramid Texts* of King Unas in the 5th Dynasty and, most probably, earlier since these texts are derived from earlier works. *Pyramid Texts* 316, 462, 892, 1188, 1219, 1238 and Utterances 265-6 all indicate some form of judgment on the king. *Pyramid Texts* 462, 892 and 1238 also look like the later negative confessions of the *Book of the Dead* and indicate a general judgment of the king.

Spells:

> 316—He wishes to be [justified] by his deeds.
> 462—There is no word...no crime...among men or gods.
> 1188—Who ferriest over the just...King Pepi is just.
> 1219—[King has a celestial afterlife because of] righteousness...reverence.
> 1238—There is no evil which the King has done.
> Utt. 265-6—Pepi is justified.

Regardless of the fine points of the above comments, it remains that conduct and behavior counted very much from the earliest written records for both king and commoner. Thus, by the end of the Old Kingdom, both groups appear to have been subject not only to any judicial proceedings that may have arisen after death, but also a more fully-developed general judgment.

CHAPTER 8

A Comparison Between the Afterlife Judgment Concepts in Ancient Greece And Egypt: Conclusions

αἰθὴρ μὲν ψυχὰς ὑπεδέξατο σώματα δὲ χθών.

> For the fallen at Potidaea,
> Greece 432 BCE[405]

My *Ba* (soul) in heaven, my corpse in the graveyard.

> Hepusonb,
> New Kingdom ca. 1400 BCE

May you recognize your soul in the upper sky, while your flesh, your corpse, is in *On*.

> Coffin Texts 44, I, 181f,
> Middle Kingdom ca. 2000 BCE

The *Akh* (spirit) belongs to heaven, the corpse belongs to the earth.

> Pyramid Texts,
> Old Kingdom ca. 2300 BCE[406]

---

[405] The air (ether) has received their souls (psyches), the earth their bodies (*CIA* i.442). Cf. Euripides "let soul release to air, body to earth" (*Suppliants* 533), "The mind of the dead does not live, yet it has eternal thought as it falls into eternal ether" (*Helen* 1014-16).

[406] Heaven (ethereal realm) has the spirit, the earth has the body. *Pyramid Text* 474, in Spell 305.

A Possible Cultural Transmission

Although the conclusions of this inquiry do not depend on a theory of any kind of a cultural transmission between the two societies of ancient Egypt and Greece, I would be remiss if I did not investigate such possible interconnections. However, keeping in mind the admonitions of Jonathan Z. Smith concerning the perils of comparative religion, one must be careful in making too much of perceived similarities.[407] There are, as we will see, some very interesting similarities that may imply a causal relationship; nevertheless, for the conclusions of this study the evolution of the Egyptian and Greek afterlife beliefs will be treated as independent and parallel developments.

Our investigation of ancient Greece opens with the writings of Homer and Hesiod (ca. 800-700 BCE). By this time the Egyptian Book of the Dead had been in existence for at least 700 years and the Pyramid Texts for at least 1500 years. The civilizations of palatial Minoan Crete and Mycenae had come and gone respectively during ca. 2000-1470 BCE and ca. 1450-1200. Greece had been influenced by the successive invasions of northern Indo-European speakers from 2000 BCE on and then influenced by the Minoan civilization from around 1500 BCE.[408]

The ancient religion of the Cretans and Mycenaeans with their cults of the dead[409] had been drastically changed by various societal destructions and no longer reflected the common views of the early eastern Mediterranean civilizations. A key change that appears in Homer was the practice of cremation instead of the normal inhumation of the Cretans, Mycenaeans and Egyptians. The subterranean afterlife where one could still benefit by one's grave goods had disappeared and Homer tends to ignore the indigenous agricultural and chthonic gods in favor of the Indo-European ones.

---

[407] Jonathan Z. Smith, *Map is not Territory* (Leiden: E.J. Brill, 1978), 240-264; *Imagining Religion* (Chicago: University of Chicago Press, 1982), 19-35.

[408] See Simon Hornblower and Anthony Spawforth, eds., *The Oxford Companion to Classical Civilization* (Oxford: Oxford University Press, 1998), 310, 468, 479, 789.

[409] See Nilsson, *The Minoan-Mycenaean Religion and its Survival in Greek Religion*, 617-19.

There was, however, still an afterlife, but it was that of a 'thoughtless or powerless head;'[410] a mere shadow of the formerly living person that now existed in an undifferentiated region that held king and commoner, good and bad alike. Status and conduct in one's life no longer mattered. This situation could have reflected the beliefs of nearby Semitic cultures or the northern invaders or, perhaps, both.

However, even in Homer, we see glimpses of a residual religious belief that was inherited from the earliest inhabitants of what was to become the Hellenic homeland. Some of these residual beliefs are thought to have been inherited from Egypt by way of Crete and Mycenae.[411]

Some Scholars' Views

In 1908 Maspero believed that the gods Demeter and Dionysis had evolved from the Egyptian Isis and Osiris since he accepted Foucart's[412] research that showed that "the Eleusinian mysteries are Egyptian by execution and intention; Egyptian thought dominates them, and the manner in which the thought is expressed is Egyptian."[413] This view is advanced later by others, including A. A. Barb in 1971,[414] but is rejected by Griffiths.[415]

---

[410] When the soul leaves the body it becomes an ἀμενηνός κάρηνον or strengthless head (*Od.* 10.520, 535, 11.29, 49), while the body becomes κωφὴ γαῖα or, literally, "dumb earth" (*Il.* 24.54). Achilles is mistreating the body of Hector and the gods are angry at him for dishonoring his remains, metaphorically, "mindless dirt".

[411] See Nilsson, *The Minoan-Mycenaean Religion*, 625, passim.

[412] Maspero called this area of study a hazard region and praised P. Foucart for venturing there. He extensively references P. Foucart, "Recherches sur l'origine et la nature des mysteres d'Eleusis," in *Memoires des Inscriptions et Belles Letters*, vol. xxxv, Pt. 2 (1895): passim.

[413] Maspero, *New Light on Ancient Egypt*, 54ff, 60ff, 238ff.

[414] Barb claims that the Eleusinian and Dionysiac Mysteries were indebted to Egypt. A.A. Barb, "Mystery, Myth and Magic," in *The Legacy of Egypt*, ed. J.R. Harris (Oxford: Clarendon Press, 1971), 149ff.

[415] Griffiths says that it is "disconcerting to find" Barb resurrecting these ideas and doing so "without a mention of Paul Foucart and critiques of his views" (J. Gwyn Griffiths, "The Legacy of Egypt," *The Classical Review* 25 [1975]: 307-8).

Martin Bernal makes the case for the inheritance of Egyptian culture by the Greeks in *Black Athena*,[416] but his argument, for various reasons, has not been universally well received.[417]

The fact that the Cretan Rhadamanthys, the brother of Minos, is considered a judge of the dead in Greek literature from Homer to Plato might indicate that Cretan beliefs influenced the Greeks. This fact, of course, does not show that Egypt influenced Crete.

Undoubtedly, Herodotus made the oldest of these cases for cultural dependence on Egypt where he related that Orphics and Bacchics received their ideas from Egypt (*Hist.* 2.81). He, also, was not universally well received. Gunter Zuntz denies Herodotus' claim for interdependence by emphasizing the differences in the imagery found on certain tablets buried with the deceased. For example, the guardians of the underworld are quite divergent in demeanor. The Greek guardians are hostile whereas the Egyptian ones are welcoming.[418] But, Peter Kingsley counters with the statement that "Zuntz failed to take into account: the most decisive factor of all. The discovery made in the tombs of the seventh to fifth centuries BC, in both Sardinia and Carthage, of strips of gold foil…engraved with Egyptian figures…[which] clearly testify to a curve of influence from Egypt up to southern Italy via the Phoenicians and Carthage."[419]

---

[416] Bernal makes some interesting arguments. One such is that Minoan Crete may have survived the earliest northern invasions of 2200-1900 BCE, whereas the Greek mainland did not fare so well. This survival may have left his supposedly inherited Egyptian cultus viable until the Minoan destruction by Mycenae ca. 1450. This then would have allowed a somewhat diluted cult of the dead back into Mainland Greece, which remained influential even after the fall of Mycenae. See Martin Bernal, *Black Athena*, (London: Free Association Press, 1987), passim.

[417] An excellent rebuttal and counter-rebuttal appears in John E. Coleman, "Did Egypt Shape the Glory that was Greece?" *Archaeology*, (Sept/Oct 1992), 48-77; Martin Bernal, "The Case for Massive Egyptian Influence in the Aegean," ibid, 53-86.

[418] Gunther Zuntz, *Persephone*, (Oxford: Clarendon Press, 1971), 371-6.

[419] Peter Kingsley, "From Pythagoras to the Turba Philosophorum: Egypt and Pythagorean Tradition," *Journal of the Warburg and Courtauld Institutes*, 57 (1994): 3-4.

Some examples of cultural transmission.

In particular, the Greek Isles of the Blest and the Elysian Fields look like direct descendents of the Egyptian Ialu Fields or Fields of Reeds.[420] Also, the Egyptian phrase 'true of voice' (*maa kheru*) appears to have been taken over as a loan word for the Greek word that refers to the blessed spirits of the dead (*makar, makarios*).[421] The Isles of the Blest are called μακάρων νῆσοι in Greek and are referred to by that name in Hesiod, and Homer has expressed the same concept by the name of Elysium. Herodotus records an African oasis a few days journey from Thebes as being named the Isle of the Blest (Herodotus 3.26.1).

A clear example of cultural iconic transmission is that of *Taweret* during the Egyptian 12th Dynasty. The Middle Kingdom hippopotamus demon was, according to a study by Judith Weingarten, the basis of the Minoan Genius of around 1850 BCE.[422]

Two concepts based on the Greek word for soul (psyche) also look like likely candidates for a dependency. The weighing of the soul (*psychostasia*) is common to both Egypt and Greece.[423] The leader of souls (*psychopompos*) is also a common theme in both cultures.[424]

---

[420] Vermeule says that there was "influence from abroad…natural source for such influence was Egypt" (Vermeule, *Aspects of Death in Early Greek Art and Poetry*, 62f, 69); Also see J. Gwyn Griffiths, Greece and Rome 16 (1947) 122-26.

[421] Vermeule credits William Stevenson Smith of the Museum of Fine Arts in Boston with this connection. She further references B. Hemmerdinger, "Noms communs grecs d'origine egyptienne," *Glotta* 46 (1968) 238ff.; and says, "but the equation is dismissed with contempt" in R. Pierce, "Egyptian Loan-Words in Ancient Greek," *SymbOsl* 46 (1971) 105. See her references in Vermeule, Aspects, 63, 230 n. 62.

[422] Judith Weingarten, *The Transformation of Egyptian Taweret into Minoan Genius* (Partille: Paul Astroms Forlag, 1991), 3-15.

[423] The weighing of the Achaians and Trojans and of Achilles and Hector by Zeus (*Iliad* 8.69, 22.209) looks similar to that of the weighing of the heart and *Ma'at* in the Book of the Dead. Also, Hermes is shown on a vase painting as weighing two souls in Vermeule, Aspects, 161.

[424] In Greece, Hermes and/or Charon guide the souls to Hades and the Egyptian ferryman in Pyramid Text 1188 boats the souls to the Field of Rushes.

Finally, the opening quotations to this chapter are uncanny in their similarity, and they are consistent all the way from the *Pyramid Texts* through Euripides.[425]

Many scholars[426] have drawn similar and more extensive comparisons than those briefly rehearsed here and some, but not all, argue for a direct causal relationship between Egypt and Greece. Although they may be correct in their conclusions, we need not express an opinion on the issue here since the conclusions drawn in this study need assume only a parallel development of ideas.

Taking the Larger View

Taking a broader view of the question, our two societies exhibit a great deal of similarity. We will first take this larger view of the ancient Egyptians and Greeks, and then we will examine each issue with a finer scope.

In the pre-history of Greece and Egypt, according to the archeological evidence, there was a belief that something of the person survived death and would need some familiar objects from life to help them in an afterlife. We can only surmise how this afterlife was envisioned but it seems that it would have been to inhabit the environs of the tomb or perhaps even to journey to the underworld.

With the dawn of the written record, there appears to be no significant afterlife recorded for the common people. On the other hand, the elite of the respective societies appear to fair better. The kings and heroes have advanced beyond an underground existence and they are now transformed and transported to a glorious place to live for all time in the company of the gods or god-like entities. This transformation involves multiple material and non-material elements that make up the human personality.

---

[425] See the opening citations to this chapter. Is this coincidence or evidence for dependence? We need make no hypothesis. There are many intriguing parallels, though the issue remains contested, but in any event, it is not relevant to this study's principle thesis, except as such investigation of those parallels contribute to our comparisons between the two societies' afterlife concepts.

[426] For example, Brede Kristensen discusses many parallels in his study but notes in several places that some religious ideas may be examples "of conformity in type without direct borrowing" (W. Brede Kristensen, *Life out of Death* [Louvain, Belgium: Peeters Press, 1992], 171).

The gods are directly responsible for the elite gaining this type of afterlife due to some outstanding characteristic of the person involved. The gods are also responsible for the proper ordering of the cosmos and the society and there seems to be some types of prohibited conduct that would violate that order and warrant a loss of the afterlife.

In the later writings, intermediate between the dawn of writing and our terminal texts, the ideas of conduct and behavior evolve and become more important. More people are now included in the numbers who participate in the afterlife.

With this evolution we find a significant divergence in the development of the two cultures. Egypt evolves primarily due to internal developments whereas Greece continues its evolution due to the same kind of external influences that had already modified its earlier beliefs.

By the time of the terminal writings of this inquiry we find a full-blown judgment in the afterlife based primarily on one's conduct and behavior in this life. Even though, as with many contemporary religions, there are still attempts to circumvent an unfavorable judgment with magic and other special pleadings, it is now clear that one's conduct in life will produce an automatic outcome at a post-mortem judgment.

Having taken the broader view, we now examine the issues with a finer scope.

Pre-History

In the Paleolithic period, the belief in some sort of an afterlife was common and widespread.[427]

In the Egyptian Neolithic, bodies are buried in the sand and surrounded with grave-goods that could be useful in the world to come. In Greek pre-history we find burials at Knossos and Mycenae that exhibit this same kind of expectation. Both societies' expectations of an afterlife for all were to be interrupted by future events.

---

[427] See S.G.F. Brandon, *Religion in Ancient History*, (New York: Charles Scribner's Sons, 1969), 72.

In Egypt, the development of a strong central kingship and of the Heliopolitan priesthood put a strong emphasis on the very existence of *Maat* or universal order being upheld by the king. In the *Pyramid Texts* (ca. 2300 BCE) written to support this idea there was no room for discussion about what happened to the people other than the king. Some people may even have lost faith in their former belief in an afterlife but, more probably, they held on to the custom of the spirit living on in the tomb.[428]

In Greece, the later invasions (ca. 1200 BCE) of the northern peoples brought an end to the civilization of Mycenae and of the vital link to the ancient Minoan religious cult of the dead.[429] Now humans were differentiated from the gods on the basis of their immortality in that the gods had it and humanity did not.

The Dawn of Writing

With the Pyramid Texts and with Homer and Hesiod, the common folk are simply ignored with respect to a beneficial afterlife and the pre-historic post-mortem expectations seem to have disappeared. In the Pyramid Texts only the king has an afterlife and in Hesiod no one has an afterlife except some of the heroes of an earlier age before our race of people came into existence. In Homer, the normal post-mortem expectation was the undifferentiated repose of the shades.

However, even Homer has mixed views, and he allows a beneficent afterlife to some heroes and a horrible punishment to some few others. Significantly, we see that some people who have transgressed against proper conduct can be punished in the afterlife.[430] And, even the *Pyramid Texts* have residual indications that the dead will suffer a judgment.

---

[428] As late as the 4th Dynasty we have seen a materialistic belief that the afterlife of a prince, Hardjedef, is having a well-appointed tomb in the necropolis.

[429] This assumes that the Mycenaeans received their cult from the Minoans. Regardless, the Mycenaean cult was discontinued and the main Homeric afterlife scenario became the common belief.

[430] It is often claimed that the reason for punishment is a transgression against the honor of the gods and that this should not be taken as indication of a developed ethics. That may be, but this belief was effectively used to keep order in the society. Without such consequentialist morality one could violate oaths with impunity, thereby destroying that order. Whether they be called *Maat* or *Dike*, the gods of order helped control conduct and behavior, and violations of their order meant punishment in the afterlife.

The person at these respective times (ca. 2500 BCE and 800 BCE) is believed to be a composite being. In the *Pyramid Texts* the person (king) consists mostly of a *ka, ba, akh, ib* and body and in the Homeric epics all persons consist of a *psyche, thymos, nous, menos* and body.

Whereas all of the personality elements, severally and individually, in Egypt participate in the afterlife, in Homer only the unconscious psyche persists in Hades as a shade as the common lot of almost all people. A few rare exceptions (e.g., Menelaus) are transported alive and bodily to Elysium and Tiresias retains his thymos even though he is dead and in Hades.[431]

Conduct in the dawn of writing period.

Conduct is so important to both societies that the primary god is said to maintain the proper order. Each god has a daughter who has the express purpose of seeing to it that the order of the world and the society is preserved. In Egypt, *Maat*[432] is the daughter of Re and in Greece *Dike*[433] is the daughter of Zeus and Themis. *Maat* and *Dike* both allude to the maintenance of justice, order and reality. Heraclitus (B94) had claimed that the sun would not overstep his measure for if he did, the Furies (handmaids of *Dike*) would punish him. This links the natural order of the cosmos with justice, a link that I believe existed in Egypt with the concept of *Maat* and one that Plato would later attempt to reestablish, against the Sophistic movement, by positing a higher reality on which the virtues were grounded.

Comparing the conduct and behavior that appears in the texts of both of these early periods shows that behavioral terms are of the utmost importance to their societies and are possibly necessary for the attainment of the afterlife.

---

[431] *Od.* 4.561ff, *11*.90ff.

[432] *Maat* is the ubiquitous personification or truth, justice, order, reality, etc. in all periods of Egyptian religion.

[433] In Hesiod, *Dike* is the daughter of Zeus who reports crooked judgments to him. *Dike* is the personification and deification of Justice. Zeus had wed Themis (Right) and produced three daughters: Eumonia (Good Order), Eirene (Peace) and Dike (Justice). See Hesiod *Works and Days* 256ff.

Terms in the Pyramid and Other Old Kingdom Texts[434]	Matching Terms in Homer and Hesiod
false oaths/falsity of words	Only false oaths and honor appear in their afterlife
honor to gods and parents	citations. All other of these terms appear elsewhere.[435]
lying/say that which is not	lying[436]
insolence/arrogant	insolence (*hubris*)
justice/righteousness	just (*dikaioi*)
piety/reverence	piety
wisdom/wise	wisdom
order/*maat*	cosmos/*dike*
moderation/self-control	moderation (*soaphrosune*)

Later Intermediate Developments

The idea of a beneficent afterlife in Homer and Hesiod did not resonate in mainland Greece and subsequent writers essentially followed Homer's more usual affirmation that the common lot is to join the undifferentiated shades.[437] This was to change only with the introduction of new forces, just as the pre-historic cults of the dead had changed centuries earlier.

Importing these new ideas, Pythagoras taught that the soul (ψύχη) would become more than a gibbering shade (εἴδολον) and that it is judged after death[438] and

---

[434] Ptahhotep, Henku, Hetepherakhet, Kagemni, Harkhuf, Nekhebu, Sheshi.

[435] See Appendix I: "Instances in Homer," Table 6.

[436] Achilles in *Il.* 9.310 says, hateful to me as the gates of Hades is that man that hides one thing in his mind and says another. Compare this to *Pyramid Text* 1161, "say that which is, do not say that which is not, for the god detests falsity of words." Clearly, as where many of these other virtues, truthfulness was a very early virtue, even though Homer condones Odysseus's lying elsewhere,. However, most virtues do not appear in an afterlife reference in Homer.

[437] Eleusis did seem to offer a better lot for some, but this contradicted the main current of Greek eschatological belief as epitomized by Homer.

[438] Iamblicus *Vita Pyth.* 29f. See *On The Pythagorean Life*, trans. Gillian Clark (Liverpool: Liverpool University Press, 1989).

Orphic texts taught a post-mortem judgment that is iconographically depicted where Aeacus, Triptolemus and Rhadamanthys appear as judges.[439]

In Egypt, it was not external forces that caused the change from the views of the <u>Pyramid Texts</u>. It was the desire of non-royalty to participate in the beneficent afterlife, and furthermore, that desire was aided by the diminution of the power of the kings to monopolize it. Now, all people had a soul (*ba*) and could share the celestial afterlife with the king.

Examining the conduct and behavior of this intermediate period, we see that not only was it of importance but that it was essential to the attainment of a good afterlife for the believers. But, not everyone believed.

The Doubters

It should be remembered that neither of our societies held to monolithic views and that there were always dissenters against the mainstream affirmations or denials of an afterlife in both Egypt and Greece. The following citations are indicative of those dissentions.

Greece.

> When a man comes near to the realization that he will be making an end, fear and care enter him for things to which he gave no thought before. The tales told about what is in Hades—that the one who has done unjust deeds here must pay the penalty there—at which he laughed up to then, now make his soul twist and turn because he fears they might be true…he is, at any rate, now full of suspicion and terror.
>
> Cephalus in <u>Republic</u> 330[440]

Egypt.

> I have heard the words of Imhotep and Hardedef,
> Whose sayings are recited whole.
> What of their places?
> Their walls have crumbled,

---

[439] See vase painting in Jane Harrison, *Prolegomena to the Study of Greek Religion* (Cambridge: Cambridge University Press, 1922), 599.

[440] The old man Cephalus' speech in Plato's *Republic* 330de. Translated by Bloom, *The Republic of Plato*, 6.

Their places gone,
As though they had never been!
None comes from there,
To tell of their state,
To tell of their needs,
To calm our hearts,
Until we go where they have gone!
...
Make holiday,
Do not weary of it!
Lo, none is allowed to take his goods with him,
Lo, none who departs comes back again!

The Song from the Tomb of King Intef[441]

These quotations show a panic of doubt in each of their respective principals. Cephalus is questioning the age-old Homeric belief that when one dies he goes to an undifferentiated place, Hades, where there is neither a really beneficent afterlife nor a fear of an afterlife retribution. Cephalus seems to fear the punishments attendant with the newer post-Homeric beliefs and would prefer the relatively benign oblivion of Homer. Over a thousand years earlier,[442] Intef's Harper doubted the opposite belief by questioning that there really is an afterlife and an afterlife recompense. In each case they are expressing doubts regarding long centuries of received wisdom; the one of the Homeric denial of a post-mortem place of punishment or reward and the other of Egyptian religious affirmation of a beneficent afterlife.

The Terminal Writings

The *Book of the Dead* and Plato constitute the terminal writings for this inquiry. Here we will examine a major contrast between Egypt and Greece, that of the soul, before moving on to our final comparison of conduct and behavior as determinants for an afterlife.

---

[441] A Harper's song from the tomb of a King named Intef of the Middle Kingdom (between 2000 and 1600 BCE.) Translated by Miriam Lichtheim, *Ancient Egyptian Literature*, 1.196. There is a scholarly debate on the dating of this song. Erik Hornung claims that it laments the loss of the traditional afterlife and "is a product of Akhenaten's religion of light and the deep shadows it cast" (Eric Hornung, *Akhenaten and the Religion of Light* [Ithaca: Cornell University Press, 1999], 103-4). In other words it belongs to the New Kingdom.

[442] Contra Hornung, above, Lichtheim holds to a Middle Kingdom date.

The soul.

A cursory look has the soul in Egypt and Greece appearing quite similar. In both, it is the entity or entities that complete the human personality. It is that element which achieves immortality, and in some cases (the king in the *Pyramid Texts* and everyone in Plato), is pre-existent to the body.

In both, there is a celestial or ethereal afterlife and both have instances of the soul going to reside among the stars. There the similarities end.

The Pythagorean/Orphic/Platonic soul has fallen from a lofty height and is condemned to live in the flesh due to some original sin.[443] This concept of the body being the tomb of the soul would have been abhorrent to the Egyptians who loved life in the flesh and expected the body to live eternally with the souls.

In Egypt all of the non-physical elements of the personality (*ba, ka, akh*), along with the body[444] lives on, whereas in Greece only the *psyche* does so, and the body souls (*thymos, nous, menos*) cease to exist. With Plato, the tripartite soul assumed all of the functions of the other body souls and later only the highest of the three (the reason) attained immortality.

In Platonic thought, the soul would endure a purgation period before returning once more to a body unless that soul had achieved the highest reward or punishment, whereas in Egypt there was only bliss or oblivion and no place of purgation for a return nor was there a place of punishment until quite late.[445]

---

[443] Plato explains the original sin at *Laws* 854b where he says, the impulse to evil "is a sort of frenzied goad, innate in mankind as a result of crimes of long ago that remain unexpiated." In *Laws* 701c, Plato had explained the origin of the crimes of long ago as being revealed by having people "reincarnated in themselves, the character of the ancient Titan (Τιτανικήν) of the story…and thanks to getting into the same position as the Titans did, they live a wretched life of endless misery." Of course, Empedocles had alluded to this idea much earlier.

[444] The Greeks had no concept of a resurrection of the body, but the Egyptians expected a reconstitution of the body like that of Osiris.

[445] Herodotus (2.123) had claimed that the Egyptians invented the transmigration of souls. He probably mistook their transformations for reincarnation. They indeed metamorphosed into other creatures and even into their gods, but not for a return to the flesh. The Egyptians eventually would also develop a concept of hell as a punishment for misdeeds instead of simple oblivion later in the New Kingdom.

See Table 10 in Appendix O, for a summary comparison of the Egyptian and Platonic soul. Compare tables 1, 5 and 9 for Platonic, Homeric and Egyptian soul.

Conduct in the terminal period.

In chapter 6 we analyzed the Declarations of Innocence in spell 125 of the Book of the Dead and separated the terms into two categories: Inner qualities of character and relationships with others. There, the determination was that inner qualities of character were paramount in the second (and presumably later) set of Declarations. What can we say of the terms found in Plato's myths by way of comparison? See the chart on the following page for an analysis.

Needless to say that these designations are quite subjective and it might be argued that they should be reversed or even placed in both categories. Nevertheless, let us make some observations on the chart as it stands.

Almost all of Plato's terms for conduct deserving reward are placed in the Inner Qualities of Character column, whereas the terms for conduct deserving punishment are almost evenly divided between the two catagories.

From this observation, we can conclude that he appears to have been stressing the intrinsic behaviors and claiming that 'what you are' is a reflection of the symmetry of your soul and will attain for you the reward after death. On the other hand, it is mostly the extrinsic conduct in 'what you do,' or 'how you comport yourself' that can destroy the soul's symmetry and thereby condemn you to a post-mortem punishment.

Terms in Plato's Myths Analyzed by Inner Qualities of Character and Relationships with Others

Conduct deserving reward

Term	Dictionary Form	As In Plato's Myths	Inner Qualities of Character	Relationships with Others
justly	δίκιος	δικαίως		x
piously	ὅσιος	ὁσίως		x
truth	ἀλήθεια	ἀληθείας	x	
done own work	πράσσω	πράξαντος	x	

Term	Dictionary Form	As In Plato's Myths	Inner Qualities of Character	Relationships with Others
no busybody	πολυπραγμονέω	πολυπραγμονή–σαντος	x	
good	ἀγαθός	ἀγαθός	x	
noble	καλός	καλός	x	
virtue	ἀρετή	ἀρετήν	x	
well-ordered	κόσμιος	κοσμία	x	
wise	φρόνιμος	φρόνιμος	x	
pure	καθαρός	καθαρῶς	x	
moderate	μέτριος	μετρίως	x	
wisdom	φρόνησις	φρονήσεως	x	
moderation	σωφροσύνη	σοφροσύνη	x	
justice	δικαιοσύνη	δικαιοσύνη	x	
courage	ἀνδρεία	ἀνδρείαι	x	
freedom	ἐλευθερία	ἐλευθερίαι	x	
good deeds	εὐεργεσία	εὐεργεσίας		x
piety	εὐσέβεια	εὐσεβείας	x	
philosopher	φιλοσόφος	φιλόσοφος	x	
lover of beauty	φιλοκάλος	φιλόκαλος	x	
symmetrical	ὀρθός	ὀρθός	x	
honor	τιμῆς	τιμῆς		x
shame	αἰδώς	αἰδοῦς	x	

Conduct deserving punishment

Term	Dictionary Form	As In Plato's Myths….	Inner Qualities of Character	Relationships with Others
unjustly	ἄδικος	ἀδίκως		x
godlessly	ἄθεος	ἀθέως	x	
false oaths	ἐπίορκος	ἐπιορκιῶν		x

Term	Dictionary Form	As In Plato's Myths....	Inner Qualities of Character	Relationships with Others
lying	ψεῦδος	ψεύδους	x	
boasting	ἀλαζονεία	ἀλαζονείας		x
arrogant power	ἐξουσία	ἐξουσίας		x
luxury	τρυφάω	τρυφῆς	x	
insolence	ὕβρις	ὕβρεως		x
incontinence	ἀκράτεια	ἀκρατείας	x	
asymmetry	ἀσυμμετρία	ἀσυμμετρία	x	
ugliness	αἰσχρότης	αἰσχρότης	x	
impious	ἀνόσιος	ἀνοσιώτατα		x
errors	ἁμάρτημα	ἁμαρτήματα		x
attached/body	ἐπιθυμητικός	ἐπιθυμητικῶς	x	
impure	ἀκάθαρτος	ἀκάθαρτον	x	
killings	φόνος	φόνων		x
sacrileges	ἱεροσυλία	ἱεροσυλίας		x
violence	βίαιος	βίαιον		x
pleasures	ἡδονά	ἡδονάς	x	
betrayal	προδίδωμι	προδόντες		x
caused death	θάνατος	θανάτων		x
to slavery	δούλειος	δουλείας		x
impiety	ἀσέβεια	ἀσεβείας		x
envy	φθόνος	φθόςος	x	
forgetfulness	λήθη	λήθης	x	
badness	κακία	κακία		x
crooked (asymmetrical)	σκολιός	σκολιός	x	

A Graphic Comparison of Conduct and Behavior Between Egyptian and Greek Societies

Many comparisons of conduct and behavior have already been done in this chapter. Now, this penultimate section will graphically compare the terms for conduct and behavior as they appear in texts related to the afterlife in the ancient Egyptian and the ancient Greek societies.

Comparisons Between Egypt and Greece

Comparing Plato's terms.

The first comparison will be a condensed recapitulation of the comparisons of the Platonic terms as already discussed in the preceding chapters and illustrated in Tables 4, 7 and 10 in the appendix. See the summary chart following.

SUMMARY CHART OF

Conduct and Behavior that Influences the Afterlife: Plato, Other Greeks and Egyptians
(terms as they appear in Plato's judgment myths only)

Conduct deserving reward   Afterlife/behavior citations

Term	Dictionary Form	As In Plato's Myths	Earlier Greeks	All Periods Egyptians	BOTH	NEITHER
justly	δίκιος	δικαίως	x	x	x	
piously	ὅσιος	ὁσίως	x			
truth	ἀλήθεια	ἀληθείας	x	x	x	
done own work	πράσσω	πράξαντος				x
no busybody	πολυπραγμονέω	πολυπραγμονή–σαντος				x
good	ἀγαθός	ἀγαθός	x	x	x	
noble	καλός	καλός	x			
virtue	ἀρετή	ἀρετήν	x			
well-ordered	κόσμιος	κοσμία		x		
wise	φρόνιμος	φρόνιμος	x	x	x	
pure	καθαρός	καθαρῶς	x	x	x	
moderate	μέτριος	μετρίως		x		

Term	Dictionary Form	As In Plato's Myths	Earlier Greeks	All Periods Egyptians	BOTH	NEITHER
wisdom	φρόνησις	φρονῆσεως	x	x	x	
moderation	σωφροσύνη	σοφροσύνη		x		
justice	δικαιοσύνη	δικαιοσύνη	x	x	x	
courage	ἀνδρεία	ἀνδρείαι	x			
freedom	ἐλευθερία	ἐλευθερίαι	x			
good deeds	εὐεργεσία	εὐεργεσίας	x	x	x	
piety	εὐσέβεια	εὐσεβείας	x	x	x	
philosopher	φιλοσόφος	φιλόσοφος				
lover of beauty	φιλοκάλος	φιλόκαλος				
symmetrical	ὀρθός	ὀρθός				x
honor	τιμῆς	τιμῆς	x	x	x	
shame	αἰδώς	αἰδοῦς	x			
unjustly	ἄδικος	ἀδίκως	x			
godlessly	ἄθεος	ἀθέως				x
false oaths	ἐπίορκος	ἐπιορκιῶν	x	x	x	
lying	ψεῦδος	ψεύδους	x	x	x	
boasting	ἀλαζονεία	ἀλαζονείας	x	x	x	
arrogant power	ἐξουσία	ἐξουσίας	x			
luxury	τρυφάω	τρυφῆς				x
insolence	ὕβρις	ὕβρεως	x	x	x	
incontinence	ἀκράτεια	ἀκρατείας				x
asymmetry	ἀσυμμετρία	ἀσυμμετρία				x
ugliness	αἰσχρότης	αἰσχρότης				x
impious	ἀνόσιος	ἀνοσιώτατα	x			
errors	ἀμάρτημα	ἀμαρτήματα	x	x	x	
attached/body	ἐπιθυμητικός	ἐπιθυμητικῶς				x
impure	ἀκάθαρτος	ἀκάθαρτον	x			
killings	φόνος	φόνων	x	x	x	
sacrileges	ἱεροσυλία	ἱεροσυλίας	x	x	x	
violence	βίαιος	βίαιον	x	x	x	
pleasures	ἡδονά	ἡδονάς				x
betrayal	προδίδωμι	προδόντες	x			
caused death	θάνατος	θανάτων	x	x	x	
to slavery	δούλειος	δουλείας	x			
impiety	ἀσέβεια	ἀσεβείας	x	x	x	
envy	φθόνος	φθόςος	x			
forgetfulness	λήθη	λήθης				
badness	κακία	κακία				x
crooked (asymmetrical)	σκολιός	σκολιός	x			

What can be made of this chart? Several terms of great importance to Plato were left out of both the other Greeks and the Egyptians. They can be classified under three headings:

Anti-body:
    luxury
    attached to the body
    pleasures

Inharmonious soul:
    asymmetry
    ugliness
    crooked
    symmetrical

Tripartite society and soul:
    done own work
    no busybody

The first group of terms results from the soul/flesh dualism found in the puritanical Pythagorean/Orphic tradition. We have already seen that this dualism would have been abhorrent to the Egyptians who were very much attached to the body throughout their entire history. It would not have faired much better with the earlier, pre-Pythagorean, Greeks who believed that the body was the only substantial part of a person and that the psyche was an insubstantial shade. The second and third groups are inventions of Plato to describe the harmony he wants to see among the citizens of his perfect city. He, of course, likens the harmony and symmetry of the tripartite soul with that of the three classes of the city.

Comparison of Greek to Egyptian.

The next summary chart compares the Greek authors', other than Plato, after-life/conduct and behavior terms to those found in the Egyptian texts. Matching terms will be marked with an 'x'. Non-matching terms are left blank except for the most important, which will be commented upon. See following chart on the next page.

Comparison of Greek and Egyptian Conduct Terms that Appear in Afterlife Citations

Term in Other Greeks	Is Term In Egyptian Texts?
Homer	
false oaths	x
honor	x
Homer (conduct not associated with an afterlife citation)	
prudence and justice	x
aristos, agathos (brave)	NO—brave/courage term lacks importance in Egypt*
wisdom	x
moderation	x
holiness/piety	x
honor parents	x—family very important*]
respect stranger and suppliant	NO—strangers and suppliants were not an Egyptian concern*446
crooked judgments	x
insolence	x
Pindar	
kept oaths	
injustice	x
righteous	x right-doing, right
impious	x
wrongdoing/lawless	x
just	x
errors/sins	x
courage	
wisdom	x
virtue	
pious	
Heraclitus	
falsehoods/lying	x
truth	x

446 Items marked with an asterisk will be further commented upon in the text.

Term in Other Greeks	Is Term In Egyptian Texts?
courage	
justice	x
honor	x
Empedocles	
good deeds	x
error	x
broke oaths	x
pre-natal wrong	NO—only the king had a pre-natal existence—then, no wrong*
violence	x aggressive, inspire terror
honor	x
killings	x—only in BOD*
Aeschylus	
sacrileges	x profane, defamation, merry
betrayal	
misdeeds	
just	x
piety	x
boasting	x
impiety	x
ignorance	
murder	x
impious to god, stranger, parents	x vs. good son
wrongs	x
hubris	x
mistake	x
lose wits	
blindness	
impetuous	?—suppress desires*
foolish	x
pride	x
rashness	
unnatural act	x
violate sanctuary	NO—sanctuary was not an issue*
honor	x

Term in Other Greeks	Is Term In Egyptian Texts?
Sophocles	
honor	x
piety	x
manly courage	
crimes	x
justice	x
truth	x
noble	
wise	x
freedom	
good deeds	x graciousness, giving,
shame	
killings	x
Euripides	
courage	
noble	
generous	x
good	x
blasphemy	x
honor father	x
murder	x
honorable defeat	
justly	x
pious	
justice	x
wise	x
piety	x
unjust	
insolence	x
impiety	x
crimes	x
Aristophanes	
wronged stranger, parents	x
perjury	x

Term in Other Greeks	Is Term In Egyptian Texts?
parricide	
foolish	x
factionalism	
disagreeable	
civil strife	
bribes	
betrayal	
smuggles	
defiles	x
purity	x vs. unclean
righteousness	x
pious	
justice	x
piety	x

Note that some terms and concepts, which were important in Greece, were not even a consideration in Egypt.

Sanctuary for strangers and suppliants was not an issue because Egypt was so isolated that the concept of guest friendship and sanctuary did not develop there.

There was no term for courage in the afterlife citations probably because in a relatively pacific society, it was not the high virtue that it would become in belli-cose Greece. Although the Egyptians did have occasional internal strife, there were such extended periods of peace that the martial virtues did not evolve as they did in places like Greece where the warrior was held in honor.

Finally, there could be no pre-natal wrong because the Egyptians did not have a dualistic outlook on life; they were not souls fallen from a better place into the punishment of the flesh. Although the king was presumed to have a pre-natal existence in the *Pyramid Texts*, no one else did, and the king was not a fallen soul; rather he was an incarnated god.

But some terms, such as being a good son, were equally important to both societies. Among the first of the unwritten laws of the gods in Greece was the admonition to honor and show piety toward one's parents. In Egypt a good son was one who insured a proper burial for the dead parent and who considered it important to his quality of afterlife to be beloved of his mother, father and sister.

Some other concepts regarding family existed equally in both societies. The idea of the sins of the fathers being visited on succeeding generations was powerful in both. Punishing the children for the sins of the fathers figured heavily in Greece until such time as they recognized the injustice of the concept and were able to replace it with a punishment, still in the future, but now in an afterlife.

We find this concept already in Homer at *Il.* 4.160, Hesiod at *Works* 280ff, Solon at fragment 2.15 and finally with Theognis at 731-52 where he protests its injustice.

In Egypt, in spite of having an afterlife in which to insure that only the guilty party would be punished with oblivion, we still see this sins-of—the-fathers type of punishment in *Pyramid Text* 1278-9 where it is said, "he will be nowhere and his house will be nowhere."

Comparison of Egyptian to Greek.

For the last of the summary charts, we shall compare the terms in the Egyptian texts of the Old Kingdom (with comments on later periods) to those in the Greek authors.

The most important terms will be associated with the first Greek author to use it in an afterlife citation, the others with an x. An exception will be some non-after-life citations of Homer in order to show that the behavioral concept was important at that early time (Homer-nal). See the chart starting on the following page.

Already in the Old Kingdom the Egyptians recognized most of the terms that would later appear in the *Book of the Dead*[447] and among the early Greeks.

---

[447] Some obvious ones are missing in the Old Kingdom citations, such as murder, but these will appear with the Book of the Dead.

Comparison of Egyptian and Greek Conduct Terms that Appear in Afterlife Citations

	Positive Conduct	In the Greek Texts?	Negative Conduct	In the Greek Texts?
Ptahhotep:				
	wise	Soph.	arrogant	Homer-nal
	self-control	Homer-nal	aggressive	Emped.
	seek-good thing		transgress	
	truth	Heracl.	rapacious	
	rightdoing	x	baseness	
	straight forward	x	wrongdoing	Pindar
	kindly hearing		inspire terror	Emped.
	propitiate friends		plunder	
	quiet		calumny	
	control self	x	distortion of truth	x
	wisdom	Homer-nal, Pindar	angry speech	
	good will		boast	Aesch.
	true judgment	Homer-nal	speak ill	
	friendly		errs	Emped.
	graciousness		disobeys	
	good deed	Emped.	defies	
	good	Emped.	babbles	
	right	x	covetous	x envy
	devoid of falsehood	Heracl.	selfish	
	honored	Homer	repeat slander	
	justice	Heracl.	hot temper	
	suppress desires	Aesch.	theft	
	patient		quarrelsome	
	good son	Aesch.	haughty	x
	acts rightly	x	anger	
			one-sided	
			rob	
			steal	
			copulate with woman boy	NO*
			hostility	
			ill-tempered	
			frivolous	
			notorious	
			error	Emped.
			fool	Aesch.
			give offense	

	Positive Conduct	In the Greek Texts?	Negative Conduct	In the Greek Texts?
Henku:				
	gave bread[448]	Eurip.	oppressed	
	clothed	x	lie	Heracl.
	spoke good		allow fear	
	gave cattle	x		
	beloved	NO*		
Hetepherakhet:				
	own means		took property	
	treat people well		force	
	guard others things		unclean	Arist.
			evil	x
Kagemni:				
	Respectful	x honor	chatter	
	Restraint	x	blunder	
	Modest	x	fault	x
	Silent	x	gluttony	
	Quiet	x	covet	x
	Gentle		greed	
	Timid		drunkard	
			boast	Aesch.
Harkhuf:				
	gave bread	x	speak evilly	
	clothed	x		
	help boatless	x		
	speak fairly			
Nekhebu:				
	pacifier	NO*	beat people	
	gave bread	x	enslave	x
	clothed	x	angry	
	beloved		speak evil	
			profane	Aesch.
			destroy	

---

448 This is subsumed under the term beneficence, as are the other gifts.

	Positive Conduct	In the Greek Texts?	Negative Conduct	In the Greek Texts?
Sheshi:				
	done justice	x		
	spoke truly	x		
	did right	x		
	spoke fairly			
	judged well	x		
	rescued weak	NO*		
	gave bread	x		
	clothed	x		
	helped boatless	x		
	buried sonless			
	respected parents	Homer-nal Eurip.		
	raised siblings			
The Pyramid Texts:				
	righteousness	x	oppose king	
	reverence piety	Homer-nal, Soph.	defamation of goddess	x
	just by deeds	x	merry in sanctuary sacrilege	Aesch.
	say that which is	x	say that which is not	x
	just	x	falsity of words	Homer
			commit wrong	Pindar
			crime	x
			evil	x
			violate the king's tomb	

Some important terms that do not appear in the Greek afterlife citations are:

kindly hearing
pacifier
rescued weak
friendly
quiet
good will
gentle
timid
patient
beloved of father, mother

treat people well
speak fairly
helping, feeding, clothing others
all of the concepts of Hetepherakhet

Obviously, some of these terms do appear in Greek texts, just not in the afterlife citations. However, a few like 'pacifier' and 'rescued weak' are totally absent from the extant texts of ancient Greece.

The last item on the above list deserves special consideration since it contains the germ of an idea that was not to be developed in Greece until the era of Plato. Even then it was not to become the categorical imperative until the time of Kant some four thousand years after the autobiography of Hetepherakhet was written—in the twenty-fourth century BCE.

Hetepherakhet claims that he is making his tomb of his own means and not taking from another's tomb in order to do so. He clearly recognizes that in order to expect his tomb to be well treated, he must treat others' in the same way. It is not much of a stretch to formulate his statement as a rule thus: 'Treat another's property as you would have him/her treat yours.' Nor is it much more of a stretch to the great modern philosophical imperative: 'Do only that which you would wish to become a universal law.' (See **Appendix P** for a comparison to Jewish and Christian terms of conduct and behavior).

We can see that this list contains the cooperative virtues of a relatively pacific state, where benevolence was considered important. These virtues, dependent on the order (*Maat*) of the universe, existed in Egypt some 2000 years before Plato was to make his valiant attempt to resurrect them with an appeal to a higher reality. But, even he did not include them in his eschatological myths.

Conclusions

In the earliest periods, we have seen that the texts dealing with an afterlife appear to be concerned only with the elite: the king in Egyptian 5th Dynasty *Pyramid Texts* and the heroes in Homeric and Hesiodic Greece. This study has argued that there is some evidence in the early texts of both societies for a belief that the common people could also be rewarded or punished in an afterlife. In later periods both societies religious texts dealing with the afterlife exhibit a much more developed democratization.

As post-mortem beliefs became more democratic, conduct and behavior grew in importance. However, from the earliest time periods, both societies believe that the gods, primarily *Maat* in Egypt and *Dike* in Greece, are responsible for the proper ordering of the cosmos and that violations of that order will call down the most dire consequence—the loss of a beneficent afterlife.

The considerations discussed here and in the earlier chapters should be sufficient to prove my thesis that, not only were conduct and behavior of utmost importance to maintaining the proper order of our ancient societies but that furthermore, from the earliest times, they were significant determinants for a favorable or unfavorable judgment in an afterlife.

Appendices

A. *Plato's Eschatological Myths*

Plato's escatological myths may be found in any number of sources. An excellent free on-line source is:

http://www.perseus.tufts.edu/

B. *Additional Investigation of Plato's Psyche*

It is clear that Plato did not invent the immortality concept, but in what way is Plato's soul different from what we will see in earlier writers' concepts? In order to arrive at a conclusion to this question we will first have to determine the attributes of the Platonic soul. This will involve not only reviewing the eschatological myths but also looking at various other places in the Platonic corpus. I will cite descriptions[449] of soul attributes and then summarize them in a tabular format.

As Halliwell points out concerning the <u>Republic</u>:

It is imperative to keep in mind the various facets of *psuche*, 'soul'—as (a) the principle of life, animating the body; (b) the powers of mind and consciousness; (c) the locus of ethical responsibility, i.e. the cause of justice or injustice in the person.[450]

Halliwell goes on to use <u>Rep</u> 1.353 for examples of the above: a) "What of living? Isn't that a function of a soul" (353d); b) "Some functions of a soul...taking care of things, ruling, deliberating" (353d); c) "Bad soul rules...badly...a good soul...well...justice is a soul's virtue, and injustice its vice"(353e).

<u>The soul is reincarnated</u>:

"The human soul is immortal...never destroyed, and one must live one's life as piously as possible...As the soul is immortal, has been born often and has seen all things here and in the underworld, there is nothing which it has not learned" (<u>Meno</u> 81bc).

"Coming to life again in truth exists, the living come to be from the dead, and the souls of the dead exist" (<u>Phaedo</u> 72d).

"Each soul chooses the life it wants...a human soul can enter a wild animal, and a soul that was once human can move from an animal to a human being again" (<u>Phaedrus</u> 249b).[451]

---

[449] All translations, unless otherwise noted, in this section are from John M. Cooper, ed., Plato: Complete Works (Indianapolis: Hackett Publishing Company, 1997).

[450] S. Halliwell, Plato: Republic 10, 157.

[451] Cf. Rep 617.

"If a person lived a good life throughout the due course of his time, he would at the end return to his dwelling place in his companion star...but if he failed in this, he would be born a second time, now as a woman" (Tim 42b).

The entire myth of Er is about reincarnation in Rep 614-21, especially where it is said: "Ephemeral souls, this is the beginning of another cycle that will end in your death" (617d).

The harmonia theory of the soul is refuted:

"If then the soul is a kind of harmony [of the body, when the body is destroyed]...the soul must immediately be destroyed" (Phaedo 86bc);[452] This is refuted by Plato's doctrine of recollection, since "the theory of recollection...was based on [the preexistence of the soul, before it was placed into a body]" (92d).

Soma/sema—the body is the prison/tomb of the soul:

"Perhaps in reality we're dead...our bodies are our tombs" (Gorg. 493c).

"In the language of the mysteries, that we men are in a kind of prison" (Phaedo 62b).[453]

"Some people say that the body is the tomb of the soul" (Crat. 400bc).[454]

There is a dualism of the soul/body:

"So the soul is more like the invisible than the body, and the body more like the visible" (Phaedo 79bc).

---

[452] This theory is said to come from Pythagoreanism by way of Empedocles according to John Burnet, Plato's Phaedo, 82. But Rowe claims that this idea "is incompatible with any known Pythagorean belief about the soul" (C.J. Rowe, Plato: Phaedo, 205).

[453] See Dodds, Gorgias, 297-8, 300, 373-6.

[454] This is one of the few times that Plato's Socrates refers to his predecessors; in this case the Orphics. They were credited with the idea that the soul is imprisoned until a penalty for some pre-natal wrong is paid.

<u>Death is a separation of soul from body</u>:

"Do we believe that there is such a thing as death?...Is it anything else than the separation of the soul from the body" (<u>Phaedo</u> 64c)?

<u>There is remembrance (anamnesis) of the forms (*eide*)</u>:

"On the way around [the place beyond heaven] it has a view of Justice...Self-control...Knowledge" (<u>Phaedrus</u> 247cd).

The soul is implanted with rules before incarnation (<u>Tim</u>. 42).

<u>The soul is tripartite—λογιστικόν, θυμοειδές, ἐπιθυμητικόν</u>:

These represent the rational, appetitive and spirited parts which are associated with wisdom, temperance and courage.[455]

"And we'll call him wise because of that small part of himself that rules...advantageous for each part and for the whole soul, which is the community of all three parts" (<u>Rep</u>. 442d).[456]

"The soul of each individual is divided into three parts, in just the same way that a city is" (<u>Rep</u>. 580d).

The human being is like the Chimera of the old legends; a tripartite composite inside covered by a likeness of just the human part (<u>Rep</u>. 588cd).

"Let us liken the soul to the natural union of a team of winged horses and their charioteer" (<u>Phaedrus</u> 246a).[457]

"Remember how we divided each soul in three..." (<u>Phaedrus</u> 253c).

---

[455] Note that Plato's tripartite soul follows the three lives of Pythagoras: curious (rational), covetous (appetitive), and ambitious (spirited).

[456] Cf. Rep 435bc. Dodds claims that tripartition first appears here in the Republic. Dodds, Plato: Gorgias, 300.

[457] Cf. Rep 439e.

The immortal part of the soul was fused with a body and two mortal parts of the soul (Tim. 69-72).[458]

At Gorg. 506, the praise of order in the soul may imply that there are parts to be ordered. This could be a first indication of Plato's Republic tripartite theory.

Of the three souls, the Logistikon (reason) is the immortal part:

The immortal [part of the soul]...encased within a round mortal body" (Tim. 69a).

"But it isn't easy for anything composed of many parts to be immortal if it isn't put together in the finest way, yet this is how the soul appeared to us [both composite and immortal]" (Rep. 611b).

And, the ethical part:

"Isn't it appropriate for the rational part to rule, since it is really wise [a cardinal virtue]" (Rep. 441e)?

"When the charioteer sees that face [of the boy] his memory is carried back to the real nature of Beauty, and he sees it [beauty]...on the sacred pedestal next to Self-control" (Phaedrus 254b).

And, the cognitive part:

"Whenever a soul is bound within a mortal body, it first lacks intelligence...but as the stream that brings growth...[the soul] regains composure...render intelligent the person" (Tim. 44ab).

There are types of soul, each molded into a different type of marrow—the divine part into the head (Tim. 73bc).

---

[458] Cf. Rep. 611b-612a, Pol. 309a-c.

The soul is divine:

"But if these creatures [the mortals] came to be and came to share in my life by my hand, they would rival the gods" (Tim. 41c). Cf. Phaedo 81a below.

The soul is similar to things known:

The soul is most akin to forms (*eide*)" (Phd. 78b-79b).

The soul is the facility that knows the *eide* (Phaedo 65a-67b).

"A soul…makes its way to the invisible, which is like itself, the divine and immortal and wise…as is said of the initiates, truly spend the rest of time with the gods" (Phaedo 81a).

The soul "departs for what resembles it" in Damascius 349 on Phaedo 81a.[459]

'Always in motion' defines the soul:

"But since we have found that a self-mover is immortal, we…declare that this [self-motivation] is the very essence and principle of a soul." That which moves the body is soul, therefore the soul is immortal. (Phaedrus 245e).

The parts of the soul are really individual souls:

In the Timaeus, the tripartite soul is redefined by claiming that there are kinds of soul where: "within the body they built another kind of soul as well, the mortal kind" (Tim. 69ab).

In the Laws, there is confusion about this: "about the soul: one of the constituent elements (whether 'part' or 'state' is not important) to be found in it" (Laws 863b).

Socrates insists that we describe the soul with absolute precision—"whether it is one and homogeneous by nature or takes many forms" (Phaedrus 271a). Cf. 253c, 256be, 277c.

---

[459] My argument in Chapter 1 has it this would not be the gods, but rather the Forms.

The soul is fallen from a higher place:

After quoting Euripides, Plato goes on to say that "perhaps in reality we're dead...our bodies are our tombs, and that part of our souls in which our appetites reside..." (Gorg. 493a).[460]

If the soul could not keep up with the train of the gods and see the Forms, it is "weighed down, sheds its wings and falls to earth" (Phaedrus 248cd).

There is a Titanic original sin on the soul:

"They cease to care about oaths and promises and religion in general. They reveal, reincarnated in themselves, the character of the ancient Titans of the story [and will suffer] a wretched life of endless misery" (Laws 701c). Cf. 854b, where an evil force bred of ancient unexpiated wrongdoing prompts evil action in people.

---

[460] Plato here refers to a part of the soul. Is this an early intimation of the tripartite theory? It would seem so to this writer. It also seemed so to Taylor and Burnet but Dodds disagrees. A.E. Taylor, Plato the Man and his Works, 120n1; Burnet, Early Greek Philosophy, 296n2; E.R. Dodds, Plato: Gorgias, 300.

C. _TABLE 1:_ Table of Attributes and Features of the Platonic Soul

Attributes and Features of the Platonic[461] Soul

Attribute	Plato
allows death when separates from body	yes for all
motivates the body	attributes
principle of life	
immortal	
immaterial	
powers of mind and consciousness	
locus of ethics	
never destroyed	
reincarnated	
been born often	
pre-natally sees the Forms	
anamnesis from pre-natal existence	
chooses its next life	
dwells in its companion star	
like the invisible	
consists of mortal and immortal parts	
not a harmony	
soma is sema	
a unity	
tripartite (rational, appetitive, spirited)	
divine	
similar to Forms	
always in motion	
fallen to earth	
covered in human form	
contains Titanic substance	

---

[461] This tabular format will be used to compare Plato's soul to some other Greek authors and Egyptian texts discussed in this study.

D. *TABLE 2:* Summary of the Four Myths

The four eschatological myths of Plato are summarized in the following table:

The Four Platonic Myths Summarized

Element of Myth	Gorgias	Phaedo	Republic	Phaedrus
marks on soul	yes, from life	no	yes, from judge	no
who judges	three heroes	not specified	not specified	not specified
how judged	automatic	automatic	not specified	self-destruct (great cycle) not specified (small cycle)
where judged	meadow	where the dead are gathered	between openings to heaven & earth by meadow	plain of truth (great cycle) not specified (small cycle)
judgment final	yes	only for incurables	no	no
no. paths to judgment	one	many	one	not mentioned
no. afterlife destinations	2-Tartarus & Isles of Blest	3-Tartarus, true earth, highest abode	2-under earth & heaven	3-under earth, heaven, realm of Forms
Tartarus for	incurables	both incurables & curables	incurables	not mentioned
Isles of Blest for	just, pious	not mentioned	not mentioned	not mentioned
Hades for	curables	all—that certain place	all—the meadow at xroads would be in Hades—618d	not mentioned
how punished	Tartarus eternal, suffer in prison	Tartarus eternal, Tartarus then curables go to Acherusian, the average to Acherusian	under earth	lose wings & take bodies, beneath earth (great and small cycle)
time incurables punished	eternity	eternity	eternity	no incurables

how rewarded	grow wings & ascend to Forms, heaven (great and small cycle)	heaven	Acheron then true earth, highest abode	Isles eternal
souls led by genius	not mentioned	not mentioned	to & back again	not mentioned
genius assigned	not mentioned	no, chosen	yes	not mentioned
reincarnation	yes	yes	yes	not mentioned
who is reincarnated	everyone	all but incurables	all but phil. & incurables	no one
true earth	not mentioned	not mentioned	yes	not mentioned
free will	n/a	attempted	n/a	n/a
punishment-remedial/deterrent/retributive	remedial	remedial under retributive for incurables	remedial & deterrent for curables	remedial for curables, retributive for incurables
soul simple or compound	compound	compound	simple	simple
anamnesis of Forms	yes	no	yes	no
reason to be just	consequences	consequences -vs- Republic non-myth justice for itself	consequences	consequences
"hell"	none	under earth	Tartarus	Tartarus
"heaven"	celestial & super-celestial realms	heaven	true earth, highest abode	Isles of Blest
"purgatory"	prisons under earth	in the earth	Acherusian, Acheron	place of custody

E. _TABLES 3 and 4:_ Tables of Conduct and Behavior Words In Greek and English Translation

The terms denoting conduct and behavior in the eschatological myths of Plato are presented in tabular format. The first table is of all the terms in all of the myths. The second table displays the occurrence of any such term across all myths.

The following Table 3 is intended to summarize the various specific definitions of conduct and behavior, as interpreted by various modern translators of the Greek, that figure in the afterlife in the eschatological myths of Plato.

It can be seen from the foregoing text and this table that Plato groups all of his conducts and behaviors stated in the myths under five major categories each; those:

deserving reward	deserving punishment
just	unjust
good	bad
pious	godless
wise	
well-ordered	
	polluted
	impure

The Greek terms in the first Table are listed exactly as they appear in the myths of Plato. However, all subsequent Tables list these terms in the nominative (or the dictionary form).

TABLE 3

Conduct and Behavior that Influences The Afterlife: Plato
(terms as they appear in Plato's judgment myths only)

Work	Conduct deserving punishment		Conduct deserving reward	
Gorgias	godless & unjust		just & pious	
	523b		**523b**	
	unjustly	ἀδίκως	justly	δικαίως
	godlessly	ἀθέως	piously	ὁσίως
	525a-525d		**526c-527d**	
	false oaths	ἐπιορκιῶν	piously	ὁσίως
	injustice	ἀδικίας	truth	ἀληθείας
	lying	ψεύδους	done own work	πράξαντος
	boasting	ἀλαζονείας	no busybody	πολυπραγμονήσαντος
	arrogant power	ἐξουσίας	good	ἀγαθός
	luxury	τρυφῆς	noble	καλός
	insolence	ὕβρεως	virtue	ἀρετήν
	incontinence	ἀκρατείας		
	asymmetry	ἀσυμμετρίας		
	ugliness	αἰσχρότητος		
	impious	ανοσιώτατα		
	errors	ἁμαρτήματα		
Phaedo	polluted & impure		well-ordered & wise	
	108a-b		**108a-c**	
	attached/body	ἐπιθυμητικῶς	well-ordered	κοσμία
	impure	ἀκάθαρτον	wise	φρόνιμος
	unjust	ἀδίκων	pure	καθαρῶς
	killings	φόνων	moderate	μετρίως

Work	Conduct deserving punishment		Conduct deserving reward	
	113e-114e		114b-115a	
	sacrileges	ἱεροσυλίας	pious	ὁσίως
	murders	φόνους	purified (by phil)	καθηράμενοι
	violence	βιαίον		
	errors	ἁμαρτήματα	virtue	ἀρετῆς
	pleasures	ἡδονάς	wisdom	φρονήσεως
			moderation	σοφροσύνη
			righteousness	δικαιοσύνη
			courage	ἀνδρεία
			freedom	ἐλευθερία
			truth	ἀληθεία
Republic	unjust		just	
	615b-c		615b-c	
	injustice	ἀδίκηαιος		
	betrayal	προδόντες	good deeds	εὐεργεσίας
	caused deaths	θανάτων	just	δίκαιοι
	to slavery	δουλείας	holy	ὅσιοι
	impiety	ἀσεβείας	piety	εὐσεβείας
	murder	αὐτόχειρος – φόνου		
Phaedrus	bad		good	
	246e-8e		246b-9b	
	ugly	αἰσχρῶ	noble	καλός
	bad	κακῶ	good	ἀγαθός
			wise*	σοφόν
	envy	φθόςος	justice	δικαιοσύνην
	badness	κακία	moderation	σωφροσύνην
	forgetfulness	λήθης	philosopher	φιλοσόφου
	unjustly	ἀδίκως	lover of beautiful	φιλοκάλου
			justly	δικαίως
			truth	ἀλήθειαν

Work	Conduct deserving punishment		Conduct deserving reward	
	253d-e		253d-e	
	badness	κακία	virtue	ἀρετή
	crooked (asymmetrical)	σκολιός	straight in form (symmetrical)	εῖδος ὀρθός
	wantonness	ὕβρεως	honor	τιμῆς
	boasting	ἀλαζονείας	moderation	σωφροσύνης
			shame	αἰδοῦς
			truthful	ἀληθινῆς

* The cardinal virtue of wisdom (as σοφόν) occurs just after the myth at 250d.

NOTE: The earlier myths contain terms that we today might consider immoralities that harm only the self such as luxury, body attachment and pleasures, whereas, the later myths lack these in favor of actions that infringe on others' rights. Did Plato leave them out of the later myths deliberately as he departed from his earlier Puritanism (as he indeed did in the Phaedrus)? Or, can any conclusion be drawn from the use or non-use of certain terms? See note on TABLE 4 for a possible suggestion.

The next Table 4 is an inverse index of the previous Conduct and Behavior table. It is formatted to show which terms appear in more that one myth. However, for this purpose only root words are shown, generally ignoring parts of speech (e.g., pious, piously and holy are considered a single instance of the term, but piety is a separate, albeit synonymous, word)

The nominative case, or dictionary form, will be used for all subsequent inverse index tables for the earlier Greeks and the Egyptians.

TABLE 4

Conduct and Behavior that Influences The Afterlife: Plato Inverse Index
(terms as they appear in Plato's judgment myths only)

Conduct deserving reward   Myths' terms in afterlife/behavior citations

Word in Plato	Dictionary Form	Gorgias	Phaedo	Republic	Phaedrus
justly	δίκιος	x		x	x
piously	ὅσιος	x x	x	x	
truth	ἀλήθεια	x	x		x x
done own work	πράσσω	x			
no busybody	πολυπραγμονέω	x			
good	ἀγαθός	x			x
noble	καλός	x			x
virtue	ἀρετή	x	x		x
well-ordered	κόσμιος		x		
wise	φρόνιμος		x		synonym
pure	καθαρός		x		
moderate	μέτριος		x		
wisdom	φρόνησις		x		syn.
moderation	σωφροσύνη		x		x
justice	δικαιοσύνη		x		x
courage	ἀνδρεία		x		
freedom	ἐλευθερία		x		
good deeds	εὐεργεσία			x	
piety	εὐσέβεια			x	
wise	σοφός		syn.		x
philosopher	φιλοσόφος				x
lover of beauty	φιλοκάλος				x
straight in form (symmetrical)	εἶδος ὀρθός				x
honor	τιμῆς				x
shame	αἰδοῦς				x

Conduct deserving punishment[462] Myths' terms in afterlife/behavior citations

Term in Plato	Dictionary Form	Gorgias	Phaedo	Republic	Phaedrus
unjustly	ἄδικος	x x	x	x	x
godlessly	ἄθεος	x			
false oaths	ἐπίορκος	x			
lying	ψεῦδος	x			
boasting	ἀλαζονεία	x			x
arrogant power	ἐξουσία	x			
luxury	τρυφάω	x			
insolence	ὕβρις	x			x
incontinence	ἀκράτεια	x			
asymmetry	ἀσυμμετρία	x			synonym
ugliness	αἰσχρότης	x			x
impious	ἀνόσιος	x	syn.	syn.	
errors	ἁμάρτημα	x	x		
attached/body	ἐπιθυμητικός		x		
impure	ἀκάθαρτος		x		
killings	φόνος		x x	x	
sacrileges	ἱεροσυλία		x		
violence	βίαιος		x		
pleasures	ἡδονά		x		

---

462 These 'virtues' and 'vices' deal with internal character matters and on how the person has dealt with others and the gods (based on law of the universe). Absent from the list, in general, are the extremely relative types of behavior based on societal custom. Plato certainly discusses the societal norms elsewhere, but not where it counts for the salvation of one's soul. Examples of those relative societal norms are: gluttony, drunkenness, prodigality, gambling, sexual enjoyment or anything that gratifies or gains mastery over only the doer (victimless crimes). It is possible that Plato left out the more obvious, and harder to defend, societal customs in order to strengthen his case that the law was above both convention and nature. Here he is countering the φύσις vs. νόμος argument of the Sophists.

Term in Plato	Dictionary Form	Gorgias	Phaedo	Republic	Phaedrus
betrayal	προδίδωμι			x	
caused death	θάνατος			x	
to slavery	δούλειος			x	
impiety	ἀσέβεια	syn.	syn.	x	
envy	φθόνος				x
forgetfulness	λήθη				x
badness	κακία				x
crooked (asymmetrical)	σκολιός				x

F. The Question of Interpolation in Homer

The following discussion of Homeric interpolation considers the claims of modern scholars in the chronological order of their writings. At the end of this discussion I give my own thoughts on the matter of interpolation.

Thomas Day Seymour, in 1907, following the ancient doubters said: "This passage (λ 576-600) [11.576-600] has no organic connection with the story of Odysseus's visit to Hades, and cannot have been an original part of it...the sufferings of Tantalus and his associates have nothing to do with Odysseus, and are not even made out to be characteristic of the place."[463]

James Adam, in 1908, was a little less dogmatic where he comments on "the *Nekyia* of the *Odyssey*, which, though doubtless later than the bulk of the poem, represents at least a very early stage of Greek belief about the future life."[464]

However, by 1951 E.R. Dodds was declaring that "no one, I suppose, now believes that the 'great sinners' in the Odyssey are an 'Orphic interpolation'."[465] He even states that the scholar Wilamowitz had maintained this "in his rash youth, but he recanted later."[466]

Walter Burkert, in 1985, had acknowledged that there is a problem with the passage in book 11; that "lines 11.565-627 were athetized by Aristarchos and were called the 'Orphic interpolation' by Wilamowitz."[467]

Heubeck, in 1989, is insistent that the *Nekyia* is an organic part of the <u>Odyssey</u> and says that "the overall structure of the book guarantees the place of these disputed lines."[468] The Heracles passage of lines 601-27 has long been thought to be a Pisistratian addition by Onomacritus in the sixth century. Nevertheless, Heubeck argues against this position by claiming "that the poet did not wish to suppress the idea of Heracles' divine status...but was unwilling to forego the scene [of Odysseus meeting Heracles] and so attempted a compromise between the popular belief about the hero and the ei)/dwlon concept fundamental to the rest of the book."[469]

---

[463] The ancient doubters are, among others, the scholars of the Alexandrian school such as Aristophanes and Aristarchus. Seymour, Life in the Homeric Age, 468 n. 1.

[464] Adam, The Religious teachers of Greece, 58.

[465] Dodds, The Greeks and the Irrational, 137.

[466] Dodds, The Greeks and the Irrational, 158 n. 12.

[467] Burkert, Greek Religion, 427 n. 32.

[468] Heubeck and Hoekstra, A Commentary on Homer's Odyssey, 2.111.

[469] Heubeck and Hoekstra, A Commentary on Homer's Odyssey, 2.114.

J. Gwyn Griffiths, in 1991, makes note of the fact that "many scholars, including W.B. Stanford, regard the account of the judgment in the *Odyssey* as a later interpolation derived from Orphic sources."[470] Then he goes on to ask why these same scholars do not question the stories about Elysium, since they are just as 'non-Homeric'. Although making no claim as to the account's authorship, he does allow that this one reference to posthumous punishment is not Homer's normal approach to the afterlife. The passages are contrary to usual Greek ideas of Hades and Griffiths says that both the punishment of the wicked and the reward of the just appear to "have the stamp of Cretan origin, and beyond that the impress of Egyptian ideas of Heaven and Hell."[471]

Ralph Hexter,[472] writing in 1993, was adamant that the disputed lines are an interpolation and shows how much better the story would read when they are eliminated. The poem would now read:

11.563   But he [Ajax] gave no reply, and turned away, following other ghosts toward Erebos.

11.628   But I stood fast, awaiting other great souls who perished in times past.

This has the benefit of flowing nicely from one line to the next and it also eliminates the harsh dismissal of Ajax in the disputed text. It also, of course, eliminates the only real punishment scene in the Odyssey.

Timothy Gantz, also in 1993, disagreed with Dodds and and says that "the *Nekuia* (precisely that section of it most likely to be a post-Homeric addition)" is the only place in Homer that punishment of any mortals occurs.[473] Furthermore, the lines following (Od. 11.630-31) may even be an interpolation added to an interpolation as Plutarch claims in Thes. 20.2 that, according to Hereas of Megara in the 4th or 3rd cent, the Athenian tyrant Pisistratus inserted the lines in order to mention Theseus of Athens.[474]

---

[470] Griffiths, The Divine Verdict, 294.

[471] We will look at the ramifications of this statement in more detail in chapters 6, 7 and 8 on Egyptian religion. Griffiths, The Divine Verdict, 294.

[472] Ralph Hexter, A Guide to the Odyssey (New York: Vintage Books, 1993), 156-8.

[473] Timothy Gantz, Early Greek Myth (Baltimore: Johns Hopkins University Press, 1993), 130.

[474] Timothy Gantz, Early Greek Myth, 852 n. 24.

In 1995, Christine Sourvinou-Inwood agreed with Dodds concerning the authenticity of the passage in book 11. She believes it to be an organic part of the whole work, although she admits that many other scholars believe Odyssey 11.568-627 to be interpolated by the "Continuator of books 23.297ff and 24." Additionally, she does agree with the "overwhelming majority of scholars" that book 24 is a later addition; "a Continuation (sic) written in the archaic period."[475]

I would argue that the disputed lines in book 11 are an interpolation not only because of the many reasons given by many scholars holding that view, but for three additional reasons. First, I suggest that they are an interpolation based on a textual analysis of the disputed passages. In the non-disputed text, all mentions of dead persons are always referenced as 'the ghost of X' (e.g., ψυχὴ Θηβαίου Τειρεσίαο). However, in the disputed passages, the dead are simply spoken of as 'X', omitting the qualifier, 'ghost of'. This may be a minor point of textual analysis, but it indicates a likelihood that another hand could be at work in writing these lines. This same argument may be made for the likewise disputed catalogue of heroines in lines 225-332. There, just as in the 'sinners' passages, the heroine is referenced by name only, omitting the qualification, 'ghost of' the heroine. This could indicate that the same hand may have been involved in both of the alleged interpolations.

A second argument for accepting these lines as an interpolation is that they simply conflict with the rest of the Homeric afterlife belief, which would certainly show that they represent a different stratum of religious beliefs.[476]

---

[475] Sourvinou-Inwood claims that the 'shades' of book 24 "are intermediate chronologically between the Homeric and the fifth-century ones" (Christine Sourvinou-Inwood, 'Reading' Greek Death [Oxford: Clarendon Press, 1995], 70, 84, 106); Also see idem, "To die and Enter the House of Hades: Homer, Before and After," in Mirrors of Mortality, ed. Joachim Whaley (Rochester: Stanhope Press, 1981), 16.

[476] One question is, would a final Homer redactor have accepted all these vastly varying and contradictory religious strata? The final redactor obviously did, since he could not just throw out centuries of well-known texts in order to promote his later views. A later promoter would have to incorporate his new views beside the old ones. The question is, could the same poet simultaneously hold to an afterlife judgment while also rejecting any beneficial afterlife elsewhere in his own writings? I think not. However, one should remain open to the possibility that this stratum may actually be earlier rather than later than the rest of Homer; that it is an echo of a remote forgotten time.

My final argument is that even his slightly later contemporary, Hesiod, does not indicate any such afterlife beliefs as is found in the Od. books 11 and 24. If Homer had already known of the afterlife beliefs then they should have been known to Hesiod also.[477]

---

[477] However, it could have been just that Hesiod's peasant social background kept him from acknowledging such a belief. This notion would make my final argument less viable. These considerations of chronology, social background and even geographical location will be explored further in the next chapter.

G. *TABLE 5: Attributes and Features of the Homeric Soul*

Attributes and Features of the Homeric[478] Soul

Attribute in Plato	Homer
allows death when separated from body	yes
motivates the body	yes
principle of life	yes
immortal	something survives death
immaterial	no
powers of mind and consciousness	the nous
locus of ethics	no
never destroyed	no
reincarnated	no
been born often	no
pre-natally sees the Forms	no
anamnesis from pre-natal existence	no
chooses its next life	no
dwells in its companion star	no
like the invisible	no
consists of mortal and immortal parts	no
not a harmony	n/a
soma in sema	no
a unity	no
tripartite (rational, appetitive, spirited)	multiple (nous, thymos, psyche)
divine	no
similar to Forms	no
always in motion	no
fallen to earth	no
covered in human form	yes
contains Titanic substance	no

---

[478] This tabular format is being used to compare the Homeric multiple souls with Plato's ψύχη.

H. Passages from Greek Authors Concerning the Afterlife

Chapter 2: Homer

Iliad 3.276
Father Zeus…and you who under the earth take vengeance on dead men, whoever among them has sworn to **falsehood**,[479] you shall be witnesses, to guard the **oaths of fidelity**.

Iliad 13.415
Asios lies not now all unavenged. I think rather as he goes down to Hades of the Gates, the strong one, he will be cheerful at heart, since I have sent him an escort.

Iliad 19.256
Let Zeus first be my witness…and Earth, and Helios the Sun, and the Furies, who underground avenge dead men, when any man has **sworn to falsehood**.

Iliad 23.100
Even in the house of Hades there is left something, a soul and an image, but there is no real heart of life in it.

Iliad 23.178
Good-bye, Patroklos. I hail you even in the house of the death god.

Odyssey 4.561
[Menelaus is to be sent to Elysium]

Odyssey 11.90
Now came the soul of Tiresias the Theban, holding a staff of gold, and he knew who I was, and spoke to me.

Odyssey 11.300
Kastor, breaker of horses, and the strong boxer, Polydeukes. The life-giving earth holds both of them, yet they are still living, and, even underneath the earth,

---

[479] Conduct and Behavior terms are emphasized by bold type.

enjoying the **honor** of Zeus, they live still every other day; on the next day they are dead, but they are given <u>honor</u> even as the gods are. [also see <u>Il</u>. 3.235].

<u>Odyssey</u> 11.476
    To Hades place, where the senseless dead men dwell, mere imitations of perished mortals.

<u>Odyssey</u> 11.576
    [Tityos, Tantalus and Sisyphus suffering in Hades.]

<u>Odyssey</u> 11.601
    [Heracles' phantom in Hades, himself among the immortal gods].

<u>Odyssey</u> 23.333
    Kalypso who detained him [Odysseus] with her, desiring that he should be her husband, in her hollow caverns, and she took care of him and told him that she would make him ageless all his days, and immortal.

<u>Odyssey</u> 24.4
    [Hermes leads the spirits, they follow gibbering].

<u>Odyssey</u> 24.98
    Now as the spirits were conversing thus with each other, there came approaching them [Achilles and Agamemnon] the courier Argeiphontes, leading down the souls of the suitors killed by Odysseus. These two in wonderment went up to them as they saw them.

Chapter 3: From Homer to the Orphic Tablets

Hesiod

<u>Works and Days</u> 166
    But when earth had covered this generation also, Zeus the son of Cronos made yet another, the fourth, upon the fruitful earth, which was **nobler** and more **righteous**, a god-like race of hero-men who are called demi-gods, the race before our own, throughout the boundless earth. Grim war and dread battle destroyed a part of them, some in the land of Cadmus at seven-gated Thebes when they fought for the flocks of Oedipus, and some, when it had brought them in ships

over the great sea gulf to Troy for rich-haired Helen's sake: there death's end enshrouded a part of them. But to the others father Zeus the son of Cronos gave a living and an abode apart from men, and made them dwell at the ends of earth. And they live untouched by sorrow in the islands of the blessed along the shore of deep-swirling Ocean, happy heroes for whom the grain-giving earth bears honey-sweet fruit flourishing thrice a year, far from the deathless gods, and Cronos rules over them; for the father of men and gods released him from his bonds. And these last equally have **honor** and glory.

And again far-seeing Zeus made yet another generation, the fifth, of men who are upon the bounteous earth.

Heraclitus of Ephesus

Fragments

(21) [the dead are awake and the living sleep]

(24-5) Gods and men **honor** those who are slain in battle. Greater deaths win greater portions.

(26) Man kindles a light for himself in the night-time, when he has died but is alive. The sleeper, whose vision has been put out, lights up from the dead; he that is awake lights up from the sleeping.

(27) There awaits men when they die such things as they look not for nor dream of.

(28) The most esteemed of them knows but fancies, and holds fast to them, yet of a **truth justice** shall overtake the artificers of **lies** and the **false witnesses**.

(62) Mortals are immortals and immortals are mortals, the one living the others' death and dying the others' life.

(63)…that they rise up and become the wakeful guardians of the quick and dead.

(66) [the world judged in fire]

(88) And it is the same thine in us that is quick and dead, awake and asleep, young and old; the former are shifted and become the latter, and the latter in turn are shifted and become the former.

(89) The waking have one common world, but the sleeping turn aside each into a world of his own.

Empedocles of Acragas

Fragments

(15) A man who is wise in such matters would never surmise in his heart that as long as mortals live what they call their life, so long they are, and suffer good and ill; while before they were formed and after they have been dissolved they are just nothing at all.

(112) Friends, that inhabit the great town looking down on the yellow rock of Acragas, up by the citadel, busy in **goodly works**, harbors of **honor for the stranger**, men **unskilled in meanness**, all hail. I go about among you an immortal god, no mortal now, **honored** among all as is meet, crowned with fillets and flowery garlands.

(115) There is an oracle of Necessity, an ancient ordinance of the gods, eternal and sealed fast by broad oaths, that whenever one of the daemons, whose portion is length of days, **has sinfully polluted his hands with blood, or followed strife and forsworn himself,** he must wander thrice ten thousand seasons from the abodes of the blessed, being born throughout the time in all manners of mortal forms, changing one toilsome path of life for another…One of these I now am, an exile and a wanderer from the gods, for that I put my trust in insensate strife.

(117) For I have been ere now a boy and a girl, a bush and a bird and a dumb fish in the sea.

(118) I wept and I wailed when I saw the unfamiliar land.

(119) From what **honor**, from what a height of bliss have I fallen to go about among mortals here on earth.

(121) [now in a joyless place].

(124) [earth is the scene of sorrow]

(126)…clothing them with a strange garment of flesh.

(146) But, at the last, they appear among mortal men as prophets, song-writers, physicians, and princes; and thence they rise up as gods exalted in **honor**, sharing the hearth of the other gods and the same table, free from human woes, safe from destiny, and incapable of hurt.

Pindar

Olympian 2.5

Theron…must be proclaimed—a man **just in his regard for guests**, bulwark of Akragas, and foremost upholder of the city.

Olympian 2.16

Once deeds are done, whether in **justice** or **contrary to it**, not even Time, the father of all, could undo their outcome…under the force of noble joys the pain dies and its malignancy is suppressed, whenever divine Fate sends happiness towering upwards. This saying befits of Kadmos' fair-throned daughters who suffered greatly; but grievous sorrow subsides in the face of greater blessings. Long-haired Semele lives among the Olympians after dying in the roar of a thunderbolt; Pallas loves her ever and father Zeus.

Olympian 2.28

They say, too, that in the sea, Ino has been granted an immortal life.

Olympian 2.53

Truly, wealth embellished with **virtues** provides fit occasion for various achievements by supporting a profound and questing ambition; it is a conspicuous lodestar, the truest light for a man. If one has it and knows the future, that the helpless spirits of those who have died on earth immediately pay the penalty— and upon **sins** committed here in Zeus' realm, a judge beneath the earth pronounces sentence with hateful necessity; and in equal days, good men receive a life of less toil, for they do not vex the earth or the water of the sea with the strength of their hands to earn a paltry living. No, in company with the **honored** gods, those who joyfully **kept their oaths** spend a tearless existence, whereas the others endure pain too terrible to behold.

But those with the **courage** to have lived three times in either realm, while keeping their souls free from all **unjust deeds,** travel the road of Zeus to the tower of Kronus, where ocean breezes blow round the Isle of the Blessed, and flowers of gold are ablaze, some from radiant trees on land, while the water nurtures others; with these they weave garlands for their hands and crowns for their heads, in obedience to the **just** counsels of Rhadamanthys, whom the great father keeps ever seated at his side, the husband of Rhea, she who has the highest throne of all. Peleus and Kadmos are numbered among them, and Achilles too, whom his mother brought, after she had persuaded the heart of Zeus with her entreaties.

Nemean 10.54
[The fate of the Dioscuri].

Fragment 129-30
For them [the **pious**] shines the might of the sun below during the nighttime up here...some take delight in horses and exercises...complete happiness blooms and flourishes. [But, for the **unholy**,] From there sluggish rivers of gloomy night belch forth an endless darkness.

Fragment 131
The body of all men is subject to overpowering death, but a living image of life still remains, for it alone is from the gods. It slumbers while the limbs are active, but to men as they sleep, in many dreams it reveals and approaching decision of things pleasant or distressful.

Fragment 133
But, for those from whom Persephone accepts requital for the ancient grief, in the ninth year she returns their souls to the upper sunlight; from them arise proud kings and men who are swift in strength and greatest in **wisdom**, and for the rest of time, they are called **sacred** heroes by men. [Quoted in Meno 81b.]

Fragment 137
Blessed is he who **sees them** [**mysteries**] and goes beneath the earth; he knows the end of life and knows its Zeus-given beginning [of a new life?].

Fragment 214
[For beautifully, O Socrates, did he [Pindar] say that whoever lives his life **justly** and **piously**,] with him lives sweet Hope, heart-fostering nurse of old age, which most of all steers mortals' much-veering judgment.

Chapter 4: The Dramatists

Aeschylus

Choephori 324
Chorus
My child, the fire's ravening jaw does not overwhelm the wits of the dead man, but afterwards he reveals what stirs him. The **murdered** man has his dirge; the

guilty man is revealed. Justified lament for fathers and for parents, when raised loud and strong, makes its search everywhere.

Eumenides 95
[Clytemnestra suffers shame and verbal abuse in the underworld.]

Eumenides 175
That man shall never be free; though he flee beneath the earth, he shall never gain his liberty. He shall come stained with the guilt of **murder**.

Eumenides 255
Look everywhere, so that the **matricide** will not escape by secret flight, with his debt unpaid!

Yes, here he is again with a defense; his arms twisted around the image of the immortal goddess, he wishes to be tried for his debt. But that is not possible; a mother's blood upon the earth is hard to recover—alas, the liquid poured on the ground is gone.

But you must allow me in return to suck the red blood from your living limbs. May I feed on you—a gruesome drink! I will wither you alive and drag you down, so that you pay atonement for your murdered mother's agony.

Eumenides 267
And if any other mortal who has **wronged a god or a stranger**, with **impious** action, **or his dear parents**, you shall see how each has the reward **Justice** ordains. For Hades is mighty in holding mortals to account below the earth, and with mind that records them in its tablets he surveys all things.

Eumenides 338
That after mortals to whom has come wanton **murder** of their own, I shall follow, until they descend below the earth; and after death no wide liberty is theirs.

Eumenides 387
...mindfull of **wrongs**...and will punish sighted and sightless alike in the sunless slime.

Eumenides 441
[the **hubris** of Ixion]

<u>Persians</u> 620

But friends, sing over these libations to the dead songs of good omen, and conjure up the Spirit of Darius.

<u>Persians</u> 640

O Earth, and you other rulers of those who dwell in the nether world, ensure, I implore, that the glorious spirit, the god of the Persians, whom Susa bore, may quit his abode. Send to the upper world him the likes of whom the Persian earth has never entombed.

<u>Persians</u> 673-827

[The raising of the ghost of Darius. These passages contain **many conduct and behavior words** in the context of an afterlife scenario].

<u>Suppliant Maidens</u> 158

Yet, if she will not, we, a dark, sun-burned race, with suppliant boughs will invoke the underworld Zeus, Zeus the great host of the dead; for if the gods of Olympus hear us not, we will hang ourselves.

<u>Suppliant Maidens</u> 225

And one who **preys** upon a girl against her will, and mine, can he be cleansed? Never!

Even after death there is no flight for him: he shall be charged for an **unnatural act**, and **wrong** shall be avenged. Rumor says there is another Zeus who sits in Hades and chars final vengeance into all who have worn out their earthly lives. [or, holds a last **judgment** upon **misdeeds**].

<u>Suppliant Maidens</u> 413

King

Surely there is need of deep and salutary counsel; need for a keen-sighted eye, not confused, to descend, like some diver, into the depths; that to the state above all things this matter may not work mischief, but may end well for us; that strife may not seize you for its prize, **nor yet that we surrender you from these seats of sanctuary**, and bring upon ourselves the dire, abiding **vengeance of the all-destroying god**, who, **even in the realm of Death, does not set his victim free**…Take counsel, and, as is your sacred duty, prove yourself to our sacred champion. Do **not betray the fugitive** who has been **impiously** cast out.

Sophocles

<u>Fragment</u> 837

Thrice blessed are those mortals who have witnessed these **initiation** rites and departed to Hades. For it is permitted to them alone to live there, while the rest fare badly in all things.

<u>Antigone</u> 74

Antigone

I will bury him—it would honor me to die while doing that. I shall rest with him, loved one with loved one, a **pious** criminal. For the time is greater that I must serve the dead than the living, since in that world I will rest forever [An alt. trans: for there will be a longer span of time for me to please those below than there will be to please those here.] But if you so choose, continue to dishonor what the gods in **honor** have established...

If you mean that, you will have my hatred, and you will be subject to punishment as the enemy of the dead. But leave me and the foolish plan I have authored to suffer this terrible thing, for I will not suffer anything so terrible that my death will lack honor.

<u>Antigone</u> 449

Creon

And even so you dared overstep that law?

Antigone

Yes, since it was not Zeus that published me that edict, and since not of that kind are the laws which **Justice** who dwells with the gods below established among men. Nor did I think that your decrees were of such force, that a mortal could override the **unwritten and unfailing statutes given us by the gods**. For their life is not of today or yesterday, but for all time, and no man knows when they were first put forth. Not for fear of any man's pride was I about to owe a penalty to the gods for breaking these. Die I must, that I knew well (how could I not?). That is true even without your edicts. But if I am to die before my time, I count that a gain. When anyone lives as I do, surrounded by evils, how can he not carry off gain by dying?

<u>Antigone</u> 891

Antigone

Tomb, bridal-chamber, deep-dug eternal prison where I go to find my own, whom in the greatest numbers destruction has seized and Persephone has welcomed among the dead! Last of them all and in by far the most shameful circumstances, I will descend, even before the fated term of my life is spent. But I cherish strong hopes that I will arrive welcome to my father, and pleasant to you, Mother, and welcome, dear brother, to you. For, when each of you died, with my own hands I washed and dressed you and poured drink-offerings at your graves. But now, Polyneices, it is for **tending your corpse** that I win such reward as this. And yet I **honored** you **rightly**, as the **wise** understand.

Electra 244

For if the dead man is to lie there as earth nothingness, unhappy one, and they are not to pay the penalty, murdered in their turn, that would be the end of reverence and the piety of all mortals.

Electra 236
Electra

But what limit has nature begot for my affliction? Tell me, how can it be **right** to **neglect the dead**? Has such a seed been sown in any mortal? May I never have such men's esteem; never, when I am close to prosperity, may I dwell in ease, hindering the wings of shrill lamentation so as to deprive my begetter of his honors! For if the dead is to lie a wretch, merely dust and nothingness, while his slayers do not pay back to him blood for blood in penalty, then **shame** and **reverence** will vanish from all humanity.

Electra 417

They say that she was once more in company with your father and mine, who had come to the world of light.

Electra 442
Electra

Consider whether you believe that the dead in his tomb will welcome this tribute with affection towards her, by whose hand he died dishonored and was mutilated like an enemy? She, who, as if to wash herself clean, wiped off the bloodstains on his head? Surely you do not believe that your bringing these things will absolve her of the **murder**?

Electra 453

Then fall down and pray that he himself may come in **kindness** to us from the world below, a helper against our enemies; and that young Orestes may live to set his foot upon our enemies in superior might, so that hereafter we may crown our father's tomb with wealthier hands than those with which we honor him now.

I think, yes, I think that he too had some part in sending her these appalling dreams. Still, sister, do yourself this service and help me, and him, too, that most beloved of all men, who rests in Hades' domain, our shared father. The girl's words are **pious**; and if you are **wise**...

Electra 965
Electra

But if you will follow my plans, first you will win praise for **piety** from our dead father below, and from our brother, too; next, you shall be called hereafter **free**, just as you were born, and shall find a worthy marriage. For **noble** natures draw the gaze of all...

At festivals, and wherever the citizenry is assembled, let these two be honored by all men for their **manly courage**. Thus will every one speak of us, so that in life and in death our glory shall not fail.

Come, dear sister, be persuaded! Toil with our father, share the burden of your brother, put an end to my troubles and an end to yours, keeping in mind that a **shameful** life brings **shame** upon the **noble-born**.

Oedipus Tyrannus 1370

With what eyes could I have faced my father in the house of the dead, or my poor mother.

Oedipus Colonus 1645

[The apotheosis of Oedipus]

Philoctetes 1140

For **piety** dies not with men; in their life and in their death, it is immortal.

Euripides

Alcestis 357

...wait for me, then, in that place, till I die, and make ready the room where you will live with me.

<u>Alcestis</u> 742
Chorus-Leader

Alas, alas! O resolute in **courage**, heart **noble** and **generous**, farewell! May Hermes of the Underworld and Hades receive you kindly! And if in that place the **good** have any advantage, may you have a share in it and sit as attendant beside Hades' bride!

<u>Bacchae</u> 1338
Dionysus speaking to Cadmus

...changing your form, you will become a dragon, and your wife, Harmonia, Ares' daughter, whom you though mortal held in marriage, will be turned into a beast, and will receive in exchange the form of a serpent...but Ares will protect you and Harmonia and will settle your life in the land of the blessed.

That is what I, Dionysus, born not from a mortal father, but from Zeus, say. And if you had known how to be **wise** when you did not wish to be, you would have acquired Zeus' son as an ally, and would now be happy.
Kadmos

Dionysus, we beseech you, we have acted **injustly**.
Dionysus

You have learned it too late; you did not know it when you should have.
Kadmos

Now we know, but you go too far against us.
Dionysus

Yes, for I, a god by birth, was **insulted** by you.
Kadmos

Gods should not resemble mortals in their anger.
Dionysus

My father Zeus approved this long ago.
Agave

Alas! A miserable exile has been decreed for us, old man.
Dionysus

Why then do you delay what must necessarily be?
Kadmos

Child, what a terrible disaster we have all come to—unhappy you, your sisters, and unhappy me. I shall reach a foreign land as an aged immigrant. Still it is foretold that I shall bring into Hellas a motley barbarian army. Leading their spears, I, having the fierce nature of a serpent, will bring my wife Harmonia, daughter of Ares, to the altars and tombs of Hellas. I will neither rest from my troubles in my misery, nor will I sail over the downward flowing Acheron and be at peace.

<u>Helen</u> 1014
Theonoe

My nature and my inclination lean towards **piety**; and I respect myself, and I would not **defile** my father's fame, or gratify my brother at the cost of seeming infamous. There is a great temple of **justice** in my nature; and having this heritage from Nereus, I will try to keep it, Menelaos...

For truly there is retribution for these things, both among the dead and among all men living. The mind of the dead does not live, yet it has eternal thought as it falls into eternal ether...

And you, my own dead father, never, as far as I have strength, shall you be called **impious** instead of **pious**.

<u>Helen</u> 1676
Dioscouri

And it is destined by the gods that the wanderer Menelaos will dwell in the islands of the blessed; for deities do not hate the **well-born**, but the sufferings of the multitude are greater.

<u>Rhesus</u> 962
Hector

I knew it; it needed no seer to say that he had perished by the arts of Odysseus. Now I, when I saw the Hellene army camped in my land, of course would not hesitate to send heralds to my friends, bidding them come and help my country; and so I sent, and he as in duty bound came to share my toils. I do not at all rejoice to see him dead. And now I am ready to raise a tomb for him and burn at his pyre great store of fine raiment; for he came as a friend and in sorrow he is going away.
Muse

He shall not go into earth's dark soil; so earnest a prayer will I address to the bride of the nether world, the daughter of the goddess Demeter, giver of increase, to release his soul; and, debtor as she is to me, show that she honors the friends of Orpheus. And to me for the rest of time he will be as one who is dead and does not see the light; for never again will he meet me or see his mother; but he will lie hidden in a cavern of the land with veins of silver, restored to life, a deified man, just as the prophet of Bacchus dwelt in a grotto beneath Pangaeus, a god whom his votaries honored.

Suppliants 532

…let soul release to air, body to earth…Their bodies have melted into ash and fire, to the Underworld they have flown.

Suppliants 1138

The boundless air now wraps them round, turned to ashes by the flame; they have winged their flight to Hades.

Frag 484

[Man is a fallen creature but contains a divine spark.]

Frag 852

A man who **reverences his parents** in life is, while both **alive and dead, dear to the gods.**

Aristophanes

Frogs 145

Dionysus

Don't frighten me or make me scared. You won't turn me aside.

Heracles

And then a vast sea of mud and ever-flowing dung, in which there lies anyone who has ever, say, **broken the laws of hospitality**, or slyly **grabbed back a rent-boy's money** while having it with him, or **struck his mother**, or **given his father a sock in the jaw**, or sworn a **perjured oath**, or had someone copy out a speech by Morsimus.

Frogs 274

[**Father-beaters** and **perjurers** punished in the afterlife]

Frogs 354

CHORUS-LEADER:

Let all speak fair, and let these stand out of way of our dances whoever is unfamiliar with words such as these—or has thoughts that are **not clean**—or has not seen or danced in the secret rites of the true-bred Muses nor been initiated in the Bacchic verbal mysteries of bull-devouring Cratinus—or delights in words of **buffoonery** from men who choose the wrong time to behave thus—or does not endeavor to resolve the internal **strife** that threatens us and is **not peaceable** towards other citizens, but **stirs it up and fans its flame** out of a desire for private advantage—or is an office-holder who takes **bribes** to harm the city when it's struggling in heavy seas—or **betrays** a fort or a fleet—or is a damnable five-per-cent-collector like Thorycion who **exports contraband [smuggles]** from Aegina, sending oarport-leathers, flax and pitch across to Epidaurus—or induces anyone to **supply money for our adversaries' navy**—or is a soloist in cyclic choral performances who **shits on the offerings to Hecate [sacrilege]**—or is a politician who goes and nibbles away at the fees of poets after having been satirized in the course of the ancestral rites of Dionysus. To these I proclaim, and again I proclaim the ban, and again a third time do I proclaim the ban, that they stand out of the way of the initiates' dances, but do you awaken the voice of song and begin the all-night revels which befit this our festival.

Frogs 454

For on us alone do the sun
and the daylight shine,
all of us who are **initiated**
and who led a **righteous [eu/sebh=]**
way of life towards strangers
and towards ordinary folk.

Peace 374

Please lend me a sucking-pig; I must get initiated before I die.

Peace 832

That when we die we become stars in the sky.

I. *TABLE 6: Instances in Homer of Important Conduct and Behavior not Associated with an Afterlife*

The following are a sampling of some passages that deal with Homeric concepts of conduct and behavior (some of which will be very important for Plato) but do not link such behavior to an afterlife:

Cardinal virtues:

Justice—not named as dikaiosune but is there in concept. See Od 2.282f, 3.132f where one is prudent (νοήμωνες) and just (δίκαιοι). Also Od. 11.571.

Courage—no andreia term, but bravery (aristos, agathos) is paramount.

Wisdom—Il. 1.258, 2.202, 2.273, 9.53.

Temperance—Soaphrosune at Od. 23.13, 30. Il. 9.255.

Holiness—do not be impious Od. 5.447.

Unwritten laws of the gods:

Honor parents Od 9.270.

Respect stranger and suppliant Od. 14.404; Od. 6.207-8, 9.269-71, 14.57-8, 14.283-4, Od. 5.447.

At Od. 14.284   Zeus, the stranger's god, indignant at evildoers—here not in the afterlife.

Hospitality Od. 14.158, 1.119, 4.3ff.

At Il. 4.160   Zeus punishes oath breakers now or future generations— here, not in the afterlife. Cf. Hesiod Works 283ff and many later Greek writers holding this view

But hubris against non-suppliant may not be rewarded Od 3.205ff.

At Od 17.484-7   the gods behold the violence and righteousness of men.

At Il 9.457   Zeus of the netherworld and Persephone along with the Erinyes fulfill a father's curse.

At Il 16.387 -   punishment for crooked judgments in this life.

At <u>Od</u> 8.329 -   ill deeds do not win out, god pays back good.

At <u>Od</u> 14.83 -   gods reward justice and virtuous action—here, not in the afterlife.

At <u>Od</u> 23.62 -   gods slay for insolence—here, not in afterlife.

At <u>Il</u>. 18.98 -   shame.

J. Egyptian Chronological Summary Chart

<u>Chronology of Times and Issues of Importance to this Inquiry</u>[480]

Period	Date	Event
<u>Paleolithic</u>	before 10,000 BCE	
<u>Neolithic or Pre-Dynastic</u>	4800-3100 or 3000	
Badarian	4800-4200	- grave goods, buried facing west
Naquada I	4200-3700	
Naquada II/III or Gerzean	3700-3000*	
Archaic, Thinite or <u>Early Dynastic</u>	3000-2705*	
1st Dynasty Narmer-Menes		
		- Narmer Palette
Djer		- *ka* inscriptions
		- *akh* inscriptions
Djet		
2nd Dynasty		
Reneb		- cult of sun-god established
<u>Old Kingdom</u>	2705-2180*	
3rd Dynasty	2705-2640*	
Djoser		- first pyramid built
4th Dynasty	2640-2520*	
Sneferu		
Khufu		- Great Pyramid built
Djedefre		- 1st king called 'son of Re'

---

[480] Major dates marked with an "*" are from Erik Hornung, Idea into Image: Essays on Ancient Egyptian Thought, 187-188; The Ancient Egyptian Books of the Afterlife, xxi-xxii. Other dates are from: D'Aria, Mummies and Magic, 9.

Khafra
Menkaura
5th Dynasty   2520-2360*

                                                  - nobles' autobiographies

Unas
                                                  - Henku inscription
                                                  - Hetepherakhet inscription

                                                  - Pyramid Texts (2350?-2180?)
                                                  - *ba* first noted

6th Dynasty   2360-2195*

                                                  - Ptahhotep instruction
                                                  - Kagemni instruction

Teti
Pepy I
Merenra

                                                  - early Coffin Texts prototypes
                                                  - Harkhuf inscription

Pepy II
7/8 Dynasties
Ibi

                                                  - last of the Pyramid Texts

1st Inter. Period   2180-1987*

9/10 Dynasties
Merikare

                                                  - Coffin Texts (after 2200?)

Middle Kingdom   1987-1640*

11th Dynasty   1987-1938*
12th Dynasty   1938-1759*
13th Dynasty   1759-1640*

                                                  - heart scarab with Book of the
                                                    Dead's spell 30

2nd Inter. Period   1640-1530*

14-17 Dyn.

                                                  - Hyksos rule Egypt

<u>New Kingdom</u>	1540-1075*	
18th Dynasty	1540-1292*	
		- classical judgment scene
Akhenaten		- failed attempt at monotheism
Tutankamun		
19th Dynasty	1292-1190*	
		- devourer of dead added to judgment scene
		- <u>Papyrus of Ani</u>
Ramses II		
20th Dynasty	1190-1075*	
Ramses III-XI		
<u>3rd Inter. Period</u>	1075-664*	
<u>Late Period</u>	664-332*	
<u>Greek Period</u>	332-30*	
<u>Roman Period</u>	30-642*	

K. _TABLE 7:_ Conduct and Behavior that Influences the Afterlife: Greek Authors

Conduct and Behavior that Influences The Afterlife: Greek Authors Inverse Index (terms as they appear in Plato's judgment myths only)[481]

Conduct deserving reward   Other Greek writers in afterlife/behavior citations

Term in Plato	Dictionary Form	Homer	Heracl.	Emp.	Pind.	Aesch.	Soph.	Eur.	Aris.
justly	δίκιος				x	x		x	
piously	ὅσιος				x		x	x	
truth	ἀλήθεια		x						
done own work	πράσσω								
no busybody	πολυπραγμονέω								
good	ἀγαθός							x	
noble	καλός						x	x	
virtue	ἀρετή				x				
well-ordered	κόσμιος								
wise	φρόνιμος						x	x	
pure	καθαρός								x
moderate	μέτριος								
wisdom	φρόνησις				x				
moderation	σωφροσύνη								
justice	δικαιοσύνη	x			x		x	x	x
courage	ἀνδρεία	x			x		x	x	
freedom	ἐλευθερία							x	
good deeds	εὐεργεσία			x			x	x	
piety	εὐσέβεια					x	x	x	x
philosopher	φιλοσόφος								
lover of beauty	φιλοκάλος							x	
symmetrical	ὀρθός								
honor	τιμῆς	x	x	x	x	x	x	x	
shame	αἰδοῦς						x		

---

481 These terms appear in the four myths of Plato and are counted for the other Greek authors only if they appear in passages that allude to a reward or punishment in some form of an afterlife. Synonymous concepts are also included.

Conduct deserving punishment   Other Greek writers in afterlife/behavior citations

Term in Plato	Dictionary Form	Homer	Heracl.	Emp.	Pind.	Aesch.	Soph.	Eur.	Aris.
unjustly	ἄδικος				x			x	x
godlessly	ἄθεος								
false oaths	ἐπίορκος	x	x	x	x				x
lying	ψεῦδος		x						
boasting	ἀλαζονεία					x			
arrogant power	ἐξουσία								
luxury	τρυφάω								
insolence	ὕβρις				x	x		x	
incontinence	ἀκράτεια								
asymmetry	ἀσυμμετρία								
ugliness	αἰσχρότης								
impious	ἀνόσιος					x	x		
errors	ἁμάρτημα			x	x	x	x		
attached/body	ἐπιθυμητικός								
impure	ἀκάθαρτος								
killings	φόνος			x		x	x	x	
sacrileges	ἱεροσυλία					x		x	x
violence	βίαιος			x					x
pleasures	ἡδονά								
betrayal	προδίδωμι					x			x
caused death	θάνατος			x		x		x	
to slavery	δούλειος								
impiety	ἀσέβεια				x	x			
envy	φθόνος								
forgetfulness	λήθη								
badness	κακία								
crooked (asymmetrical)	σκολιός								

L. *TABLE 8:* *Synopsis of Scholars' Conclusions Concerning the Dating of the Egyptian Judgment of the Dead*

Synopsis of Scholars' Conclusions Concerning the Dating of the Egyptian Judgment of the Dead

AUTHOR	DATE OF PUBLICATIONS REVIEWED		Comment:
Favor Post-OLD KINGDOM:		J/G*	Comment:
Spiegel	1935, 53	-	1st Intermediate Period
Wilson	1951	-	not before Merikare
Anthes	1961	-	in Instruction of Merikare
Yoyotte	1961, 88	-	traces in 5&6th Dynasty, but multiple aspect in 9&10th
Assman	1989	-	end of 3rd millennium
Quirke	1992	J/G	judicial in Coffin Texts, gen. in 2nd Intermediate Period (c. 1600)
Hornung	1971, 89, 95	J/G	judicial in Pyramid Texts, gen. after the end of the Old Kingdom
Favor OLD KINGDOM Dating:			
Erman	1885	-	evolution complete by time of Pyramid Texts
Petrie	1898	-	conscience in 5th dynasty relate to BOD
Moret	1927	-	by king Unas in 5th dynasty
Breasted	1912, 33	-	late 5th dynasty
Junker	1949	G	general judgment is in Pyramid Texts
Morenz	1960	G	general judgment traced to Ptahhotep
Zandee	1960	J	in 5th dynasty, but always judicial
Brandon	1962, 67	J	in Pyramid Texts, but judicial
Griffiths	1960, 75, 80, 82, 83, 88, 91	J/G	judicial in Pyramid Texts, gen. in Ptahhotep
Grieshammer	1970	J/G	judicial in Old Kingdom, gen. from Ptahhotep
Lichtheim	1973, 76, 80	-	catalog of virtues in 5th dynasty
Faulkner	1980, 93	-	in Pyramid Texts, king exempt, others not exempt from judgment
Baines	1991	J	concept started in Old Kingdom, but judicial

*Note: Scholar claims that the judgment is: J = Judicial; G = General; or - = either not specified or opinion not ascertained.

M. *TABLE 9:* *Attributes and Features of the Egyptian Soul*

Attributes and Features of the Egyptian[482] Soul

Attribute in Plato	Egypt
allows death when separated from body	n/a
motivates the body	n/a
principle of life	n/a
immortal	yes
immaterial	no
powers of mind and consciousness	n/a
locus of ethics	n/a
never destroyed	yes
reincarnated	no
been born often	no
pre-natally sees the Forms	no
anamnesis from pre-natal existence	no
chooses its next life	no
dwells in its companion star	yes
like the invisible	no
consists of mortal and immortal parts	all are immortal
not a harmony	n/a
soma in sema	no
a unity	no
tripartite (rational, appetitive, spirited	multiple (ba, ka, akh)
divine	yes
similar to Forms	no
always in motion	no
fallen to earth	no
covered in human form	no
contains Titanic substance	no

---

[482] This tabular format is being used to compare the Egyptian multiple personality elements with Plato's ψύχη.

N. Passages[483] from Egyptian Texts Concerning the Afterlife

Old Kingdom Texts

Pyramid Texts

Pyramid Text 152

O Re-Atum, this King comes to you, an imperishable spirit [*akh*]…May you traverse the sky…

Pyramid Text 167

Atum, this thy son is here,
Osiris, whom thou hast preserved alive—he lives!
He lives—this Unas lives!
He is not dead, this Unas is not dead:
he is not gone down, this Unas has not gone down: he has not been judged, this Unas has not been judged.
He judges—this Unas judges!

Pyramid Text 250

I come to you, O Nut…I have left Horus behind me, my wings have grown into those of a falcon…my soul [*ba*] has brought me…

Pyramid Text 251

Open up your place in the sky among the stars of the sky, for you are the Lone Star, the companion of Hu; look down on Osiris when he governs the spirits, for you [the king] stand far off from him, you are not among them [the other people's spirits] and you shall not be among them.

---

483 This section corresponds to the similar one from the Greek authors in Appendix H. Note the contrast between this and the Greek entries. In Greece, the references to an afterlife are rare, whereas, in Egypt, almost all passages deal with an afterlife. Thus, this appendix contains passages that are simply representative of the vast volume of available ones.

Pyramid Text 309

The King is bound for the sky, on the wind, on the wind! He will not be excluded, and there will be no session on him in the Tribunal of the God, for the King is unique, the eldest of the gods.

Pyramid Text 316

O Geb, Bull of Nut,
A Horus is Unas, the heir of his father.
Unas is he who went and came back,
The fourth of four gods
Who have brought the water, who have made a purification,
Who jubilates over the strength of their fathers.
* **He wishes to be justified [*maa kheru*]**[484]
In what [through that] he has done.
Unas, a small orphan (tefen),
Went to the law with his sister (Tefnet).
The Two Truths judged, *
While Shu was a witness.
The Two Truths have decreed
That the thrones of Geb should come to him
And that he should raise himself to what he wanted.

* Or an alternate translation has:

He wishes to be just in voice by his deeds.
Tefen and Tefnet have judged Unas;
…
Inasmuch as the Two Justices have given the verdict;
He has taken possession of the thrones of Geb, and he has raised himself there where he wished. Gathering together his flesh which was in the tomb, he joins himself to those who are in Nun, he brings the sayings of Helioplolis to fulfillment.
So Unas goes out this day, in the just form of a living Akh.

---

[484] Conduct and Behavior terms are emphasized by bold type.

Pyramid Text 462ff

There is no **word against Unas on earth among men.**
There is no **crime of Unas in the sky among the gods.**
Unas has done away with the word against him,
he has annulled it, in order to rise towards heaven.

Pyramid Text 474

The spirit (*akh*) is bound for the sky, the corpse is bound for the earth."

Pyramid Text 654

Oho! Oho! Rise up, O Teti!
Take your head,
Collect your bones,
Shake the earth from your flesh!
Take your bread that rots not,
Your beer that sours not,
Stand at the gates that bar the common people!
…
The gatekeeper…
Sets you before the spirits, the imperishable stars.

Pyramid Text 738f

Hail to you, Tait [the Divine weaver]…Guard the King's head, lest it come loose;
gather together the King's bones, lest they become loose.

Pyramid Text 892

This Pepi **blasphemes not the king,**
He **defames not [the goddess] Bastet,**
He does **not make merry in the sanctuary.**

Pyramid Text 1174c

I have removed myself from the Tribunal of the Magistrates of the Abyss at the
head of the Great Ennead.

Pyramid Text 1188

O thou who ferriest over **the just** who is without a
ship.
Ferryman of the Field of Rushes,
King Merire (Pepi) **is just** before the sky
and before the earth.
King Pepi **is just** before that island of the earth
   to which he has swum and arrived there.

Pyramid Text 1160-1:

I will set a record of myself among men and the love of me among the gods. It is
said: 'Say **that which is, do not say that which is not**, for the **god detests falsity
of words**.

Pyramid Text 1219

Thou (O Morning Star) makest this Pepi to sit down because of his **righteousness**
and to rise up because of his **reverence**.

Pyramid Text 1238

There is no **evil** in which King Pepi has done.
Weighty is this word in thy sight, O Re.

Pyramid Text 1278-9

As for anyone who **shall lay a finger on this pyramid** and this temple which
belongs to me and to my double [*ka*], he will have laid his finger on the Mansion
of Horus in the firmament, he will have **offended the Lady of the Mansion**…his
affair will be judged by the Ennead and he will be nowhere and his house will be
nowhere; he will be one proscribed, one who eats himself.

Pyramid Text 2007-9

You have your water, you have your flood, you have your efflux which issued
from Osiris; gather together your bones, make ready your members, throw off
your dust, loosen your bonds.

Old Kingdom Autobiographies

Henku (5th Dynasty)

O all ye people…who shall pass by this tomb…
I **gave bread** to all the hungry of the
Cerastes—mountain;
I **clothed** him who was naked therein;
I **filled** its shores with large cattle,
and its lowlands with small cattle…
I **never oppressed** one in possession of
his property, so that he complained
because of it to the god of my city;
I **spake and told that which was good**;
never was there one fearing because of one
stronger than he,
So that he complained because of it to the god.
I **speak no lie**, for I was one
beloved of his father, praised of his mother,
Excellent in character to his brother,
and amiable to his sister.

Inscription of Hetepherakhet (5th Dynasty)

I **made this tomb by my very own means**,
I **never took the property** of anyone.
All persons who worked at it for me,
they worked **praising god for me** greatly for it.
They worked this for me for bread, for beer,
For clothes, for ointment, for much barley and
emmer,
I **never did anything by force** against anyone.
…
The Senior Elder of the Portal, Hetep-her-akhet,
he says:
I made this tomb on the side of the West,
in a clean place where no person's tomb was,
in order to guard the possessions of one who went
to his *ka*.
Any persons who would enter this tomb **uncleanly**,

and do something **evil** against it—
they shall be judged for it by the great god.

The Autobiography of Harkhuf (6th Dynasty)

An offering which the king gives and Osiris…
May he journey in peace on the holy ways to the West…
May he ascend to the god, lord of heaven…
…
I gave bread to the hungry,
Clothing to the naked,
I brought the boatless to land.
O you who live upon this earth,
Who shall pass by this tomb
Going north or going south,
Who shall say: "a thousand loaves and beer jugs
For the owner of this tomb,"
I shall watch over them [who make offerings]
in the necropolis.
I am an excellent equipped spirit (*akh*),
A lector-priest who knows his speech.
As for any man who enters this tomb unclean,
I will seize him by the neck like a bird,
He will be judged for it by the great god!
I was **one who spoke fairly, who repeated what was**
liked,
I **never spoke evilly against any man to his**
superior,
For I wished to stand well with the great god.

The Autobiography of Nekhebu (6th Dynasty)

Never did I **beat a man**…
Never did I **enslave any people**…
It was I who **pacified them.**
I never spent the night **angry**…
It was I who **gave clothing, bread, and beer to**
all the naked and hungry among them.
I am one **loved of** all people,
I **never spoke evil to king or potentate about**

anyone.

...

O you who are alive on earth,
who shall pass by this tomb!
If you wish to be favored by the king,
And honored by the great god,
Enter not this tomb profanely, uncleanly!
Anyone who enters it <u>profanely</u> despite this—
I will be judged with him by the great god!

...

Not shall you **destroy a thing in this tomb,**
I am a spirit [potent] and equipped!
Anyone who destroys a thing in this tomb—
I will be judged with them by the great god!
I am one who speaks the good, repeats the good,
I never spoke evil against anyone.

<u>Inscription of Sheshi</u> (6th Dynasty)

I have come from my town,
I have descended from my nome,
I have done **justice** for its lord,
I have satisfied him with what he loves.
I spoke truly, I did right,
I spoke fairly, I repeated fairly,
I seized the moment,
So as to stand well with the people.
I judged between two so as to content them,
I rescued the weak from one stronger than he
as much as was in my power.
I gave bread to the hungry, clothes <to the
naked>,
I brought the boatless to land.
I buried him who had no son,
I made a boat for him who lacked one.
I respected my father, I pleased my mother."
I raised their children.
So says he whose name is Sheshi.

Instruction Texts

<u>The Maxims of Ptahhotep</u> (6th Dynasty)

If you are a man that leads,
Who controls the affairs of the many,
Seek out every **beneficent deed**,
That your **conduct may be blameless**.
Great is **justice**, lasting in effect,
Unchallenged since the time of Osiris.
One punishes the **transgressor of laws**,
Though the **greedy** overlooks this;
Baseness may seize riches,
Yet **crime** never lands its wares;
In the end it is justice that lasts…
…
The wise feeds his *ba* with what endures,
So that it is happy with him on earth.

<u>The Instruction to Kagemni</u> (6th Dynasty)

The **respectful** man prospers,
Praised is the **modest** one,
The tent is open to the **silent**,
The seat of the **quiet** is spacious.
Do **not chatter!**
Knives are sharp against the **blunderer**,
Without hurry except when he **faults**.

When you sit with company,
Shun the food you love;
Restraint is a brief moment,
Gluttony is base and is reproved.
A cup of water quenches thirst,
A mouthful of herbs strengthens the heart;
A little something stands for much.
Vile is he whose belly **covets** when (meal)-time has passed,
He forgets those in whose house his belly roams.
When you sit with a **glutton**,
Eat when his **greed** has passed;

When you drink with a **drunkard**,
Take when his heart is content.

…

He who is **gentle**, even **timid**,
The harsh is kinder to him than to his mother,
All people are his servants.

Let your name go forth
While your **mouth is silent**.
When you are summoned, don't <u>boast</u> of strength
Among those your age, lest you be opposed.
One knows not what may happen,
What god does when he punishes.

<u>Post-Old Kingdom Texts</u>

The Instruction for King Merikare

The Court that judges the <u>wretch</u>,
You know they are not lenient,
On the day of judging the <u>miserable</u>,
In the hour of doing their task.
It is painful when the accuser has knowledge,
Do not trust in the length of years,
They [the judges] view a lifetime in an hour!
When a man remains over after death,
His **deeds**[485] are set beside him as treasure,
And being yonder lasts forever.
A <u>fool</u> is who does what they reprove!
He who reaches them without **having done wrong**
Will exist there like a god,
Free-striding like the lords forever!

…

A man should do what profits his *ba*.

…

So the *ba* goes to the place it knows.

…

Divine are they who follow the king!

---

[485] One's good deeds are a treasure for a favorable judgment.

Coffin Texts

Coffin Text Spell 8, I, 24

Hail to you, Tribunal of the God who **shall judge me concerning what I have said [and did]**, I being ignorant at ease and having no care. O you who surround me and stand at my back. May I be vindicated in the presence of Geb, chiefest of the gods. Yonder god **shall judge me according to what I know**. I have arisen with my plume on my head and my **righteousness** on my brow, my foes are in sorrow, and I have taken possession of all my property in vindication.

Coffin Text Spell 44, I, 181-185

The doors of the sky are opened because of your **goodness**; may you ascend and see Hathor, may your **complaint [evil]** be removed, may your **sin [iniquity] be erased** by those who weigh in the balance on the day of **reckoning characters**.
…
May you sail southward in the Night-bark and northward in the Day-bark; may you recognize your soul [*ba*] in the upper sky, while your flesh, your corpse, is in On.

The Book of the Dead

Spell 30

O my heart which I had from my mother! O my heart which I had from my mother! O my heart of my different ages! Do not stand up as a witness against me, do not be opposed to me in the tribunal, do not be hostile to me in the presence of the Keeper of the Balance, for you are my ka which was in my body, the protector who made my members hale. Go forth to the happy place whereto we speed; do not make my name stink to the Entourage who make men. Do not tell lies about me in the presence of the god; it is indeed well that you should hear!
Thus says Thoth, judge of truth, to the Great Ennead which is in the presence of Osiris: Hear this word of very truth. I have judged the heart of the deceased, and his soul stands as a witness for him. His **deeds are righteous** in the great balance, and **no sin** has been found in him. He did **not diminish the offerings in the temples, he did not destroy what had been made, he did not go about with deceitful speech while he was on earth.**
Thus says the Great Ennead to Thoth who is in Hermopolis: This utterance of yours is true. The **vindicated** Osiris N is **straightforward, he has no sin, there is no accusation against** him before us, Ammit shall not be permitted to have

power over him. Let there be given to him the offerings which are issued in the presence of Osiris, and may a grant of land be established in the Field of Offerings as for the Followers of Horus.

Thus says Horus son of Isis: I have come to you, O Wennefer, and I bring N to you. His **heart is true**, having gone forth from the balance, and he has **not sinned against any god or any goddess**. Thoth has judged him in writing which has been told the Ennead, and Maat the great has witnessed. Let there be given to him bread and beer which have been issued in the presence of Osiris, and he will be for ever like Followers of Horus.

Thus says N: Here I am in your presence, O Lord of the West. There is **no wrong-doing in my body**, I have **not wittingly told lies**, there has been **no second fault**. Grant that I may be like the favoured ones who are in your suite, O Osiris, one greatly favored by the good god, one loved of the Lord of the Two Lands, N, vindicated before Osiris.

Spell 125

Hail to you, great god, Lord of justice! I have come to you, my lord…I know the names of the forty-two gods…who live on those who cherish **evil** and who gulp down their blood on that day of reckoning of characters in the presence of [Osiris]…I have come to you, I have brought you **truth**, I have expelled **falsehood** for you…I have not [the **first list of evils*** followed by—]

I am pure, pure, pure, pure!

[then a **second list of evils***—described as the "negative confession" or the "declaration of innocence"].

* There are two of these lists, both of which may be called declarations of innocence in Chapter 125. See the details in chapter 6.

New Kingdom Text

Hepusonb (ca. 1400 BCE)

My *Ba* (soul) in heaven, my corpse in the graveyard.

Compare this to a similar saying in Greece 1000 years later: For the fallen at Potidaea, Greece 432 BCE:

αἰθὴρ μὲν ψυχὰς ὑπεδέξατο σώματα δὲ χθών.[486]

---

[486] The air (ether) has received their souls (psyches), the earth their bodies.

O. _TABLE 10:_ Conduct and Behavior that Influences the Afterlife: Egyptian

Conduct and Behavior that Influences The Afterlife: Egyptian Texts Inverse Index (terms as they appear in Plato's judgment myths only)

Conduct deserving reward   Egyptian Texts: in afterlife/behavior citations[487]

Term in Plato	Dictionary Form	Pyramid Texts	Ptahhotep	Other Old Kingdom	Book of Dead
justly	δίκιος	x	x	x	x
piously	ὅσιος				
truth	ἀλήθεια	x	x	x	x
done own work	πράσσω				
no busybody	πολυπραγμονέω				
good	ἀγαθός		x		
noble	καλός				
virtue	ἀρετή				
well-ordered	κόσμιος	x		x	
wise	φρόνιμος		x		
pure	καθαρός				x
moderate	μέτριος			x	
wisdom	φρόνησις		x	x	
moderation	σωφροσύνη		x	x	
justice	δικαιοσύνη	x	x		x
courage	ἀνδρεία				
freedom	ἐλευθερία				
good deeds	εὐεργεσία	x	x	x	x
piety	εὐσέβεια	x			x
philosopher	φιλοσόφος				
lover of beauty	φιλοκάλος				
symmetrical	ὀρθός				
honor	τιμῆς		x	x	
shame	αἰδοῦς				

---

487 These terms appear in the four myths of Plato and are counted for the Egyptian texts if they appear in passages that allude to a reward or punishment in some form of an afterlife. Synonymous concepts are also included.

Term in Plato	Dictionary Form	Pyramid Texts	Ptahhotep	Other Old Kingdom	Book of Dead
unjustly	ἄδικος				
godlessly	ἄθεος				
false oaths	ἐπίορκος	x			x
lying	ψεῦδος	x	x	x	x
boasting	ἀλαζονεία		x	x	
arrogant					
power	ἐξουσία		x		x
luxury	τρυφάω				
insolence	ὕβρις		x		
incontinence	ἀκράτεια				
asymmetry	ἀσυμμετρία				
ugliness	αἰσχρότης				
impious	ἀνόσιος				
errors	ἁμάρτημα	x	x	x	x
attached/body	ἐπιθυμητικός				
impure	ἀκάθαρτος			x	
killings	φόνος				x
sacrileges	ἱεροσυλία	x		x	x
violence	βιάιος			x	x
pleasures	ἡδονά				
betrayal	προδίδωμι				
caused death	θάνατος				x
to slavery	δούλειος			x	
impiety	ἀσέβεια				x
envy	φθόνος			x	x
forgetfulness	λήθη				
badness	κακία				
crooked (asymmetrical)	σκολιός				x

P. A Comparison of Conduct and Behavior: Egyptian and Greek with Jewish and Christian Religions

A simple comparison between the ancient Egyptians and the ancient Greeks in terms of the types of conduct and behavior that was important to them would be an interesting project in itself. If compared within the context of a widely known set of values, some of which are extra-Egyptian or Greek, it would be even more enlightening. With that in mind, I shall use various sets of conduct and behavior values as templates, starting with the Biblical Ten Commandments. Then we shall compare with the Golden Rule and the Cardinal Virtues.

The first resemblance that we notice between the Biblical Ten Commandments and Egyptian <u>Book of the Dead</u> texts is that they are both stated primarily in the negative. Only two of the Ten are stated in the positive.

The Ten Commandments of the Hebrew Bible[488]

I am the Lord your God, who brought you out of the land of Egypt.

I.   You shall have no other gods before me.

In any polytheistic society, there was usually not a problem with this one. However, in Egypt, Re and Osiris vied for supremacy and in Greece, Zeus let it known that he alone was primary and would not allow any other gods before himself. Briefly, in the 18th Dynasty, Akhenaten created monotheism in Egypt and denied the other gods.

II.   You shall not make for yourself an idol…for I the Lord your God am a jealous God, punishing children for the iniquity of parents, to the third and fourth generation.

The interesting comparison here is not the fact of having no idols since both Egypt and Greece obviously did. The part of this commandment of interest is the punishing of the children for the sins of the fathers. This figured heavily in Greece until such time as they

---

[488] Exodus 20:1-17. The historical setting of the Ten Commandments is during the Egyptian 19th Dynasty (c. 1350-1200), but the actual text would have been composed much later. All Biblical texts are from The New Revised Standard Version unless otherwise noted.

recognized the injustice of this concept and were able to replace it with a punishment, still in the future, but now in an afterlife.

We find this concept already in Homer at Il. 4.160, Hesiod at Works 280ff, Solon at fragment 2.15 and finally with Theognis at 731-52 where he protests its injustice.

In Egypt, in spite of having an afterlife in which to insure that only the guilty party would be punished with oblivion, we still see this sins-of—the-fathers type of punishment in Pyramid Text 1278-9 where it is said, "he will be nowhere and his house will be nowhere."

III.   You shall not make wrongful use of the name of the Lord your God.

In Greece this is the earliest recorded injunction. At Homer Il. 3.276 and 19.256, the gods will punish those who have vainly used the gods in an oath. This wrongful use of the god's name was both an affront to the honor of the god and a violation of societal order. Also see: Hesiod, Works, 280, Heraclitus frag 28b, Empedocles 115, Pindar Ol. 2, Aristophanes Frogs 135ff and Plato Gorg. 525a.

In Egypt, this conduct was enjoined in the Book of the Dead spell 125.

IV.   Remember [Observe] the Sabbath day, and keep it holy.

This commandment is very religion specific, however, both Egypt and Greece recognized days that were set aside in honor of the deity. (i.e., see Book of the Dead spell 125).

V.   Honor your father and mother, so that your days may be long [, and that it may go well with you][489] in the land.

This is a universal commandment and appears very early in both Egypt and Greece. Some instances are: Hesiod Works 185, Plato Rep. 615c in the Myth, and extensively in the Dramatists. Isocrates phrased it as a rule where he says, "conduct yourself toward your parents as you would have your children conduct themselves toward you" (Isoc. 1.14).[490] Egypt has this in Henku and Sheshi.

---

[489] Deuteronomy 5:16. The [text] in Deuteronomy is almost exactly the same as in Exodus. It is thought to have been composed c. 650 BCE. Note the consequentialist ethics. Cf. Harkhuf, "I wished to stand well with the great god."

[490] One could phrase this as: act as though you would wish your act to be a universal law of the gods. This could pass for a categorical imperative if only they had known Kant.

VI.   You shall not murder.

This is another universal commandment some examples of which are: Empedocles 115, Phaedo 108b, 113e, and Rep. 615b. Egypt has it in the Book of the Dead spell 125 and others.

VII.   You shall not commit adultery.

This does not appear in any of Plato's eschatological myths but is noted at Rep. 443a. However, it is rare in all of the Greek writers as well as in Egypt but does appear in the Book of the Dead spell 125.

VIII.   You shall not steal.

Stealing is prohibited during all time periods. It shows up in all of the Greeks and in Book of the Dead spell 125 and Ptahhotep.

IX.   You shall not bear false witness against your neighbor.

Lying about or bearing false witness against members of one's community was condemned at: Heraclitus 28 and Plato Gorg. 525a, and elsewhere in Greece. In Egypt most of the texts condemn it: Pyramid Text 1160, Ptahhotep, Henku, Harkhuf, Nekhebu and Book of the Dead spells 30 and 125.

X.   You shall not covet [desire] your neighbor's house...wife [field]... slave...or anything that belongs to your neighbor.

In Homer, Agamemnon is accused of being covetous at Il. 122. Plato in the Phaedo Myth at 108a has the word used for lusting after things of the body that will result in an afterlife punishment. In Egypt, covetousness is condemned by Kagemni and Ptahhotep.

Thus we see an instance of each of these commandments in the conduct and behavior admonitions of both ancient Egypt and Greece.

The Golden Rule

We tend to think of the Golden Rule as expressing the highest morality in a most succinct manner. Can we find it in our two societies which many modern writers have claimed lack that quality of morality?

The two classical statements of the Golden Rule are:

Hillel (ca. 60 BCE—10 CE). What is hateful to you, do not do to your fellow creatures (b. sabb. 31a).

Jesus (ca. 4 BCE—30 CE). In everything do to others as you would have them do to you (Matthew 7:12).

However we do find it in the Greece of the 5th century as formulated by a contemporary of Plato, the:

Orator Isocrates (436-338 BCE). He phrases it: Do not do unto others that which angers you when they do it to you (Isoc. 3.61).

Finding the Rule thus formulated in Egypt of 2300 BCE would be asking a great deal. Nevertheless, we see the germ of such a rule with the autobiography of:

Hetepherakhet (twenty-fourth century BCE). He claims that he is making his tomb of his own means and not taking from another's tomb in order to do so. He clearly recognizes that in order to have his tomb well treated he must treat others' in the same way. It is not even much of a stretch to formulate his rule thus: "Treat another's property as you would have him/her treat yours."

The Cardinal Virtues[491]

The Cardinal Virtues would become the foundation of later Christian morality when combined with the Pauline enjoinder to faith, hope and charity. We have seen that they were created by the Greeks and codified by Plato. Our remaining question is, can we also find them in the Egyptian texts that deal with an afterlife reward or punishment?

Justice. Like *Dike* in Greece, *Maat* was the personification of Justice. This virtue is found in Pyramid Texts 316, 1219, Ptahhotep, Sheshi and the Book of the Dead spell 30.

Moderation. This virtue is in Ptahhotep and Kagemni.

---

[491] See Table 10 in the appendix for a complete comparison of Egyptian texts with all of Plato's conduct and behavior terms.

Courage. This virtue is not found in the texts we have reviewed in our inquiry. Bravery is noted in some texts dealing with war, but the generally peaceful Egypt did not bring this virtue to the fore.

Wisdom. The virtue of wisdom is in Ptahhotep.

Piety or holiness. This virtue is in the Pyramid Text 892 and the Book of the Dead spells 30 and 125.

Four of the five concepts seem to be just as important in Egypt, over 2000 years before Socrates, as they would later become with Plato and our own society.

Bibliography

Adam, James. <u>The Religious Teachers of Greece</u>. Clifton: Reference Book Publishers, 1965.

Adkins, Arthur W. H. <u>Merit and Responsibility</u>. Oxford: Clarendon Press, 1960.

Allen, Michael J.B. <u>The Platonism of Marsilio Ficino</u>. Berkeley: University of California Press, 1984.

Allen, James P., "The Cosmology of the Pyramid Texts." In <u>Religion and Philosophy in Ancient Egypt</u>. Ed. William Kelly Simpson, 1-28. New Haven: Yale University Press, 1989.

_____, "Funerary Texts and Their Meaning." In <u>Mummies and Magic: The Funerary Arts of Ancient Egypt</u>. Eds. Sue D'Auria, Peter Lacovara and Catharine H. Roehrig. Boston: Museum of Fine Arts, 1988.

Anthes, Rudolf. "Egyptian Theology in the Third Millennium B.C." <u>Journal of Near Eastern Studies</u> 18, no. 3 (1959): 170-212.

_____. "Mythology in Ancient Egypt." In <u>Mythologies of the Ancient World</u>. Ed. Samuel Noah Kramer, 17-92. Garden City, New York: Anchor Books, 1961.

_____. "The Original Meaning of mAa xrw" Journal of Near Eastern Studies 13 (Jan-Oct 1954): 21-51.

Annas, Julia. <u>An Introduction to Plato's Republic</u>. Oxford: Clarendon Press 1981.

_____. "Plato's Myths of Judgment." <u>Phronesis</u> XXVII, no. 2 (1982): 119-143.

Apostle, Hippocrates G. Trans. <u>Aristotle's Ethics</u>. Bloomington Indians: University Press,------.

Aristotle. <u>Metaphysics</u>. Trans. Hugh Tredennick. Cambridge: Harvard University Press, 1989.

_____. Trans. Francis H. Eterovich. <u>Aristotle's Nichomachean Ethics</u>. Washington: University Press of America, 1980.

Assmann, Jan., "Death and Initiation in the Funerary Religion of Ancient Egypt." In <u>Religion and Philosophy in Ancient Egypt</u>. Ed. William Kelly Simpson, 135-159. New Haven: Yale University Press, 1989.

Baines, John, "Society, Morality, and Religious Practice." In <u>Religion in Ancient Egypt: Gods, Myths and Personal Practice</u>, Ed. Byron E. Shafer, 123-200. Ithaca, New York: Cornell University Press, 1991.

_____. "Origins of Egyptian Kingship." In <u>Ancient Egyptian Kingship</u>. Eds. David O'Conner, and David Silverman. Leiden: E.J. Brill, 1995.

Barb, A.A. "Mystery, Myth and Magic." In <u>The Legacy of Egypt</u>, Ed. J.R. Harris. Oxford: Clarendon Press, 1971.

Barnes, Jonathon. <u>The Presocratic Philosophers</u>. Vol 2. London: Routledge & Kegan Paul, 1979.

Barrett, W.S. <u>Euripides: Hippolytos</u>. Oxford: Clarendon Press, 1992.

Bernal, Black Athena. London: Free Association Press, 1987.

_____. "The Case for Massive Egyptian Influence in the Aegean." <u>Archaeology</u>, (Sept/Oct 1992): 53-86.

Bhaktivedanta Swami, A.C. <u>Bhagavad-Gita: As It Is</u>. Los Angeles: Bhativedanta Book Trust, 1977.

Bloom, Allen. <u>The Republic of Plato</u>. USA: Basic Books, 1991.

Bostock, David. <u>Plato's Phaedo</u>. Oxford: Clarendon Press 1986.

Bowra, C.M. <u>Early Greek Elegists</u>. Cambridge: Harvard University Press, 1938.

_____. Pindar. Oxford: Clarendon Press, 1964.

Brandon, S.G.F. Man and His Destiny in the Great Religions. Toronto: University of Toronto Press, 1962.

_____. The Judgment of the Dead: The Idea of Life After Death in the Major Religions. New York: Charles Scribner's Sons, 1967.

_____. "The Origin of Death in some Ancient Near Eastern Religions." Religious Studies I, no. 2 (1966): 217-228.

_____. Religion in Ancient History: Studies in Ideas, Men and Events. New York: Charles Scribner's Sons, 1967.

Brandwood, Leonard. The Chronology of Plato's Dialogues. Cambridge: Cambridge University Press, 1990.

Braun, Richard Emil. Euripides: Rhesos. New York: Oxford University Press, 1978.

Breasted, James Henry. The Dawn of Conscience. New York: Charles Scribner's Sons, 1934.

_____. Development of Religion and Thought in Ancient Egypt. London: Charles Scribner's Sons, 1912.

_____. Ancient Records of Egypt. 5 vols. Chicago: University of Chicago Press, 1906.

Bremmer, Jan. The Early Greek Concept of the Soul. Princeton: Princeton University Press, 1983.

Brisson, Luc. Platon, les mots et les mythes. Paris: la Decouverte, 1994.

Burkert, Walter. Ancient Mystery Cults. Cambridge: Harvard University Press, 1987.

_____. Greek Religion. Trans. John Raffan. Cambridge: Harvard University Press, 1985.

_____. Lore and Science in Ancient Pythagoreanism. Trans. Edwin L. Milnar, Jr. Cambridge: Harvard University Press, 1972.

Burnet, John. Plato's Phaedo. 1911. Reprint, Oxford: Clarendon Press, 1959.

Cairns, Douglas L. Aidos. Oxford: Clarendon Press, 1993.

Charlesworth, James H. and Loren L. Johns. Eds. Hillel and Jesus. Minneapolis: Fortress Press, 1997.

Cooper, John M. Plato: Complete Works. Cambridge: Hackett Publishing Company, 1997.

Coleman, John E. "Did Egypt Shape the Glory that was Greece?" Archaeology (Sep/Oct 1992): 48-86.

Cross, R.C. and A.D. Woozley. Plato's Republic. London: MacMillan & Co, 1964.

D'Auria, Sue, Peter Lacovara and Catharine H. Roehrig. Mummies and Magic. Boston: Museum of Fine Arts, 1988.

Dale, A.M. Euripides: Helen. Oxford: Clarendon Press, 1967.

Damascius. The Greek Commentaries on Plato's Phaedo. Ed. L.G. Westerink. Amsterdam: North-Holland Publishing Company, 1977.

Davies, W. Vivian and Louise Schofield. Eds. Egypt, the Aegean and the Levant: Interconnections in the Second Millennium BC. London: British Museum Press, 1995.

Dawson, Christopher M. The Seven Against Thebes. Englewood Cliffs: Prentice-Hall, 1970.

Derchain, Philippe. "Death in Egyptian Religion." In Mythologies. Vol. 1, ed. Yves Bonnefoy, 111-115. Chicago: The University of Chicago Press, 1991.

de Strycker, E. Plato's Apology of Socrates. Ed. S.R. Slings. Leiden: E. J. Brill, 1994.

DeVries, G.J. A Commentary on the Phaedrus of Plato. Amsterdam: Adolf M. Hakkert, 1969.

Diels, H. and W. Krantz. <u>Die Fragmente der Vorsokratiker</u>. 6th edition. Zurich: Wiedmann, 1968.

Dieterich, Albrecht. <u>Nekyia</u>. Stuttgart: B.G. Teubner, 1969.

Dietrich, B. C. <u>The Origins of Greek Religion</u>. Berlin and New York: Walter De Gruyter, 1974.

Dimock, George. <u>Homer: The Odyssey</u>. Cambridge: Harvard University Press, 1995.

Diodorus Siculus. <u>Etudes Preliminares Aux Religions Orientales Dans L'Empire Romain</u>. Ed. Anne Burton. Leiden: E.J. Brill, 1972.

Dodds, E.R. <u>Euripides: Bacchae</u>. Oxford: Clarendon Press, 1960.

_____. <u>Plato: Gorgias</u>. Oxford: Clarendon Press 1959.

_____. <u>The Greeks and the Irrational</u>. Berkley: University of California Press, 1951.

Dover, Kenneth. <u>Aristophanes: Frogs</u>. Oxford: Clarendon Press 1997.

_____. <u>Greek Popular Morality</u>. Berkley: University of California Press, 1974

Easterling, P. E. and J. V. Muir, Eds. <u>Greek Religion and Society</u>. Cambridge: Cambridge University Press, 1985, repr. 1992.

Edelstein, L. "The Function of Myth in Plato's Philosophy." <u>Journal of the History of Ideas</u> X, no. 4 (Oct 1949): 463-481.

Erman, Adolf. <u>Life in Ancient Egypt</u>. Translated by H.M. Tirard. New York: Benjamin Blom, 1969. First published as <u>Aegypten</u> in 1885 and translated into English in 1894.

_____. <u>The Ancient Egyptians: A Sourcebook of their Writings</u>. New York: Harper and Row, 1966.

_____. <u>Die agyptische religion</u>. Berlin: G. Reimer, 1905.

Faulkner, Raymond O. The Ancient Egyptian Book of the Dead. Austin: The University of Texas Press, 1993.

_____. The Ancient Egyptian Coffin Texts. 3 vols. Warminster: Aris & Phillips 1973, 1977, 1978.

_____. The Ancient Egyptian Pyramid Texts. Oxford: Clarendon Press, 1969.

_____. Review of The Origins of Osiris and His Cult, by J. Gwyn Griffiths. Journal of Egyptian Archeology 57 (1971): 207-209.

Fagles, Robert. Bacchylides: Complete Poems. New Haven: Yale University Press, 1961.

Ferguson, John. Moral Values in the Ancient World. New York: Barnes & Noble, 1959.

Forman, Werner and Stephen Quirke. Hieroglyphics and the Afterlife. Norman: University of Oklahoma Press, 1996.

Frankfort, Henri. Kingship and the Gods. Chicago:, 1948.

_____. Ancient Egyptian Religion. New York: Harper & Brothers, 1948.

Fitzgerald, William. "Pindar's Second Olympian." Helios 10. no. 1 (spring 1983): 50.

Foley, Helene P. The Homeric Hymn to Demeter. Princeton: Princeton University Press, 1994.

Frankle, Hermann. Early Greek Poetry and Philosophy. New York: Harcourt Brace Jovanovich, 1973.

Freeman, Kathleen. The Pre-Socratic Philosophers. Oxford: Basil Blackwell, 1949.

_____. Ancilla to the Pre-Socratic Philosophers. Oxford: Basil Blackwell, 1948.

Frutiger, Perceval. Les Mythes de Platon. Paris: Librairie Felix Alcan, 1930, repr. 1976.

Gallop, David. Plato: Phaedo. Oxford: Clarendon Press, 1990.

Gantz, Timothy. Early Greek Myth. Baltimore: Johns Hopkins University Press, 1993.

Gardiner, Alan. Egypt of the Pharaohs: An Introduction. Oxford: Clarendon, 1961.

Garvie, A.F. Aeschylus' Supplices: Play and Trilogy Cambridge: University Press, 1969.

Gottfried, Bruce. "Plato's use of Myth." In Plato's Dialogues, Ed. Gerald A. Press, 177-195. Lanham MD: Rowman & Littlefield Publishers, 1993.

Grieshammer, Reinhard. Das Jenseitsgericht in den Sargtexten. Wiesbaden: Otto Harrassowitz, 1970.

Griffiths, J. Gwyn. Atlantis and Egypt, Cardiff: University of Wales Press, 1991.

_____. The Conflict of Horus and Seth. Liverpool: Liverpool University Press, 1960.

_____. The Divine Verdict: A Study of Divine Judgement in the Ancient Religions. Leiden: E.J. Brill, 1991.

_____. The Divine Tribunal. University College of Swansea, 1975.

_____. "The Faith of the Pharonic Period." In Classical Mediterranean Spirituality. Ed. A. H. Armstrong, 3-38. New York: Crossroad, 1986.

_____. "The Idea of Posthumous Judgement in Israel and Egypt." In Fontes Atque Pontes. Wiesbaden: Harrassonitz, 1983.

_____. "Motivation in Early Egyptian Syncretism." In Studies in Egyptian Religion (for Jan Zandee), Ed. M. Heerma van Voss et al., 43-55. Leiden: E.J. Brill, 1982.

_____. The Origins of Osiris and His Cult. Leiden: E.J. Brill, 1980.

_____. Greece and Rome 16 (1947) 122-26.

_____. "The Legacy of Egypt." The Classical Review XXV, no. 2 (Nov 1975).

_____. "The Idea of Posthumous Judgment in Israel and Egypt." In Fontes Atque Pontes. Ed. Manfred Gorg. Wiesbaden: Otto Harrassowitz, 1983.

_____. Apuleius of Madauros: The Isis-Book. Leiden: E.J. Brill, 1975.

Graf, Fritz. "Dionysian and Orphic Eschatology: New Texts and Old Questions." In Thomas H. Carpenter and Christopher A. Faraone, Masks of Dionysis. Ithaca: Cornell University Press, 1993.

Grimm, Laura. Definition in Plato's Meno. Oslo: Oslo University Press, 1962.

Grube, G.M.A. Plato's Meno. Indianapolis: Hackett, 1976.

_____. "Apology." In Plato: Complete Works, Ed. John M. Cooper, 17-36. Cambridge: Hackett Publishing Company, 1997.

_____. "Phaedo." In Plato: Complete Works, Ed. John M. Cooper, 49-100. Cambridge: Hackett Publishing Company, 1997.

Guthrie, W. K. C. Orpheus and Greek Religion. London: Methuen, 1935.

_____. The Revolution in the Mind. Westwood MA: Paperbook Press, 1991.

Halliwell, S. Plato: Republic 10. Wiltshire: Aris & Phillips, 1988.

Hampe, Roland. "Zur Eschatologie in Pindar's zweiter olympischer Ode." In Hermenia-Festschrift fuer Otto Regenbogen, 46-65.

Harrison, Jane. Prolegomena to the Study of Greek Religion. Cambridge: Cambridge University Press, 1922.

Herodotus. The Histories. Trans. Aubrey de Selincourt. Baltimore: Penguin Books, 1966.

Heubeck, Alfred, Stephanie West, J.B. Hainsworth. A Commentary on Homer's Odyssey. Vol. 1. Oxford: Clarendon Press, 1988.

Heubeck, Alfred and Arie Hoekstra. A Commentary on Homer's Odyssey. Vol 2. Oxford: Clarendon Press, 1989.

Hexter, Ralph. A Guide to the Odyssey (New York: Vintage Books, 1993.

Hicks, Robert Drew. Trans. Aristotle: De Anima. New York: Arno Press, 1976.

Hopfner, Theodor. <u>Griechisch-Agyptischer Offenbarungszauber</u>. Amsterdam: Adolf M. Hakkert, 1990.

Hornblower, Simon and Anthony Spawforth, Eds. <u>The Oxford Companion to Classical Civilization</u>. Oxford: Oxford University Press, 1998.

Hornung, Erik. <u>Akhenaten and the Religion of Light</u>. Ithaca: Cornell University Press, 1999.

_____. <u>The Ancient Egyptian Books of the Afterlife</u>. Trans. David Lorton, Ithaca: Cornell University Press, 1999.

_____. "Ancient Egyptian Religious Iconography." In <u>Civilizations of the Ancient Near East</u>. Vol. III, Ed. Jack M. Sasson, 1711-1731. New York: Charles Scribner's Sons, 1995.

_____. <u>Conceptions of God in Ancient Egypt: The One and the Many</u>. Trans. John Baines. Ithaca: Cornell University Press, 1982; London: Routledge & Kegan Paul, 1983. First published as <u>Der Eine und die Vielen: Agyptische Gottesvorstellungen</u>. Darmstadt: Wissenschaftliche Buchgesellschaft, 1971.

_____. <u>Idea into Image: Essays on Ancient Egyptian Thought</u>. Trans. Elizabeth Bredeck. Timkin Publishers, 1992. First published as <u>Geist der Pharaonenzeit</u>. Zurich and Munich: Artemis, 1989.

Iamblicus. <u>On The Pythagorean Life</u>. Clark, Gillian. Trans. Liverpool: Liverpool University Press, 1989.

Irwin, Terence. <u>Plato: Gorgias</u>. Oxford: Clarendon Press, 1979.

_____. <u>Plato's Moral Theory</u>. Oxford: Clarendon Press, 1977.

Isocrates. <u>Isocrates</u>. Trans. George Norlin. Cambridge: Harvard University Press, 1928.

Jebb, R. C. <u>Sophocles: The Plays and Fragments</u>. Cambridge: University Press, 1907.

Junker, Hermann. <u>Pyraminenzeit</u>. Zurich: Koln, 1949.

Kingsley, Peter. Ancient Philosophy, Mystery, and Magic: Empedocles and Pythagorean Tradition. Oxford: Clarendon Press 1995.

_____. "From Pythagoras to the Turba Philosophorum: Egypt and Pythagorean Tradition." Journal of the Warburg and Courtauld Institutes. 57 (1994): 1-13.

Kirk, G.S., J.E. Raven and M. Schofield. The Presocratic Philosophers. Cambridge: Cambridge University Press, 1983.

Kovacs, David. Euripides. Cambridge: Harvard University Press, 1984.

Knox, Bernard M. Oedipus the King. New York: Washington Square Press, 1972.

Kraut, Richard. Ed. The Cambridge Companion to Plato. Cambridge: Cambridge University Press, 1992.

Kristensen, W. Brede. Life out of Death. Louvain, Belgium: Peeters Press, 1992.

Lattimore, Richard. The Complete Greek Tragedies. Eds. David Grene and Richard Lattimore, Vol. 3. Chicago: University of Chicago Press, 1992.

Lembke, Janet. Aeschylus: Suppliants. New York: Oxford University Press, 1975.

Lesko, Leonard H. "Ancient Egyptian Cosmogonies and Cosmology." In Religion in Ancient Egypt: Gods Myths and Personal Practice, Ed. Byron E. Shafer, 88-122. Ithaca, New York: Cornell University Press, 1991.

_____. "Death and the Afterlife in Ancient Egyptian Thought." In Civilization of the Ancient Near East, Ed. Jack M. Sasson, vol. III. New York: Charles Scriebner's Sons, 1995.

_____. "Egyptian Religion: History of Study." In Encyclopedia of Religion. Vol. 5, Ed. Mircea Eliade. New York: Macmillan Publishing Company, 1987.

_____. "Egyptian Religion." In Religions of Antiquity, ed. Robert M. Seltzer, 34-61. New York: Macmillan Publishing Company, 1989.

Lichtheim, Miriam. <u>Ancient Egyptian Autobiographies Chiefly of the Middle Kingdom</u>. Gottingen: Vandenhoeck & Ruprecht, 1988.

————. <u>Ancient Egyptian Literature: A Book of Readings, 3 Vols.</u> Berkeley: University of California Press, 1973, 1976, 1980.

————. <u>Maat in Egyptian Autobiographies and Related Studies</u>. Gottingen: Vandenhoeck & Ruprecht, 1992.

————. <u>Moral Values in Ancient Egypt</u>. Gottingen: Vandenhoeck & Ruprecht, 1997.

Liddell, Henry George, Robert Scott and Henry Stuart Jones. <u>A Greek-English Lexicon</u>. Oxford: Clarendon Press, 1996.

Linforth, Ivan M. "Philoctetes, the Play and the Man." In <u>Studies in Sophocles</u>. Berkeley: University of California Press, 1963.

Lloyd-Jones, Hugh. <u>The Eumenides by Aeschylus</u>. Englewood Cliffs: Prentice-Hall, 1970.

————. <u>The Libation Bearers</u>. Englewood Cliffs: Prentice-Hall, 1970.

————. <u>Sophocles</u>, 2 vols. Cambridge: Harvard University Press, 1994.

Lloyd, Alan B., "Psychology and Society in the Ancient Egyptian Cult of the Dead." In <u>Religion and Philosophy in Ancient Egypt</u>, Ed. William Kelly Simpson. New Haven: Yale University Press, 1989.

MacIntyre, Alasdair. <u>A Short History of Ethics</u>. New York: MasMillan Co, 1966.

————. <u>After Virtue</u>. Notre Dame: University of Notre Dame Press, 1984.

Maspero, Gaston. <u>New Light on Ancient Egypt</u>. London: T. Fisher Unwin, 1908.

Mikalson, J.D. <u>Athenian Popular Religion</u>. Chapel Hill: University of North Carolina Press, 1983.

————. <u>Honor Thy Gods</u>. Chapel Hill: University of North Carolina Press, 1983.

Moors, Kent F. <u>Platonic Myth</u>. Washington DC: University Press of America, 1982.

Morenz, Siegfried. Egyptian Religion. Translated by Ann E. Keep. London: Methuen; Ithaca: Cornell University Press, 1973. First published as Agyptische Religion. Religionen der Menschheit 8. Stuttgart: Kohlhammer, 1960.

Moret, Alexander. The Nile and Egyptian Civilization. Trans. M. R. Dobie. London: Kegan Paul, Trench, Tubner & Co.; New York: Alfred A. Knopf, 1927.

Morrow, Glenn R. Plato's Cretan City. Princeton: Princeton University Press, 1960.

Morwood, James. Euripides. Oxford: Clarendon Press, 1997.

Mulroy, David. Early Greek Lyric Poetry. University of Michigan Press, 1992.

Murnane, William J. "Taking It With You: The Problem of Death and Afterlife in Ancient Egypt." In Death and Afterlife: Perspectives of World Religions, Ed. Hiroshi Obayashi, 35-48. New York: Greenwood Press,1992.

Murray, Gilbert. The Agamemnon of Aeschylus. New York: Oxford University Press, 1920.

Nichols, James H. Jr. Gorgias: and Phaedrus: Rhetoric, philosophy, and Politics. Ithica: Cornell University, 1998.
_____. Plato: Gorgias. Ithica: Cornell University, 1998.
_____. Plato: Phaedrus. Ithica: Cornell University, 1998.

Nilsson, Martin P. Minoan-Mycenaean Religion and its Survival in Greek Religion. Lund: C.W.K. Gleerup, 1950.

Nisetich, Frank J. "Immortality in Acragas." Classical Philology, Vol. 83 No 1 (Jan 1988): 6-12.
_____. Pindar and Homer. Johns Hopkins University Press, 1989.
_____. Pindar's Victory Odes. Baltimore: Johns Hopkins University Press, 1980.

North, Helen. From Myth to Icon. Ithaca: Cornell University Press, 1979.

Norwood, Gilbert. Pindar. Berkeley: University of California Press, 1945

Nussbaum, Martha. The Fraglity of Goodness. Cambridge: Cambridge University Press, 1986.

Olympiodorus. Commentary on Plato's Gorgias. Trans. Robin Jackson, Kimon Lycos, Harold Tarrant. Leiden: Brill, 1998.

Ostwald, Martin. Trans. Nicomachean Ethics. New York: Bobbs-Merrill, 1962.

Parker, Robert. "Early Orphism." In The Greek World. Ed. Anton Powell. Routledge: New York, 1995.
_____. Miasma: Pollution and Purification in Early Greek Religion. Oxford: Clarendon Press 1983.

Petrie, W.M. Flinders. Religion and Conscience in Ancient Egypt. New York: Benjamin Blom, 1972. First published in 1898.

Philbin, William J. Trans. To You Simonides. Dublin: Dolmen Editions, 1977.

Piankoff, Alexandre. The Pyramids of Unas. Princeton: Princeton University Press, 1968.

Places, Edouard des. Lexique de Platon. In Platon Oeuvres Completes. Tome XIV. 2 Vols. Paris: Societe d'Edition Les Belles Lettres, 1964.

Plato. Complete Works. Ed. John M. Cooper. Indianapolis: Hackett Publishing Company, 1997.
_____. Loeb Classical Library. Eds, E. Capps, T.E. Page, W.H.D. Rouse. 12 Vols. New York: G.P. Putnam's Sons, 1913.

Plutarch. Plutarch's Moralia. Trans. Frank Cole Babbitt. Cambridge: Harvard University Press, 1949.

Podlecki, Anthony J. The Persians by Aeschylus. Englewood Cliffs: Prentice-Hall, 1970.

Quirke, Stephen. Ancient Egyptian Religion. London: British Museum Press, 1992.

Race, William H. Pindar. 2 Vols. Cambridge: Harvard University Press, 1997.

Renouf, Peter Le Page. The Life Work of Sir Peter Le Page Renouf: Volume IV, The Book of the Dead. Paris: Ernest Leroux, 1907.

Rice, David G. and John E. Stambaugh. Sources for the Study of Greek Religion. Missoula: Scholars Press, 1979.

Robinson, Richard. Definition. Oxford: Clarendon Press, 1954. reprint 1962.

Robinson, T.M. Heraclitus. Toronto: University of Toronto Press, 1987.

Rogers, Benjamen Bickley. Aristophanes, Vol. 2 Cambridge: Harvard University Press, 1989.

Rohde, Erwin. Psyche. Trans. W.B. Hillis. New York: Harcourt, Brace & Company, 1925.

Romano, James A. Death, Burial, and the Afterlife in Ancient Egypt. Pittsburg: The Carnegie Museum of Natural History, 1990.

Ross, David. Plato's Theory of Ideas. Oxford: Clarendon Press, 1951.

Rowe, C.J. An Introduction to Greek Ethics. New York: Barnes & Noble, 1976.
_____. Plato: Phaedrus. Wiltshire: Aris & Phillips, 1986.
_____. Plato: Phaedo. Cambridge: Cambridge University Press, 1993.

Seaford, Richard. Reciprocity and Ritual: Homer and Tragedy in the Developing City-State. Oxford: Clarendon Press 1994.
_____. Euripides: Bacchae Warminster: Aris & Phillips, 1996.

Seymour, Thomas Day. Life in the Homeric Age. New York: Macmillan, 1907.

Shorey, Paul. "Plato's Ethics." In Gregory Vlastos. <u>Plato: A Collection of Critical Essays</u>. Notre Dame: University of Notre Dame Press, 1978.

_____. The Republic, vol 1. Reprint 1978. Cambridge: Harvard University Press, 1937.

_____. <u>The Unity of Plato's Thought</u>. Chicago: University of Chicago Press, 1903.

_____. <u>What Plato Said</u>. Chicago: University of Chicago Press, 1933.

Silverman, David P. "The Nature of Egyptian Kingship." In <u>Ancient Egyptian Kingship</u>, ed. David O'Connor and David P. Silverman. Leiden: E.J. Brill, 1995.

_____. <u>Divinity in Religion of Ancient Egypt</u>.------

Silverman, David P. "Divinity and Deities in Ancient Egypt." In <u>Religion in Ancient Egypt</u>. Ed. Byron E. Shafer. Ithaca: Cornell University Press, 1991.

Smith, Jonathan Z. <u>Imagining Religion</u>. Chicago: University of Chicago Press, 1982.

_____. <u>Map is not Territory</u>. Leiden: E.J. Brill, 1978.

Smyth, Herbert Weir. <u>Aeschylus</u>, Vol. 2 London: William Heinemann, 1926.

Sneath, E. Hershey. <u>Religion and the Future Life</u>. London: Fleming H. Revell, 1922.

_____. <u>The Evolution of Ethics</u>. New Haven: Yale University Press, 1927.

Sommerstein, Alan H. <u>Aeschylus: Eumenides</u>. Cambridge: Cambridge University Press, 1989.

_____. <u>Peace</u>. Warminster: Aris & Phillips, 1985.

Sourvinou-Inwood, Christine. "To Die and Enter the House of Hades." In <u>Mirrors of Mortality</u>. Ed. Joachim Whaley. Rochester: Stanhope Press, 1981.

_____. <u>'Reading' Greek Death: To the End of the Classical Period</u>. Oxford: Clarendon Press 1995.

Spencer, A.J., <u>Death in Ancient Egypt</u>. New York: Penguin Books, 1982.

Spiegel, Joachim. <u>Die Idee vom Totengericht in der agyptischen Religion</u>. Leipziger Agyptologische Studien, 2. Gluckstadt, 1935.

_____. <u>Das Werden Der Altagyptischen Hochkultur</u>. Heidelberg: F.H. Kerle Vertag, 1953.

Stewart, H.M., <u>Egyptian Stelae, Reliefs and Paintings, Part Two</u>. Warminster: Aris & Phillips, 1979.

Stewart, J.A. <u>The Myths of Plato</u>. Ed. G. R. Levy. Carbondale: Southern Illinois University Press, 1960.

Statman, Daniel. Ed. <u>Virtue Ethics</u>. Edinburg: Edinburg University Press, 1997.

Sutton, Dana Ferrin. <u>The Lost Sophocles</u>. Lanham: University Press of America, 1984.

Taylor, A. E. <u>A Commentary on Plato's Timaeus</u>. New York: Garland, 1987.

_____. <u>Plato the Man and his Works</u>.------

Taylor, C.C.W. <u>The Atomists: Leucippus and Democritus</u>. Toronto: University of Toronto Press, 1999.

Tessitore, Aristide. <u>Reading Aristotle's Ethics</u>. Albany: State University of New York, 1996.

Te Velde, Herman. "Funerary Mythology." In <u>Mummies and Magic: The Funerary Arts of Ancient Egypt</u>. Eds. Sue D'Auria, Peter Lacovara and Catharine H. Roehrig. Boston: Museum of Fine Arts, 1988.

_____. "Theology, Priests, and Worship in Ancient Egypt." In <u>Civilization of the Ancient Near East</u>, Ed. William Kelly Simpson, vol. III. New York: Charles Scriebner's Sons, 1995.

Thompson, J.A.K. <u>Studies in the Odyssey</u>. Oxford: Clarendon Press, 1966.

Trigger, Bruce G. <u>Early Civilizations: Ancient Egypt in Context</u>. Cairo: The American University in Cairo Press, 1993.

Vermeule, Emily. <u>Aspects of Death in Early Greek Art and Poetry</u>. Berkeley: University of California Press, 1979.

Vlastos, Gregory, ed. <u>Platonic Studies</u>. Princeton: University Press, 1981.

_____. <u>Studies in Greek Philosophy</u>. Ed. Daniel W. Graham. Princeton: Princeton University Press, 1995.

_____. Ed. <u>Plato: A Collection of Essays</u>. Vol 2. Notre Dame: University of Notre Dame Press, 1978.

Warren, Rosanna and Stephen Scully. <u>Euripides: Suppliant Women</u> (New York: Oxford University Press, 1995.

Waterfield, Robin. <u>Plato: Gorgias</u>. Oxford: University Press, 1994.

_____. <u>Plato: Republic</u>. Oxford: University Press, 1993.

_____. <u>Plato: Symposium</u>. Oxford: University Press, 1994.

Weingarten, Judith. <u>The Transformation of Egyptian Taweret into Minoan Genius</u>. Partille: Paul Astroms Forlag, 1991.

Wente, Edward F. "Funerary Beliefs of the Ancient Egyptians." <u>Expedition</u> (Winter 1982): 17-26.

West, M.L. <u>Early Greek Philosophy and the Orient</u>. Oxford: Clarendon Press, 1971.

_____. <u>Euripides: Orestes</u>. Warminster: Aris & Phillips, 1987.

_____. <u>Greek Lyric Poetry</u>. Oxford: Clarendon Press, 1993.

_____. <u>Hesiod: Theogony and Works and Days</u>. Oxford: Oxford University Press, 1988.

_____. <u>Hesiod: Works and Days</u>. Oxford: Clarendon Press, 1978.

_____. <u>The Orphic Poems</u>. Oxford: Clarendon Press 1983.

White, David A. <u>Myth and Metaphysics in Plato's Phaedo</u>. London and Toronto: Associated University Presses, 1989.

Wiedemann, Alfred, <u>The Ancient Egyptian Doctrine of the Immortality of the Soul</u>, New York: G.P. Putnams's Sons, 1895.

Williams, R.J., "Reflections on the Lebensmude." Journal of Egyptian Archeology 48(1962): 49-56.

Wilson, John A. The Burden of Egypt: An Interpretation of Ancient Egyptian Culture. Chicago: University of Chicago Press, 1951.

_____. In Ancient Near Eastern Texts. Ed. James B. Pritchard. Princeton: Princeton University Press, 1955.

Willcock, M.M. Ed. Pindar: Victory Odes. Cambridge: Cambridge University Press, 1995.

Woodbury, Leonard. "Equinox in Acragas: Pindar, 01.2.61-2." TAPA, 97 (1966), 597-616

Woods, Michael. Trans. Aristotle: Eudemian Ethics. Oxford: Clarendon Press, 1992.

Wright, M.R. Empedocles: The Extant Fragments. New Haven: Yale University Press, 1981.

_____. The Presocratics. Bristol: Bristol Classical Press, 1985.

Xenophon. Memorabilia. Trans. E.C. Marchant. In Loeb Classical Library, Xenophon IV. Cambridge: Harvard University Press, 1923. reprt. 1992.

Yoyotte, Jean. "Le Jugement des Morts dans L'Egypte ancienne." In Le Jugement des Morts, Sources Orientales, 4, 17-80. Paris: Seuil, 1961.

_____. "The Egyptian world-picture." The Unesco Courier. No. 9 (Sept 1988): 17-25.

Zabkar, Louis V. A Study of the Ba Concept in Ancient Egyptian Text. Chicago: University of Chicago Press, 1960.

Zandee, Jan. Death as an Enemy According to Ancient Egyptian Conceptions. Leiden: E.J. Brill, 1960.

Zaslavsky, Robert. Platonic Myth and Platonic Writing. Lanham MD: University Press of America, 1981.

Zeyl, Donald J. <u>Plato: Gorgias</u>. Indianapolis: Hackett Publishing Company, 1987.

_____. "Gorgias." In <u>Plato: Complete Works</u>, Ed. John M. Cooper, 791-869. Cambridge: Hackett Publishing Company, 1997.

_____. "Timaeus." In <u>Plato: Complete Works</u>, Ed. John M. Cooper, 1224-1291. Cambridge: Hackett Publishing Company, 1997.

Zuntz, Gunther. Persephone. Oxford: Clarendon Press, 1971.

0-595-34280-9

CPSIA information can be obtained
at www.ICGtesting.com
Printed in the USA
LVHW112317160919
631310LV00001B/52/P

9 780595 342808